D1593397

Recent Titles in
STUDIES IN CRIME AND PUBLIC POLICY
Michael Tonry, General Editor

*The Ex Post Facto Clause*
*Its History and Role in a Punitive Society*
Wayne A. Logan

*Prisons and Health in the Age of Mass Incarceration*
Jason Schnittker, Michael Massoglia, and Christopher Uggen

*Ending Mass Incarceration*
*Why it Persists and How to Achieve Meaningful Reform*
Katherine Beckett

*Doing Justice, Preventing Crime*
Michael Tonry

*The Partisan Politics of Law and Order*
Georg Wenzelburger

*Of One-eyed and Toothless Miscreants*
*Making the Punishment Fit the Crime?*
Michael Tonry

*Sentencing Fragments*
*Penal Reform in America, 1975-2025*
Michael Tonry

*Unwanted Muslim Immigrants, Dignity, and Drug Dealing*
Sandra M. Bucerius

*Living in Infamy*
*Felon Disfranchisement and the History of American Citizenship*
Pippa Holloway

*Children of the Prison Boom*
*Mass Incarceration and the Future of American Inequality*
Sara Wakefield and Christopher Wildeman

*The City That Became Safe*
*New York's Lessons for Urban Crime and its Control*
Franklin E. Zimring

*The Toughest Beat*
*Politics, Punishment, and the Prison Officers Union in California*
Joshua Page

*Punishing Race*
*A Continuing American Dilemma*
Michael Tonry

*Policing Problem Places*
*Crime Hot Spots and Effective Prevention*
Anthony A. Braga and David Weisburd

*The Policing Web*
Jean-Paul Brodeur

# Policing Gun Violence

*Strategic Reforms for Controlling Our Most Pressing Crime Problem*

Anthony A. Braga and Philip J. Cook

OXFORD
UNIVERSITY PRESS

OXFORD
UNIVERSITY PRESS

Oxford University Press is a department of the University of Oxford. It furthers the University's objective of excellence in research, scholarship, and education by publishing worldwide. Oxford is a registered trade mark of Oxford University Press in the UK and certain other countries.

Published in the United States of America by Oxford University Press
198 Madison Avenue, New York, NY 10016, United States of America.



CIP data is on file at the Library of Congress

ISBN 978–0–19–992928–3

DOI: 10.1093/oso/9780199929283.001.0001

1 3 5 7 9 8 6 4 2

Printed by Sheridan Books, Inc., United States of America

# Contents

*Acknowledgments* *vii*

1. **Introduction** **1**
2. **The Social Burden of Gun Violence** **12**
3. **Regulation and Its Enforcement** **26**
4. **21st-Century Policing and Crime Control** **46**
5. **Targeted Patrol and Problem-Solving in Hot Spots** **65**
6. **Retail Deterrence of Very High-Risk Groups** **86**
7. **Strengthening the Investigation of Shootings** **115**
8. **Reducing Shootings by the Police** **129**
9. **Policing Firearms Trafficking, Theft, and Illegal Diversion** **151**
10. **There's Much to Be Done** **173**

*Notes* *185*
*Index* *219*

# Contents

# Acknowledgments

We thank Stephen Douglas for his excellent assistance in finalizing our references and producing many of the tables and figures included in this book. Jennifer Hurtgen provided able assistance in computing the new results in Chapters 4 and 8. Braga would like to thank the numerous police officers, prosecutors, corrections officials, social service providers, and community members who shared their insights and perspectives on effective gun violence prevention work over the course of his career.

# 1
# Introduction

2020 was the year from hell. Along with the coronavirus pandemic and all that entailed, there was a surge in shootings in most cities, actually doubling in New York City. Nationally, the murder rate increased by 28%, and by the end of this fateful year it approached levels in some cities not experienced since the crack cocaine era a generation earlier. This surge in gun violence occurred in an unusual economic and political context, but the legacy of the street protests against the police, the surge in gun sales, and the mental health crisis induced by the disruptions of everyday life will not subside any time soon. What we can say with confidence is that the problem of gun violence in America, always urgent, became still more so.

What can be done to control gun violence? First is to recognize its importance. Public safety is foundational to human development, economic development, and a civilized life—and communities beset by violence are deprived in all those respects. The fact that those communities are for the most part lower-income minority households makes the problem still more urgent. The "public safety gap" is one of the most egregious racial disparities.

Gun violence is a multifaceted problem requiring a multifaceted response. But an essential component of any comprehensive effort is more effective policing. Most instances in which one person shoots another are crimes. The police offer a unique capacity for violence prevention that has no good substitute from other institutions, and effective policing could prevent much of the shooting. But to accomplish that purpose, and do so in legitimate fashion that respects individual rights, is a daunting challenge. The good news is that much has been learned in recent years about how to meet that challenge, due in part to innovative police departments that have partnered with analysts such as us to try out new strategies and evaluate them.

There is no consensus with respect to this positive assessment, quite the contrary. The police do not get much respect these days. Some doubt that police departments are even concerned with protecting the communities of color that bear a vastly disproportionate share of the burden. Widespread demonstrations throughout the summer of 2020 demanded *not* that the police be reformed but, rather, that they be "defunded." This bitter attack was

*Policing Gun Violence.* Anthony A. Braga and Philip J. Cook, Oxford University Press. © Oxford University Press 2023.
DOI: 10.1093/oso/9780199929283.003.0001

triggered by the video of a Minneapolis, Minnesota, police officer using clearly excessive and cruel lethal force in arresting George Floyd. A dozen videos of other deadly encounters between police and Black suspects have circulated widely in recent years, with cumulative effect. The outrage and profound mistrust of the police fuel the "no snitching" norm, depriving police investigators of the cooperation needed to solve cases. If the police are unable to make arrests in the majority of shootings, in part due to lack of cooperation, that failure reinforces the community view that the police do not care. But given the necessary resources and direction, this vicious circle can be reversed.

A second group of skeptics includes our colleagues in criminology and public health. A prevalent view among academic criminologists circa 1990 was that the police had little effect on crime rates.[1] That was not because the police were not trying hard enough but, rather, because law enforcement was intrinsically irrelevant. In this view, crime rates were determined by "root causes" found in systemic inequality, lack of economic opportunity, inadequate schools, drug and alcohol abuse, popular culture, and so forth. At the time, violent crime rates were peaking at unprecedented levels, and police chiefs throughout the country gladly embraced the criminologists' view that the police were irrelevant and hence not to blame. But that comfortable view was ultimately undercut by a handful of police executives, most notably William Bratton. Bratton was appointed Commissioner of the New York City Police Department twice, the first time beginning in 1994. In these and other leadership positions, he accepted responsibility for reducing crime and insisted that his commanders view crime as a problem to be solved.[2] The extraordinary improvements in public safety under his watch helped reverse the "police are irrelevant" narrative.

Colleagues in public health often appear to share the pre-Bratton viewpoint. They began researching gun violence prevention in the 1980s and from the beginning asserted that gun violence was a "public health problem" and could best be addressed through the methods and perspectives of their field. They (with notable exceptions) have ignored or minimized the role of the criminal justice system.[3] In the public health perspective, violence prevention requires working as far up the causal chain as possible, which leads back to "root causes." Law enforcement is viewed as responding to crime after it occurs, rather than seeking to prevent it, and hence of marginal interest. But that reflects a profound misunderstanding. In fact, the primary reason why police investigate crimes and arrest perpetrators is to prevent future crimes.

Sir Robert Peel, the father of British policing (hence the nickname "bobbies"), is credited with nine principles formulated in 1829 to guide the new police force. His first principle is the following: "The basic mission for which the police exist is to prevent crime and disorder."[4] The two principal mechanisms by which reactive policing can prevent crime are *deterrence* and *incapacitation*. Some individuals may be deterred from shooting another person during a robbery, gang dispute, or domestic argument by the perceived threat of arrest and punishment. If shooters are routinely convicted and imprisoned, that threat will have reality and be transmitted more effectively to the relevant individuals (members of violent gangs and other high-risk individuals). And if the police are successful in solving a shooting crime, locking up the shooter will prevent him from continuing his violent career. Arrests and convictions may also serve to interrupt retaliatory violence. Violence begets violence, and violence interrupted prevents future violence.

Police prevent violence not only by arresting shooters but also by preempting shootings through a variety of proactive methods. Because most shootings take place outside the home, one important preemptive strategy has been to enforce regulations that limit gun carrying in city limits. That is not a new idea: In the 1880s cow-town marshals of the Wild West sought to enforce local bans on gun carrying in city limits, which famously led to "the shootout at the OK Corral" in Tombstone, Arizona. Although important for public safety, police actions to deter illegal carrying must be carefully focused to avoid violating individual rights. "Focus" is also a guiding principle for directing proactive police efforts in other domains, including developing effective interventions for calming volatile gang rivalries and cooling violent "hot spots" in the city.

Advocates for the public health perspective have been among the leading voices for gun control. Stringent regulation of guns is warranted, in this view, because without guns, violent encounters tend to be far less deadly. But although there is much to be said for regulating firearms, this approach has limited scope in the American context. The political tide has swept away much of the state and local regulations during the past 50 years. That process was accelerated by a U.S. Supreme Court ruling in 2008 that for the first time found a personal right to "keep and bear arms" in the Second Amendment. Gun sales surged throughout 2020, adding fuel to the fire created by civil unrest and a fraught presidential campaign. No regulation stood in the way, and both the Court and the current political reality are likely to preclude more stringent legislation. Federal and some state regulations remain in place and are helpful, but for the purpose of gun violence prevention, they cannot serve as an alternative to enforcement of criminal law. More than that, these existing regulations are only effective to the extent that they are enforced—bringing us back to the importance of the police in the prevention effort.

Just to be clear, we are entirely supportive of addressing the fundamental socioeconomic conditions that are associated with serious violence. Reversing systemic racism, growing economic inequality, and child poverty is in the public interest, regardless of whether there is a direct connection to crime and violence. But we are confident that serious violence rates can change dramatically even without fundamental social change. Recent history proves the point. During the Great Crime Drop, from 1993 to 2014, the national homicide rate halved, led by reductions in gun violence. Yet this dramatic improvement in public safety was not the result of improvements in the usual list of root-cause conditions.[5] Indeed, during that same period, the distribution of income became even more unequal, racial disparities in education and employment remained distressingly large, and "safety net" antipoverty programs were no less deficient. Yet every large city became dramatically safer and the quality of life thereby improved. Low-income minority neighborhoods, where gun violence is concentrated, were the particular beneficiaries. Here is our bottom line: We are committed to pursuing an equitable and just society, and also committed to pursuing public safety. Progress on either goal is much to be desired. The two goals are related, but not quite in the way sometimes suggested by progressive rhetoric. A more economically just society is obviously desirable but not a prerequisite for a safer society. And creating a safer society would reduce one of the great and unjust disparities.

The unprecedented surge in gun violence in 2020 killed and injured tens of thousands more than in the previous year—and most of the victims were Black. Communities of color, whose elders were particularly hard hit by the coronavirus pandemic, found their youth targeted by this second outbreak. The consequences of the surge in violence for these communities that already had high rates of endemic violence have been dire. We do not offer any easy answers but can provide guidance on how to make the law enforcement more effective in preventing gun violence. Experience, and systematic evaluation of that experience, helps point the way.

## Introducing Ourselves

What we have to offer in this book is based in part on our own research and experience, so allow us to introduce ourselves. We have been researching gun violence prevention for a long time—Philip Cook for 45 years and Anthony Braga for 30 years. Braga's career in particular has benefited from the willingness of some police chiefs to invite academics to participate in documenting and evaluating reform efforts, to run experiments, and even to help shape programs and policy. Early in his career, starting in late 1994, he worked at Harvard's Kennedy School of Government, where he and several colleagues were tasked with assisting the Boston Police Department in reversing the epidemic of gang violence in Boston. The program they developed and helped implement, known as Operation Ceasefire, was highly effective at reducing shootings and became a widely imitated model for other cities.

The best known element of Ceasefire was an innovation called focused deterrence, in which the Boston Police "called in" the members of a violent gang and warned them that they were all subject to enhanced enforcement if any members were known to be involved with guns. At the same time, street outreach workers and social service providers attending the call-in offered help in redirecting their lives. The community, and particularly Black churches, provided vital support to this dramatic intervention. A key conceptual insight was that youths caught up in drug dealing and gang violence were capable of making better choices, and they would do so if it appeared worthwhile. The possibility of arrest, always real, was made personal and hence more influential on that choice.

Braga's career of "action research" continued during his faculty appointments at Harvard, Rutgers, Northeastern, and now Penn. For example, in the City of Lowell, Massachusetts, he organized and ran a promising field experiment in which the police were coached to identify hot spots of crime and develop interventions that could help gain control by limiting crime opportunities at these problem places. Between 2007 and 2013, he served as Chief Policy Advisor to former Boston Police Commissioner Edward F. Davis and worked with his command staff and line-level officers on community policing and crime prevention initiatives, including a series of reforms that were effective in reducing gun violence and increasing homicide clearance rates. When New York City settled a lawsuit challenging its "stop, question, and frisk" program to get guns off the street, Braga was appointed a member of the federal monitor team to oversee compliance, giving him a close-up view of the reforms implemented by the New York Police Department.

Cook has pursued a somewhat more conventional academic career path as a professor of public policy at Duke University. He was one of the first scholars of any discipline (he is an economist) to develop a research program in gun violence prevention. He and Braga met early in Braga's career, and they have worked together on a variety of projects ever since. In recent years, Cook has become convinced that the least developed area of gun violence research (relative to its potential payoff) has been policing, particularly research on how to increase the effectiveness of the police in solving gun assaults and murders. He is heading up a research team at the University of Chicago to understand the secular decline in homicide arrest rates (in Chicago and nationwide) and explore ways to reverse that trend. In one project, he is evaluating the Chicago Police Department Bureau of Detectives' new "technology centers" that facilitate the acquisition and use of video evidence in cases of serious violence.

So what the two of us have to offer is informed by both experience and research in the field. We are motivated by a shared belief that gun violence is a serious problem and that the police and criminal justice system must be an important part of the solution.

## A Focus on Routine Violence

Our primary concern is with the violence associated with routine assaults and robberies. This sort of violence rarely gets the headlines. But it accounts for the vast majority of gun homicides and nonfatal gunshot injuries each year nationwide, including more than 100,000 victims in 2020. The neighborhoods in which gun violence is concentrated suffer far-reaching consequences. First, the threat of violence drives away families who can afford to live elsewhere and discourages investment so that retail outlets and other employers are scarce. Those who do live there—children especially—are fearful, even traumatized, by the sounds of gunfire and by knowing people who have been shot, and daily activities are limited by the effort to avoid becoming a victim. Fortunately, these processes can be reversed, as evident in the renaissance in low-income neighborhoods in New York City and other large cities during the Great Crime Drop that began in 1993 and ended in 2014. Effective violence prevention is fundamental to community and economic development, mental health, and a decent quality of life. And prevention of this endemic violence is a matter of racial justice and basic fairness. More than 60% of victims nationwide are African American, and the impacted neighborhoods are predominantly minority and poor.

We are also concerned with shootings by law enforcement officers. Approximately 1,000 people each year are shot dead by officers on duty. Most, but not all, of these shootings are justified by the circumstances, in which the officer or someone else was being attacked or threatened. But a handful of well-documented cases in which the shooting is not justified and involves a Black victim have served to exacerbate distrust of the police. Many other cases may be legally justified could have been avoided with different tactics. Reducing the incidence of excessive use of force by police must be a priority in any plan to improve police effectiveness and to reduce the social costs of policing. The situation is not hopeless. Indeed, some departments are doing much better than others. Phoenix, Arizona, and Dallas, Texas, for example, are similar cities (commercial hubs, similar size and crime rate, lax gun controls, and large Hispanic population), but Phoenix has more than five times the per capita rate of fatal shootings by police compared to Dallas. The likely difference can be found in management practices by the police department.

Two other categories of gun violence are prominent in the national conversation about gun violence, although they are not our main focus here. First, mass shootings in schools and other public places account for less than 1% of gun-violence victims but have an outsize impact on our national well-being. Millions of schoolchildren have to undergo "active shooter" drills on a regular basis, ensuring that if they were not already scared, they will learn that they should be. The second category is political violence, a possibility that became vivid when a mob of White supremacists and other insurrectionists invaded the U.S. Capitol Building on January 6, 2021, seeking to block the transition from President Trump to President Biden. Although the mob did not use their guns on that occasion, we learn from their social media posts that many are heavily armed and pose an ongoing threat to public officials and institutions. Any plan to prevent mass shootings or armed insurrection requires a central role for law enforcement. But those tasks have little overlap with policing street violence and lie outside of our scope.

## Policing Offenders

We focus on three general approaches to policing gun-violence offenders. The first is through proactive police activities targeted on high-violence areas of the city. That approach has been refined by the discovery of the surprising degree to which violence is concentrated with respect to both people and places. Focusing police resources on hot spots in the city accomplishes more than does random patrol. The advantage of a focused approach is illustrated by the history of "stop, question, and frisk" programs, which were intended to help get guns off the street. At the peak of New York City's program, young men in minority neighborhoods reported they could scarcely leave their residence without at least one confrontation with the police. In response to obvious problems of overreach, not to mention lawsuits, New York, Chicago, Los Angeles, and other cities backed off of this approach, becoming much more selective. A proactive program confined to hot spots, and directed at known offenders, can be effective at much lower cost with respect to community relations. Such trade-offs must be respected in designing policy.

Targeted patrol of violent hot spots helps deter violence. Police can also play an active role in reducing the opportunity for violent crime in hot spots. Persistent concentrations of violent crime may be addressed by a variety of means: improving lighting, redirecting traffic, clearing vacant lots and empty structures, providing increased surveillance, enforcing liquor laws, and so forth. The police can serve an important role in identifying potential solutions to local problems and working with other city agencies and local business to have them adopted.

A second approach to gun violence prevention, also proactive, is to identify the most violent gangs—which in some cities account for a large portion of gun crime—and communicate to members a credible threat of legal consequences if they do not give up their guns. As mentioned above, Braga contributed to the design and implementation of the first such program, in Boston. It has been replicated in other jurisdictions. Many commentators have speculated that the threat of arrest has little effect and would have no leverage with gang members—after all, many of them already have long rap sheets and in any event have chosen to continue a life of street crime despite the considerable hazards associated with drug dealing and gang-related conflicts. But the evidence to the contrary is compelling. The success of Operation Ceasefire and similar programs not only suggests that such programs are worthwhile but also offers a more basic lesson: Contrary to the skeptics, some of these young men can indeed be swayed by a credible threat of future legal consequences for carrying and using guns in crime. That implication opens the door to other gun-violence interventions that rely on the deterrent effect of arrest and punishment. Importantly, focused deterrence programs include community mobilization and social service provision actions that help enhance police legitimacy in cities that have adopted the approach.

The third approach we consider is to increase the arrest and conviction rate for criminal shootings, both nonfatal and fatal. Following Sir Robert Peel, the primary justification here is to prevent future violence. When an individual or a gang is violently attacked, the police represent an orderly and legitimate alternative to further violence in the quest for private revenge. A successful investigation resulting in a good arrest and prosecution is in effect a service to anyone who cares about the victim and the neighborhood, whereas a failed investigation may be viewed as the result of a lack of interest or effort by the police. Distressingly, failure is much more common than success. A number of large cities have arrest rates for nonfatal shootings on the order of 10%, and only a fraction of those result in conviction. If the victim dies, the chance of an arrest is higher, partly because the police give higher priority to homicide than nonfatal shootings—but even then the arrest rate is typically less than half. In a real sense, then, the police are underserving their constituency in this key respect. The police have been vilified for doing too much in minority communities (as in the case of high-volume street stops), but in cities in which one person can shoot another with what amounts to legal impunity, they are surely doing too little.

A common barrier to successful investigation is the lack of cooperative witnesses. In many cases, the victim of a nonfatal shooting knows something about the shooter that would be helpful to the investigation, which represents an opportunity—but only if the victim can be persuaded to talk. Indeed, if the victim refuses to cooperate, it is essentially impossible to make a case that would hold up in court. It would seem that if the victim dies, the investigator's challenge is still greater because a potentially key witness is lost. But the fact that gun homicides have a higher arrest rate than nonfatal shootings indicates that investigative effort (typically much higher for fatal shootings than nonfatal shootings) matters and can overcome obstacles to investigation, including reluctant witnesses. A lighter caseload for the detectives will lead to a higher arrest rate, as will improved access to technical support and better case management. There is much that can be done if law enforcement does assign higher priority to solving cases of serious violence. The goal is to ensure that shooters are held accountable and prevented from shooting again. The ultimate goal is to serve the community by preventing gun violence.

## Motivating the Police to Do the Right Thing

The much-discussed "Ferguson effect" is relevant to the role of police in violence prevention. It has become a familiar story. A Ferguson, Missouri, police officer fatally shot Michael Brown in August 2014. The event was videorecorded and widely publicized. The resulting demonstrations against the police resulted in police disengagement in some cities, including nearby St. Louis—not necessarily as a matter of departmental policy but, rather, as a matter of choice by individual patrol officers, who have a good deal of discretion on whether to make a stop or engage with people who pose a possible threat.[6] If officers stay in their cars and avoid trouble, the result could be to facilitate violent crime. As a well-documented case in point, the release of video showing the fatal police shooting of Laquan McDonald in Chicago was followed by a drop in monthly street stops by the Chicago Police Department from 60,000 to 10,000 (October 2015 to January 2016). Chicago suffered a 50% increase in homicides in 2016. Of course, there have been other such instances, and the victims have become household names. Most prominent is George Floyd, who died after being handcuffed and held down by a Minneapolis Police Department officer kneeling on his neck in May 2020. The encounter, captured on video, instigated large protests against police brutality in more than 150 U.S. cities. Again, there have been widespread reports of police disengagement and a reasonable supposition that this contributed to the surge of community violence in that year, which killed thousands nationwide.

Effective policing requires that the police *not* withdraw—that they be fully engaged, ready and willing to confront and challenge hostile, sometimes dangerous people even in neighborhoods where they are vilified. The way forward, in our view, is to have clear rules of engagement and personnel rules that will reduce the use of lethal force by officers—coupled with an assurance of support if they are falsely accused and an accountability system if they violate the rules. These rules also need to require procedurally just encounters that can help de-escalate potentially tense situations—that is, all citizens are treated with respect and dignity when engaged by proactive police officers. Although getting the balance right may seem like a high-wire act, the use of lethal force by the police can be managed and curtailed: The fact is that similar cities have widely differing rates of law-enforcement-involved shootings.

## Policing the Underground Gun Market

In addition to deterring the illegal carrying and misuse of guns, the police also play a key role in preempting gun crime by making it more difficult for offenders to obtain a gun. Despite the fact that there are more than 300 million guns in circulation, it is not necessarily easy or quick for a teen or gang member or someone with a serious criminal record to obtain one. That is in part due to the fact that federal law places restrictions on gun transactions—retail dealers, who are required to have a federal license, are required to perform a background check on would-be buyers to determine whether they are barred due to criminal record, age, immigration status, or other characteristic. As a result, most guns used in crime are not obtained from a retail dealer but, rather, are acquired in informal (undocumented) transactions involving acquaintances or "street" sources. Theft from residences and vehicles also plays some role in arming offenders.

The supply of guns in this underground market has some structure to it, with identifiable middlemen—traffickers who move guns from less regulated to more regulated jurisdictions; brokers, who bring buyers and sellers together; straw purchasers; corrupt clerks at guns stores; and fences. A goal for law enforcement is to disrupt these transactions, perhaps by running undercover operations or by identifying sources by interviewing offenders caught with a gun. Federal agents join forces with local police because the underground market extends across state lines, with traffickers moving guns from less regulated states to the jurisdictions with tighter controls. We have learned about the underground market through analyzing case files and data from tracing confiscated guns—and from interviews with offenders. There is potential here for law enforcement to disrupt these transactions more effectively, but it will require a higher priority and more resources. The result would be to reduce the number of assaults and robberies that involve guns, and ultimately save lives.

## A Way Forward

As we write this, the COVID-era surge in deadly gun violence shows no sign of subsiding. One thing has not changed—the violence remains concentrated in low-income minority communities, impairing both economic and human development in those areas. One result is a Black–White public safety gap that contributes to economic and education gaps. Reducing serious violence, and particularly gun violence (which accounts for most homicides), must be a priority for social justice, community development, and the overall quality of life. The agency with primary responsibility for controlling serious violence is the police, and law enforcement more generally. In many violence-plagued cities and neighborhoods, the police are doing too little to address the problem of gun violence, and they could be doing more to confront this, our most important crime problem. A generation of innovation and evaluation research has helped show the way toward more effective policing that respects individual rights. There is no higher priority for law enforcement.

# 2
# The Social Burden of Gun Violence

Families who cannot afford to move to a safer neighborhood are left attempting to protect their children as best they can. The stories from violence-ridden public housing projects are particularly striking. One single mother living in Chicago's public housing reported, "At night you had to put your mattress on the floor because bullets would be coming through the windows. It was like Vietnam." In other urban neighborhoods, children are taught by their parents to hide under beds or in bathtubs at the sound of gunfire. As the *New York Times* reported, "When the leader of a Christian missionary group asked a group of children in the Cooper housing project [in New Orleans] to name some things they worry about, a 7-year-old girl raised her hand and said 'Dying.' After the class, the children ran screaming from the playground when the sound of a machine gun ripped through the air. It was 11:57 a.m." A mother in a different public housing complex in New Orleans reported, "I got a letter from this one little girl. She said her goal in life was to live to graduate high school."[1]

We were standing right there where the boy had got shot at. So then, one night they had a drive by shooting. The kids had to jump on the floor. Even the baby, she was under two year old. And then my son was coming home from school the next day—and because they didn't hit their target, they wanted to come back. I hear pow-pow-pow. My baby was laying on the bed sleeping. It was like a quarter to two. And I knew my son was coming round the corner. And I went outside and I didn't see him.[2]

"Growing up here, it just sharpens your senses. It makes you more aware of your surroundings—aware of who you're hanging out with, where you're hanging out, what time you're outside at. You always gotta be paying attention, cause a shooting can happen any time. Like if I hear a car skid off, I'm automatically ready for a drive-by. A tire pops, my mind automatically goes to a gunshot. A car's driving real slow, I'm watching it closely, you know. You really gotta be able to

*Policing Gun Violence.* Anthony A. Braga and Philip J. Cook, Oxford University Press. © Oxford University Press 2023.
DOI: 10.1093/oso/9780199929283.003.0002

> identify what's dangerous and what's not dangerous out here, just cause the stakes are so high."
>
> —Calvin.[3]

In line with these personal accounts, a report sponsored by three city-based advocacy groups puts the problem of community gun violence in a nutshell:

> Residents and leaders of America's cities face few challenges more urgent than gun violence. It takes thousands of lives, depresses the quality of life of whole neighborhoods, drives people to move away, and reduces cities' attractiveness for newcomers. It makes it harder for schools, businesses, and community institutions to thrive. Urban gun violence also reflects and worsens America's existing racial and economic disparities.[4]

Discussions of the social burden of gun violence typically begin with statistics on the number of people killed by gunfire. Such statistics are easy to understand, quite accurate, readily compared with other causes of death, and, at least for the United States, distressingly large, as we will see. The victim counts are larger yet if we add nonfatal gunshot injuries, which are more common than fatalities. But mortality statistics, even when coupled with injuries, tell only part of the story and are sometimes misleading as an indicator of the size, scope, or even nature of the problem. Indeed, much of the social cost does not stem directly from the loss or impairment of the lives of actual victims but, rather, from the public's response to the *threat* of gun violence. Individuals suffer from the trauma stemming from that threat, and the constant vigilance required to avoid victimization. For neighborhoods and whole communities, violence degrades the quality of life and drags down economic development.

This book was written while in the midst of the global lockdown instigated to reduce the flow of COVID-19 cases. As with gun violence, the burden of that pandemic is also characterized in terms of the number of deaths, but that characterization misses the cost of the massive effort undertaken to prevent still more deaths—to "bend the curve" by shutting down much of the economy and limiting normal activities. Furthermore, mortality statistics are not an adequate representation of the burden of concern for all who worry about themselves or loved ones becoming sick. In other words, in assessing the value of a vaccine or other intervention that may eliminate the virus as a threat, an analyst must count not only the value of lives saved but also the value of recovering a normal social and economic life without all the costly precautions and anxiety. The analogy to the burden of gun violence is clear.

Before developing that argument, it is useful to say more about what we do and do not learn from statistics on gunshot injuries, and explain the case for treating gunshot injuries as distinct from injuries by other weapons.

## Victimization Rates

Nearly 45,000 people were shot and killed in 2020, more than the number killed in highway crashes (Table 2.1; Figure 2.1). Most—54%—were suicides, compared with 44% that were classified as homicide. The mix of cases changes dramatically when we include gunshot survivors. Fully 71% of those injured by gunfire (fatally or not) were intentionally shot by another person, whereas only 19% of wounds were self-inflicted with the intention of committing suicide. (The comparison with highway crashes is also blown out of the water because there are approximately 2 million nonfatal injuries per year from that cause.)[5] Thus, when we add nonfatal gunshot injuries to the mix, the focus changes from suicide to interpersonal violence, most of it criminal. This is our

**Table 2.1** Gunshot Victims, 2020[a]

| Intent | Deaths | Case-Fatality Rate | Nonfatal Injuries | Total |
|---|---|---|---|---|
| Assault and homicide | 19,995<br>44% | .20 | 79,800 | 99,795<br>71% |
| Suicide | 24,292<br>54% | .90 | 2,699 | 26,991<br>19% |
| Unintentional | 535<br>4% | .04 | 12,840 | 13,375<br>10% |
| Total | 44,822<br>100% | | | 140,161<br>100% |

[a] Case-fatality rates for the assault and homicide and unintentional categories are estimated using statistics from Cook et al. (2017); that for the suicide category uses statistics from Conner et al. (2019). The numbers of nonfatal injuries were computed by applying the indicated case fatality rates to death counts. The assault and homicide category includes death from legal intervention, and the total death count excludes 400 deaths that were of undetermined circumstance.

*Sources*: Centers for Disease Control and Prevention, "Web-Based Injury Statistics Query and Reporting System (WISQARS), 2020," National Center for Injury Prevention and Control, https://webappa.cdc.gov/sasweb/ncipc/mortrate.html; Philip J. Cook, Ariadne E. Rivera-Aguirre, Magdalena Cerdá, and Garen J. Wintemute, "Constant Lethality of Gunshot Injuries from Firearm Assault: United States, 2003–2012," *American Journal of Public Health* 107, no. 8 (August 2017): 1324–1328; and Andrew Conner, Deborah Azrael, and Matthew Miller, "Suicide Case-Fatality Rates in the United States, 2007 to 2014: A Nationwide Population-Based Study," *Annals of Internal Medicine* 171, no. 12 (December 2019): 885–895.

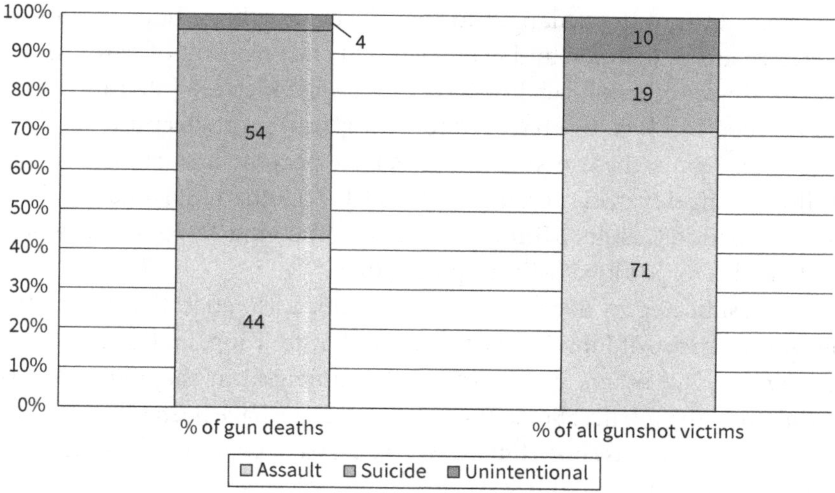


**Figure 2.1** Firearm deaths and injuries by intent, 2020. Tabulations exclude 400 fatalities with undetermined intent.

*Source*: Centers for Disease Control and Prevention, "WISQARS: Web-based Injury Statistics Query and Reporting System," 2020, National Center for Injury Prevention and Control, https://webappa.cdc.gov/sasweb/ncipc/mortrate.html.

first illustration of a basic truth—that the nature of the "problem" depends on just how it is defined and measured.

Within the category of interpersonal violence—homicide and assault—there are three subcategories that stand out. First are the mass shootings, defined here as shooting sprees in which four or more people are killed. Some of these events have become infamous household names, such as Columbine (1999), Virginia Tech (2017), Sandy Hook Elementary School (2012), a movie theater in Aurora (2012), Las Vegas Strip (2017), Marjory Stoneman Douglas High School (2018), Uvalde, Texas (2022) and Pulse Nightclub (2016). Yet despite their prominence, they account for only a small fraction of all firearms homicides: less than 1% even in the worst years. But they have the power to undermine our sense of safety in public places. Their devastating impact is indicated by the extraordinary efforts made to prepare for such events, most notably with the regular drills in schools where millions of students are taught what to do if there is a gunman roaming the school halls, shooting indiscriminately. If the kids aren't already anxious, these drills ensure they become so.

The second prominent subcategory is shootings of civilians by law enforcement officers while on duty. Since *The Washington Post* started tabulating these events in 2015, there have been just about 1,000 such deaths each year, which is to say 5–7% of all homicides. Most of these involve armed suspects who pose an imminent danger to the officer or others, but some of these shootings are unjustified and even criminal. The handful of cases in which the shooting or other officer-involved killing was video recorded and involved an unarmed Black victim have led to widespread protests and vilification of the police. Again, these notorious cases have become household names, including Michael Brown (Ferguson, MO, 2014), Laquan McDonald (Chicago, 2014), Philando Castile (Minneapolis, 2016), Breonna Taylor (Louisville, KY, 2020), and George Floyd (Minneapolis, 2020).

A third subcategory of great concern is political violence. During the 1960s, the assassinations of John Kennedy, Martin Luther King, Jr., Robert Kennedy, Malcolm X, and others were profoundly influential in shaping public concern about gun violence. Since 1963, no presidents have been killed (although President Reagan was shot), but the Secret Service spends billions each year to guard against that possibility.

The great bulk of gunshot cases are neither a mass shooting, nor an officer-involved shooting, nor a political assassination. Most deaths and injuries result when one civilian shoots another under circumstances that are not particularly newsworthy—domestic conflicts, bar room brawls, robberies, drive-by shootings by gang members seeking revenge or to "defend" territory, and so forth. These events do not become famous. But the cumulative impact on the quality of life in impacted neighborhoods is vast and demands top billing in any reasonable assessment of policing priorities.

The residents of most neighborhoods that are greatly affected by this routine gun violence are for the most part low-income, African American households. Although the quality of life for all residents is impaired, the actual victims are predominantly young men. In fact, 61% of all gun homicide victims in 2020 were Black, and 39% were Black males aged 18-34 years—a group that constitutes only 2% of the U.S. population. The stark contrasts in victimization rates by sex and race/ethnicity are illustrated in Figure 2.2. The race disparity in homicide is so great that it adds nearly 3 years to the Black–White gap in life expectancy.[6] A successful effort to reduce overall lethal violence would be of disproportionate benefit to Black males and the families and communities in which they reside.

Unsurprisingly, the shooters tend to be similar to the victims, with even greater concentration among young men. When shooters' characteristics were known to police departments submitting data to the 2019 FBI Supplementary Homicide Reports program, murderers were identified as 88% male, 56% Black, and 56% younger than age 30 years.[7] In cities in which gangs are prevalent, such as Boston, Chicago, and Los Angeles, the bulk of deadly violence

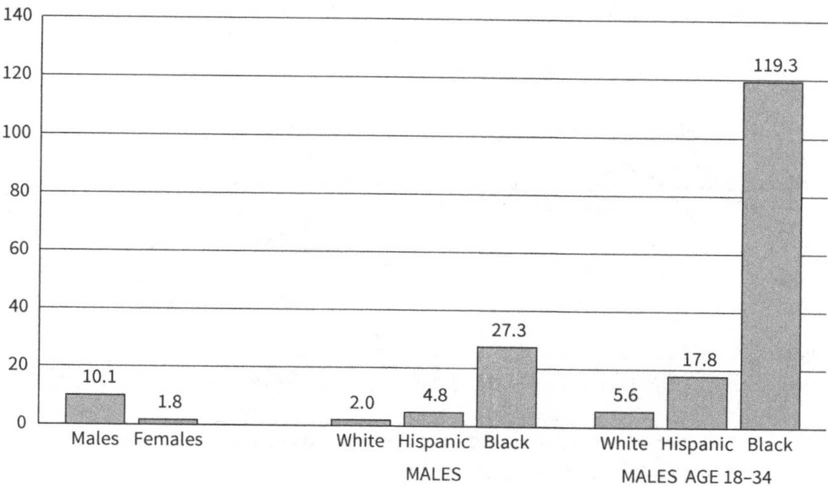


**Figure 2.2** Firearm homicide rate per 100,000 by selected demographics, 2020.
*Source*: Centers for Disease Control and Prevention, "WISQARS: Web-based Injury Statistics Query and Reporting System," 2020, National Center for Injury Prevention and Control, https://webappa.cdc.gov/sasweb/ncipc/mortrate.html.

can be attributed to members of violent gangs and crews that have ready access to guns and may be involved in the underground economy.[8]

Approximately one in seven homicides involve women as victims. For women, unlike men, the greatest danger lies within the family, especially spouses of intimate partners. However, the long-term trend for domestic violence has been favorable. The increasing independence of living arrangements gets much of the credit. Women are now far less likely to live with a man, and if they do, they have a more realistic option of moving out if the relationship becomes violent.[9] As a result, they are less likely to be killed—and much less likely to kill.[10] In the mid-1970s, there were approximately the same number of male and female domestic homicide victims, but now the victimization rate for women, although lower, is three times that of men. An enduring pattern is that when there is a gun in the home, domestic violence is more likely to escalate to murder.[11]

## The Rise and Fall (and Rise?) of Gun Violence

Although gun violence is endemic in many neighborhoods, it is not immutable. In fact, the nation as a whole experienced a remarkable rise and fall in

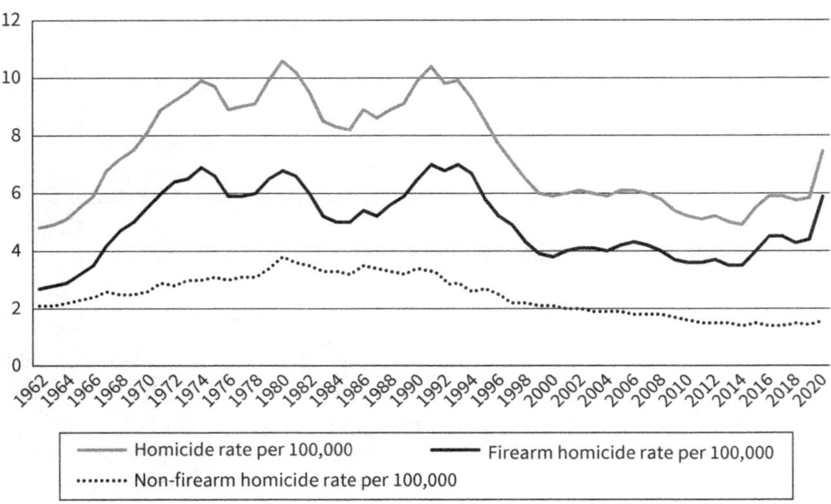


**Figure 2.3** Total, firearm, and non- firearm homicide rates, 1962–2020. Graph excludes 400 fatalities with undetermined intent.

*Source*: Centers for Disease Control and Prevention, "WISQARS: Web-based Injury Statistics Query and Reporting System," 2020, National Center for Injury Prevention and Control, https://webappa.cdc.gov/sasweb/ncipc/mortrate.html.

crime of all sorts, including gun crime, during the past six decades. Just focusing on homicide (which is measured most accurately), we see in Figure 2.3 that the homicide rate was at its lowest point in 1963 and then more than doubled during the Vietnam War era. With some variation, it stayed on a high level until the early 1990s, when it started a long and welcome decline, stretching through to 2014. During that time, the homicide rate halved, and other types of crime—robberies and assaults in particular—dropped by at least that much.[12] Gun crime dropped in step with other violent crime. Unfortunately, the tide has shifted since 2014: Although non-gun homicide has continued to decline, gun homicide has turned upward and then surged in 2020. The 28% increase in the homicide rate between 2019 and 2020 was the largest year-over-year increase since the advent of national records nearly a century ago—and the gun homicide rate increased even more, by 34%. Whether 2020 will prove to be an aberration, or the new normal, remains to be seen as we write this.

The reasons for the dramatic crime drop of 1993–2014 are not well understood, but this decline does offer some lessons:[13]

- The drop in gun homicide mirrored the drop in non-gun homicide, suggesting that both were being influenced by the same underlying factors.

- The downward turn in the early 1990s, like the increase in the years immediately before it, was closely linked to the crack cocaine epidemic.[14] Its introduction in one city after another in the 1980s was at first associated with increasing violence, but the conflicts over control of crack distribution eventually subsided, as did usage. Still, the drop in violence continued and was far broader than could be explained by changes in the crack markets alone.
- There were no obvious improvements in the "root cause" conditions during this period. The trends in income distribution, employment, poverty rates, family structure, minority status, and so forth were generally not favorable.[15]
- Although there was an increase in incarceration rates through approximately 2006, the consensus of analysts is that incarceration trends can only account for a small portion of the drop.[16]
- The resurgence of gun violence in recent years, and especially in 2020, is a source of great concern. Are we on a path to the murder rates of the 1970s and 1980s?

What we did learn, beyond the shadow of a doubt, was that the crime drop provided a great assist in making cities more livable and attractive overall, and in renewing many urban communities that had been devastated by crime and violence.

## Instrumentality

Before shifting the focus from statistics on injuries and deaths to the impact of gun violence on the community, we consider another challenge to the use of mortality statistics as a basis for judging the costs of gun violence. The question is fundamental: whether the type of weapon really even matters in violent crime. It makes little sense to treat gun homicides separately from, for example, homicides with knives if the type of weapon is an incidental detail, akin to whether the perpetrator wore a hat. In other words, if removing guns from violent encounters had no effect on the outcomes, then the fact that there were 20,000 gun homicides in 2020 would be of little distinct interest. Of course, the 25,000 total homicides (including all types of weapons) would still be of concern, but is the type of weapon of special concern? This perspective is encapsulated in the old slogan, "Guns don't kill people; people kill people." In this perspective, all that matters is the intent of the assailant. Whether the victim lives or dies from an attack causing serious injury depends on whether the attacker wanted the victim to die. Don't believe it.

The primary reason that gun use in violent crime matters is simply that of all the commonly used types of weapons—guns, knives and razors, clubs, fists—the most lethal is guns. When one person assaults another, the outcome, and especially whether the victim lives or dies, depends in large part on the type of weapon used in the attack. For an attack that results in one or more gunshot wounds, the death rate is 15–20%, and that is far higher than the likelihood of death in stabbings, where less than 3% of all serious injuries result in death (and still higher than injury inflicted with other common weapons).[17] Berkeley Law Professor Franklin Zimring coined the term "instrumentality" to indicate that the power of the weapon used in an attack has a causal effect on the likelihood of death.[18] Guns have the power to inflict lethal injury with little strength, effort, or skill on the part of the aggressor. In Zimring's pioneering research on the topic, he demonstrated the instrumentality effect in two detailed analyses of the outcome of criminal attacks that many of us found entirely persuasive. Knowing that guns are intrinsically more deadly than other weapons helps justify policies intended to separate guns from violence, including legal restrictions on carrying guns in public and state sentencing codes that specify longer prison sentences for gun robbery than knife robbery.[19]

Zimring's research, and confirmatory research since then, has not settled the issue for everyone. A recent survey of "experts" who had published on gun violence found a deep divide about whether they accepted the instrumentality argument.[20] The respondents were readily sorted into two groups based on their answers to questions about whether they personally favored "permissive" or "restrictive" regulation of firearms transactions and carrying. Interestingly, these two groups also differed on their belief about weapon substitution, which is to say instrumentality. Members of the "permissive" group indicated their belief that if regulations were effective in reducing the gun homicide rate, it would have little effect on the overall homicide rate because perpetrators would accomplish the same result using other weapons. Those in the "restrictive" group, on the other hand, indicated that an effective gun regulation would reduce the overall homicide rate on a nearly one-for-one basis with the reduction in the gun homicide rate, suggesting that the type of weapon had a large causal effect on the outcome independent of the perpetrator's intent. This clash of beliefs suggests that instrumentality remains controversial and is a foundational issue in the national gun debate.

For us, the logic behind instrumentality is compelling. It's obvious that a gun provides the means to kill someone quickly, at a distance, with little skill or strength required. It is enough that the assailant is moved to fire the gun—sustained intent is not needed. Usually in human experience, a tool that makes a task easier to complete will be completed more often. But our intuition, unfortunately, is not sufficient to sell big controversial ideas, so we were moved to do our own research.[21] Instead of comparing gun attacks with knife attacks, we compared attacks with different types of guns. We know that other things equal, more powerful guns, and particularly larger caliber guns, inflict more lethal injury. With a large data set from attacks in which the victim was shot in Boston, we found that the case-fatality rate increased dramatically with the caliber of the handgun. There was no indication that the intent or skill of the shooters differed by caliber, so it was caliber itself that made the difference. Assailants who happened to have a large-caliber gun at hand were much more likely to kill than those with a smaller caliber gun. A summary of our results: If all the handguns used in Boston shootings had been .22 caliber (the smallest in common use), instead of the actual range of calibers up to .45, the gun homicide rate would have been 40% lower. This result helps demonstrate the basic principle that the type of weapon does matter for the outcome—life or death—of a serious attack.

The type of weapons in criminal use matters in other ways as well. In robbery, a gun provides the offender with the power to take on better defended (and more lucrative) targets. Instead of mugging individual victims on the street, a gun robber can hope to rob a gas station or even a bank, controlling the confrontation well enough to complete the theft and get away.[22] But if a gun is used, the likelihood that the victim will be killed triples compared with a knife robbery. More generally, the power and range of a gun provide assailants with the capacity to threaten even well-defended targets. The right kind of gun provides the power to launch a single-handed attack with mass casualties.

Unfortunately, guns that are sold to civilians are becoming more lethal over time, with the market increasingly dominated by weapons featuring higher capacity magazines and using larger caliber ammunition.[23] In Boston, for instance, higher capacity semiautomatic pistols capable of shooting more rounds replaced revolvers as the most frequently recovered type of handgun beginning in the 1990s.[24] The transition from revolvers to semiautomatic pistols and from smaller to larger caliber handguns mirrors national trends in handgun production in the United States between the 1980s and 1990s.[25]

Another noteworthy trend has been the strong growth in sales of assault weapons—military-style semiautomatic firearms that accept a large, detachable magazine holding 50 rounds or more. These have become the predominant weapon used in mass murders.[26]

Guns make it easy to kill people. The fact that gun use in violent crime is much more prevalent in America than in other wealthy nations explains much of the observed gap in homicide rates. Successful efforts to separate guns from violence save lives and reduce the social burden of violence.[27]

## Social Cost

When a substantial proportion of robberies and assaults are committed with guns, as in the United States, the result is that the violence is intensified—it is far more deadly and difficult to avoid or defend against. The sound of gunfire can be terrifying to neighborhood residents. There are no drive-by knifings or people killed by stray clubs. The full range of such impacts is not captured by metrics based on the number of actual victims. For example, no president has been shot since 1981, yet the annual cost of protecting the president, for whom the main threat is being shot, runs to billions of dollars.[28] It is the *threat* of gun violence, and the efforts to avoid and mitigate that threat, that constitutes much of the social burden.

For routine gun violence in heavily impacted communities, the entire community experiences the threat of gun violence, which engenders anxiety or even trauma and motivates costly avoidance activities. Children who are exposed to gun violence have psychological problems and perform worse in school.[29] Mothers suffer from high blood pressure and obsess about keeping their children safe from stray bullets. Victims of gun robbery are unlikely to be shot, but the fear of that possibility is real and may cause lasting trauma. Households with the financial means of living in a safe neighborhood avoid neighborhoods where gunfire is common. And by one estimate, 70 residents move out for every homicide in a neighborhood.[30] As a result, these communities suffer from disinvestment and the resulting lack of employment and retail options. Fortunately, that process can be reversed, as suggested by the New York experience where the extraordinary reduction in violence, starting in the early 1990s, created the foundation for a new renaissance in Harlem and other impacted areas of the city.[31]

In summary, interpersonal gun violence is a public health problem but also an urban dis-amenity. It penalizes the standard of living for all who are threatened or suffer from neighborhood decline. Much of the burden is associated with the threat of gun violence—with the lack of public safety—rather than the direct casualties.

Given this understanding, the cost of homicide and gun assault is amplified relative to suicide, where others are not threatened. The same reasoning suggests that the victim count is a poor guide to the relative seriousness of mass shootings in schools. These vivid, tragic events create a source of stress for parents and schoolchildren nationwide, and they drive an enormous investment in school safety measures and disruptions of the school day for live shooter drills. Although there were only a handful of active-shooter cases in schools, more than 4 million schoolchildren were affected by a school lockdown during a recent school year (2017–2018),[32] and far more were required to rehearse such events.

For some purposes, it is useful to quantify the social burden of gun violence in dollar terms. Thomas Schelling, a Nobel Laureate in Economics, laid out the appropriate conceptual framework for placing a value on risks to life and limb. He adopted a forward-looking perspective that focuses on public safety rather than on actual victims, acknowledging that a large part of the cost is the result of chronic fear and the struggle to stay safe.[33] Placing a value on public safety is difficult but necessary in order to have a common metric for balancing costs and benefits in guiding public policy. Should a city council allocate scarce funds to a gun violence prevention program in violence-ridden neighborhoods? If effective, it would have a variety of positive consequences, including a reduction in the number of gunshot assault victims but also including the salutary effects from a reduction in the threat of gun violence to the community: reduced trauma and blood pressure, improved school performance, and the possibility of economic revitalization. The public is willing to pay for public safety, and the amount that they are willing to pay is a measure of the value of the program.

Willingness to pay could be inferred, at least in part, by increases in property value following the adoption of an effective program, although in practice analysts have difficulty sorting out the effect of a particular policy innovation from other influences on real estate markets. Instead, Cook, collaborating with fellow economist Jens Ludwig, utilized the "contingent valuation" method to determine willingness to pay, implemented through a national survey. To the questionnaire for the 1998 wave of the General Social Survey, they added several questions that followed best practice for implementing the contingent-valuation method:[34]

> Suppose that you were asked to vote for or against a new program in your state to reduce gun thefts and illegal gun dealers. This program would make it more

difficult for criminals and delinquents to obtain guns. It would reduce gun injuries by about 30% but taxes would have to be increased to pay for it. If it would cost you an extra [$50/$100/$200] in annual taxes would you vote for or against this new program?

Respondents were assigned at random to the three versions of the question, differing only by the amount of the tax increase. It was found that the likelihood of the respondent indicating a positive vote was inversely related to the specified tax increase. Based on these responses, the average household valuation of a 30% reduction in gun violence was estimated as $240. Presumably, responses reflected a judgment about the value of personal safety and safety of family and friends, as well as the respondent's sense about possible public savings in medical care and criminal justice from a reduction in gun violence. The likelihood of voting "yes" was higher for respondents with children, and it increased with household income. Multiplying up, the social cost of gun violence at the time (1998) was $80 billion; it would be far higher today due to inflation.

The contingent-valuation method is accepted in principle by economists,[35] but it is quite at odds with the standard cost of illness (COI) approach that has long been used in the public health field for monetizing the social burden of disease and injury. That approach adds the dollar amount of medical costs, lost earnings, and (in some versions) subjective value of life of those injured or killed. The COI approach is the monetary equivalent of counting victims, and it does not account for anticipation, avoidance, fear, community disinvestment, and other life-distorting consequences of the threat of gun violence.[36] The essential problem with the COI approach is not that it necessarily underestimates the magnitude of the problem; rather, the problem with the approach is that it fundamentally misrepresents the nature of the problem, and if taken literally it would be a misleading basis for directing public policy.

## Conclusion

The burden of gun violence is not just on the victims. The threat of gun violence, like the threat of COVID-19, affects all of us. Protecting our leaders from assassination costs billions of dollars every year. Drilling schoolchildren in what to do if a gunman invades their school not only disrupts education but also induces widespread fearfulness. But the great bulk of the problem of gun violence stems from the all-too-routine conflicts involving youths armed with deadly weapons, concentrated in low-income urban neighborhoods. For those who live in neighborhoods where the sounds of gunfire are common and where the threat cannot be ignored, trauma and hypervigilance are the order of the day, and the dream of moving to a better neighborhood is first and foremost a quest for safety.

Reducing gun violence is a sound investment for the city and also a matter of social justice. More effective policing can play an important role in making it happen.

# 3
# Regulation and Its Enforcement

> SAN JOSE, March 2021—Two San Jose men have been arrested for allegedly manufacturing and selling "ghost guns," including a fully automatic machine gun, out of storage facilities to known South Bay felons.
>
> Detectives said Tuesday that 34-year-old Daniel Woods and 23-year-old Praxedo Gacrama were being held in Santa Clara County jail on a variety of illegal weapons charges.
>
> Woods, who is a convicted felon, was also taken in custody for another gun trafficking case in which he is charged with conspiring to traffic firearms from Arizona to California.
>
> "This investigation sought to expose a gun trafficking network, gun manufacturers, gun purchasers, and ultimately shooters," investigators said in a news release.[1]

Commentators sometimes discuss gun control as if it were an alternative to law enforcement.[2] But in practice, regulation and enforcement go together like, for example, a light bulb and electricity. Regulations governing gun design, transactions, possession, and use are ineffective without enforcement. The reverse is also true—that police investigations of gun-violence cases are facilitated by firearms regulations.

We begin with a brief history of federal gun regulation. The underground market that is the inevitable byproduct of these regulations must be actively policed to achieve the intended effects.

## A Century of Federal Firearms Regulation

Like other valuable consumer products, firearms, when misused, can cause great harm. There is an obvious analogy here to motor vehicles and pain medication—government has sought to regulate these products so as to

*Policing Gun Violence*. Anthony A. Braga and Philip J. Cook, Oxford University Press. © Oxford University Press 2023.
DOI: 10.1093/oso/9780199929283.003.0003

reduce the harms while preserving the beneficial uses. Table 3.1 summarizes the sequence of prominent federal laws and litigation, coupled with comments on the trends in criminal violence of the time.[3] Congress first got into this arena during the Prohibition Era with its surge of gun violence. In 1927, well into the "Roaring Twenties," a ban was imposed on the use of the U.S. Mail to ship handguns. The focus on particular types of guns continued with the National Firearms Act of 1934 (NFA), which required owners of fully automatic weapons (machine guns), sawed-off shotguns, and other weapons favored by the gangsters of the day to register them with the federal authorities. All transfers were subjected to a tax of $200, which at the time was confiscatory. Finally, in 1986, Congress banned the manufacture and import of NFA weapons for civilian use, while preserving the registration requirement for older weapons of this type. There is some indication that the NFA has been effective—the use of fully automatic weapons in crime appears to be quite rare in modern times.[4] Al Capone and the Tommy gun era are distant memories.[5]

The most comprehensive federal legislation was enacted in 1968, following a surge in crime, urban riots, and political assassinations.[6] Building on similar but weaker provisions of the Federal Firearms Act of 1938, the Gun Control Act (GCA) strengthened federal licensing of firearms dealers and limited interstate shipments of guns to licensees. The goal was to protect states that opted for tighter regulation against inflows of guns from lax regulation states. In particular, the GCA banned mail-order shipments of the sort that supplied Lee Harvey Oswald with the gun he used to assassinate President Kennedy a few years earlier. The GCA also established a federal prohibition on possession by certain categories of people deemed dangerous due to their criminal record, immigration status, mental illness, or youth. "Felon in possession" was established as a federal offense, thereby creating the possibility of a partnership between local prosecutors and U.S. attorneys in combating violent crime. The GCA required that all firms in the supply chain have a federal license and keep records of gun shipments. Retail dealers in particular were obligated to screen buyers by seeing personal identification and having them complete a form attesting that they were not disqualified. This rather mild recordkeeping requirement assisted law enforcement agencies in tracing guns to their first retail sale, sometimes providing a clue to the likely possessor of a gun known to have been used in crime. Finally, the GCA banned the import of foreign-made handguns that were small or low quality and hence did not meet a "sporting purposes" test.

With the surge of violence during the 1980s associated with the introduction of crack cocaine, and a shift in the political winds in favor of the Democrats, it became politically possible to strengthen the federal regulatory scheme in

**Table 3.1** Time Line of Federal Gun Policy

| Era | Crime Patterns | Federal Crime Policy Innovations |
|---|---|---|
| 1920s | Prohibition-related gang violence | 1919: Federal excise tax on handguns (10%) and long guns (11%). |
| | Tommy-gun era | 1927: Handgun shipments banned from the U.S. Mail. |
| 1930s | End of Prohibition in 1933 | 1934: National Firearms Act: Requires registration and high transfer tax on fully automatic weapons and other gangster weapons. |
| | Declining violence rates | 1938: Federal Firearms Act: Requires anyone in the business of shipping and selling guns to obtain a federal license and record names of purchasers. |
| 1960s | Crime begins steep climb in 1963 with Vietnam War era and heroin epidemic. | 1968: Gun Control Act: Bans mail-order shipments except between federally licensed dealers (FFLs); strengthens licensing and recordkeeping requirements. |
| | Assassinations | Limits purchases to in-state or neighboring-state residents |
| | Urban riots | Defines categories of people (felons, children, etc.) who are banned from possession.<br>Bans import of "Saturday night specials." |
| 1970s | Violence rates peak in 1975 (heroin) and again in 1980 (powder cocaine era). | 1972: BATF created and located in the U.S. Department of Treasury. |
| 1980s | Epidemic of youth violence begins in 1984 with introduction of crack. | 1986: Firearm Owners Protection Act: Eases restrictions on in-person purchases of firearms by people from out of state.<br>Limits FFL inspections by BATF, and bans the maintenance of some databases on gun transfers.<br>Ends manufacture of NFA weapons for civilian use. |
| 1990s | Violence rates peak in early 1990s, then begins to subside. | 1993: Brady Handgun Violence Prevention Act: Requires licensed dealers to perform a criminal background check on each customer before transferring a firearm. |
| | School rampage shootings | 1994: Partial ban on manufacture of "assault" weapons and large magazines for civilian use.<br>1996: Congress bans the CDC from promoting gun control, and effectively stops CDC from funding research on gun violence.<br>1996: Lautenberg Amendment bans possession by those convicted of misdemeanor domestic violence. |
| 2000s | Crime and violence continue to decline. | 2004: Assault weapons ban allowed to sunset.<br>2005: Congress immunizes firearms industry against civil suits in cases in which a gun was used in crime<br>2008: *Heller v. District of Columbia* for the first time establishes personal right under the Second Amendment. |

BATF, Bureau of Alcohol, Tobacco and Firearms; CDC, Centers for Disease Control and Prevention; FFL, Federal Firearms License; NFA, National Firearms Act.

Adapted from Philip J. Cook, "The Great American Gun War: Notes from Four Decades in the Trenches," *Crime and Justice* 42, no. 1 (2013): 24–25.

one important respect—screening gun buyers. The Brady Act, implemented in 1994, required that every purchase from a federally licensed dealer be preceded by a background check, and it created a federal "instant check" system that allowed dealers to access criminal records.[7] In short, dealers could check the buyers' statement that they were not disqualified. The "lie and buy" possibility was greatly curtailed at retail outlets.

Also in 1994, Congress imposed a ban on the manufacture or import of "assault weapons" for civilian use, as well as large-capacity magazines. This ban differs in several respects from the NFA regulation of fully automatic firearms, which fire in bursts with a single trigger pull. An "assault weapon" is typically defined as a military-style firearm, but one that is restricted by design to semiautomatic fire, meaning that the shooter must pull the trigger for each round. Furthermore, and unlike the NFA, there was no restriction placed on sale or transfer of the existing stock of these guns or of the large-capacity magazines that make them so deadly. In any event, that ban on assault weapons was allowed to sunset 10 years later and only survives in the laws of a few states. Assault weapons such as the AR-15 now enjoy a large share of sales and have become the gun of choice for mass shootings.[8]

In 1996, the Lautenberg Amendment expanded the list of people proscribed from possessing a firearm to those who had been convicted of domestic violence, even at the misdemeanor level. There is compelling evidence that both this ban and the previous ban on gun possession by people subject to a domestic violence restraining order have been effective in reducing domestic homicide.[9]

In recent years, the federal "action" has shifted from Congress to the courts. Following the success of the state attorneys general in suing the tobacco industry (resulting in the Master Settlement Agreement of 1998),[10] a number of cities filed suit against the gun industry. These suits employed various theories of mass tort, but with the common goal of using the courts to do what the state legislatures would not when it came to regulating the design and marketing of firearms. In 2005, Congress intervened to stop this litigation by taking the rather extraordinary step of immunizing the gun industry from lawsuits where the damages had resulted from misuse of a gun (the Protection of Lawful Commerce in Arms Act, PL 109-92). But the courts have nonetheless become an important arena for the fight over gun control; with the *Heller v. District of Columbia* decision in 2008, the U.S. Supreme Court for the first time discovered in the Second Amendment a personal right to keep a handgun in the home for self-protection, with the suggestion that this personal right might also bar other sorts of regulations. Soon thereafter, in *McDonald v. City of Chicago* (2010), the Court ruled that the Constitutional restriction also applied to states and local governments. Gun-rights advocates brought a flood of litigation challenging most every sort of restriction on gun design, possession, transactions, and use, with no clear indication of where the Court would draw the line in defining the limits of this newfound freedom.[11] In 2022, the *Bruen* decision restricted states' ability to regulate gun carrying in public, based in part on an "historical" standard referencing 18th century practice that is likely to condition future decisions.

Following the massacre of 20 schoolchildren and 6 adults at Sandy Hook Elementary School of Newtown, Connecticut, in 2012 by a man armed with an assault weapon, former President Obama called for Congress to reinstate a federal ban on such weapons. He also called for an expansion of the background-check requirement to include not just sales by licensed dealers (which account for approximately two-thirds of all transactions) but also sales and transfers that do not involve a dealer. Nothing came of this effort, as Congress was too divided to take decisive action in either direction—a familiar story in recent years.[12]

Federal regulations, although modest in scope, have shaped firearms commerce in the United States and arguably have reduced the availability of guns to dangerous people. Still more could be accomplished within this legal framework if it was better enforced.

## Enforcing Federal Law

The principal federal agency enforcing gun laws is the Bureau of Alcohol, Tobacco, Firearms and Explosives (known by its old acronym, ATF). ATF traces its roots to America's earliest years as the agency charged with collecting alcohol taxes. It got jurisdiction over firearms in 1942, an expanded portfolio after enactment of the GCA in 1968, and independent bureau status within the Treasury Department in 1972. It has been something of a political football since its creation, as suggested by passage of the Firearm Owners Protection Act in 1986, which placed limits on ATF's ability to inspect dealers and keep records that would help identify suspicious purchasing patterns. In 2003, the ATF moved to the Justice Department as part of Congress's reorganization of the federal security apparatus following the September 11, 2001, terrorist attacks.

With respect to guns, ATF is charged with assisting local and state law enforcement with criminal investigations, a topic we return to in Chapter 9. In addition, ATF has primary responsibility for regulating firearms commerce through licensing and oversight of manufacturers, importers, distributors, and retailers. The other key federal law enforcement agency is the Federal Bureau of Investigation (FBI), which operates the National Instant Check System and processes mandated background checks on firearms sales going through licensed dealers and in some states through private sellers as well. The FBI also investigates, and U.S. attorney offices prosecute, federal crimes involving guns.

These agencies are involved in special joint operations through which the federal government provides resources to local and state law enforcement agencies to combat gun violence. In high-visibility or especially complicated cases—for example, the Washington, DC, area sniper shootings in 2002 or the Boston Marathon shooting and bombing in 2013—federal authorities play a prominent role alongside their state and local counterparts.

As the federal agency primarily responsible for enforcing federal gun laws, ATF operates, in the words of gun violence prevention advocates, "blindfolded, and with one hand tied behind the back."[13] These constraints come in many forms: legal restrictions placed on ATF's ability to fulfill its mission efficiently, vulnerability to the political crusade against gun regulation, the absence of pressure groups willing to offer support, and a lack of funding to meet its statutory obligations.[14]

Distrust of federal firearms enforcement agencies has led to enactment of several important laws limiting these agencies' ability to use data to investigate gun trafficking and other crimes. Congress has barred the federal government from saving records of successful background checks, leading critics to charge that it is virtually impossible to detect patterns in "straw purchasing," in which a legal buyer goes from store to store buying up weapons for confederates who are barred from owning them.

Congress also has placed restrictions on the use of data gathered by ATF when it traces guns used in crime. Often when local, state, or federal authorities recover a firearm at a crime scene, they ask the ATF to run a trace, which consists of tracking the supply chain for that particular firearm from manufacturer or importer to the retailer. If that dealer is still in business, ATF then calls the dealer and requests that they search through sales records to identify the initial buyer. If the dealer is out of business, however, the ATF has the records—millions of them arrive each year—and must search them manually. Since 1979, Congress has barred ATF from computerizing these records.

In 2004, Congress passed the so-called Tiahrt Amendments, sponsored by then-representative Todd Tiahrt (R-KS). These amendments barred ATF from disclosing to the public any data, either detailed or aggregated, on its traces of crime guns. The amendments also restricted law enforcement officers' access only to trace data pertaining to a specific investigation or prosecution within their own jurisdiction. Under pressure from mayors and police chiefs, Congress has since loosened these restrictions, for example, by allowing ATF to issue aggregate gun-trace reports and allowing local and state police broader access to the data.

Also in 2004, Congress barred the ATF from requiring federally licensed firearms dealers to keep an inventory of their weapons—standard practice in virtually every business. Such inventories would help agents identify "missing" guns that may have been sold illegally. Congress also barred trace data from being used as evidence in civil proceedings.

In congressional hearings after the Sandy Hook school shootings, pro-gun advocates—including senators—were openly critical of the U.S. Department of Justice for not vigorously prosecuting felons who had attempted to illegally purchase a weapon. Federal authorities argued that they had to focus their limited resources on the bad guys who had already committed a crime with their gun, not those whom the system had stopped from obtaining one. Still, it is remarkable that there were only 12 federal prosecutions stemming from 112,000 federal denials in 2017.[15]

Of particular importance is ATF's responsibility for regulating federally licensed dealers, which in 2020 numbered 130,546 (including 53,924 licensed to sell new guns, 52,466 collectors, 7,341 pawnbrokers, and the remainder belonging to manufacturer and importers).[16] The cutting edge of regulatory oversight is ATF's Firearms Compliance Inspections, in which agents make unannounced visits to licensees and scrutinize their record books and security measures, as well as conduct an inventory. ATF inspectors conducted just 4,633 such inspections in 2020, or 3.6% of all licensees. Although almost half of inspections found one or more violations, only 114 licensees gave up their license or had it revoked.[17] More commonly, the inspector used the inspection as a chance to counsel the retailer on how to bring their business operations into compliance.

## Gun Possession and Transactions in the General Population

With few exceptions, the pistols, revolvers, rifles, and shotguns used to commit criminal assault and robbery are legal commodities being put to an illegal use, and often in the hands of a person who is legally disqualified from possessing a gun due to criminal record, age, or other characteristic.[18] Guns used in crime usually originate from a legal supply chain of manufacture (or import), distribution, and retail sale. They may change hands a number of times after that first retail sale, and some of those transactions may be a theft or violate one or more regulations on gun commerce. Understanding the sources of guns to criminal use thus requires some knowledge of the supply chain of guns generally, as well as patterns of gun possession, because any possessor is a potential supplier to an offender.

The annual General Social Survey (GSS), conducted by the National Opinion Research Center, has long included questions on gun ownership (Figure 3.1). In 2016, just 31% of American households included at least one firearm, down from 47% in 1980.[19] The drop in household gun possession in part reflects the trend in household composition during this period; households are less likely to include a gun because they have become smaller and, in particular, are less likely to include a man.[20] In most cases, guns (unlike, for example, toasters) are owned by individuals rather than households, and it is meaningful to track individual ownership; the GSS reports a drop in the percentage of adults owning at least one gun from 28% (1980) to 21% (2018), in line with the trend in household prevalence. The trend among women during this period is essentially flat (10% reported owning in 1980 and 11% in 2016) so that the downward trend is due to reduced ownership by men (50% in 1980, down to 33% in 2016).[21] Between 2016 and 2021, the GSS recorded a substantial increase at both household (up to 35%) and individual (up to 26%) levels. The largest increase was for women, for whom the prevalence of gun ownership increased by 6 percentage points (up to 17%).

Figure 3.2 depicts the trend in the number of new guns shipped to U.S. retailers, where the data in this case are based on federal tax records (because there is a federal excise tax imposed on new guns). Each year's total is the sum of manufactures and imports net of exports. Figure 3.2 also documents the surge in the volume of new guns beginning in 2003 and the growing relative importance of handguns (revolvers and pistols) as opposed to long guns (rifles and shotguns). In comparing Figures 3.1 and 3.2, it is clear that if both are accurate, then the surge in new gun sales (increasing by a factor of 3.5) was absorbed by a declining number of households through 2016. To an extent, new guns replace guns that are discarded, confiscated by police, or smuggled out of the country (e.g., to Mexico and the Caribbean).[22] But it seems likely that the average number of guns per gun owner has increased, and that is confirmed by a recent survey.[23]

The cumulative number of guns in private hands in the United States is not tracked from year to year by any data system, although in 1994 and 2015 there were national surveys that went beyond the usual questions on gun ownership to inquire about the number of guns in the home—thus providing the basis for an estimate of the total private stock. The 2015 National Firearms Survey estimated that there were 270 million guns in private hands, more

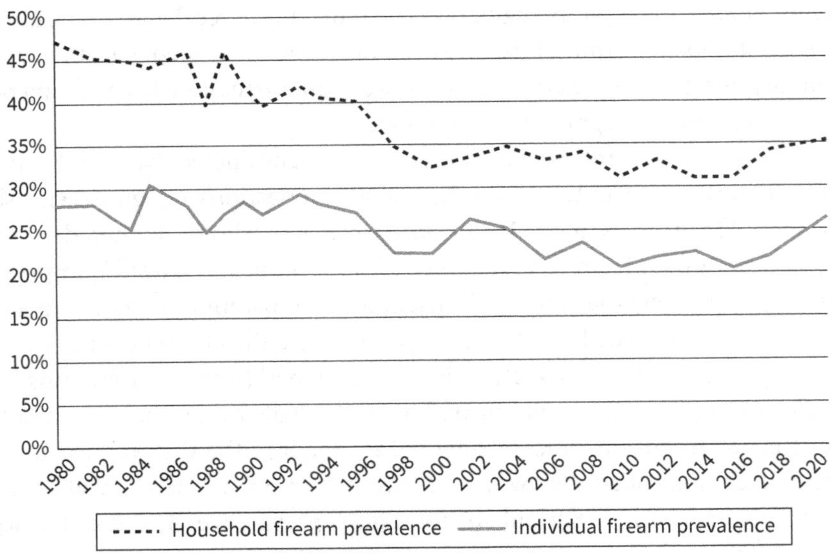


**Figure 3.1** Prevalence of gun ownership in the United States, 1980–2021.

*Sources*: Tom W. Smith and Jaesok Son, *General Social Survey Final Report: Trends in Gun Ownership in the United States, 1972–2014* (Chicago, IL: NORC at the University of Chicago, March 2015), https://www.norc.org/PDFs/GSS%20Reports/GSS_Trends%20in%20Gun%20Ownership_US_1972-2014.pdf. Data for 2016–2021 obtained from the General Social Survey cross-sectional data file, available at https://gss.norc.org/Get-The-Data.

than enough to provide one for every American adult.[24] But, in fact, gun ownership is quite concentrated, and individuals who own at least 1 gun averaged 4.9 guns in 2015.[25] That average is indeed higher than in a previous survey of this sort, conducted in 1994.[26]

Another snapshot of who owns the guns is provided by an analysis of Pew Research Center survey data for 2014.[27] An analysis of these data found that other things equal, men are much more likely to own a gun compared to women; Anglo Whites are more likely to own than minorities (Blacks and Hispanics), and low-income households are less likely to own a gun than those of the middle class. With respect to education, gun ownership peaks among those who graduated from high school but not college. After accounting for individual and household characteristics, there remains a regional effect, with the South at the high end and the Northeast at the low end. The biggest surprise is that after adjusting for education, income, and age, rural respondents do not display discernibly higher gun ownership rates that those living in urban or suburban areas.

Participation in traditional gun sports, especially hunting, has greatly declined during the past four decades, in part due to the decline in rural

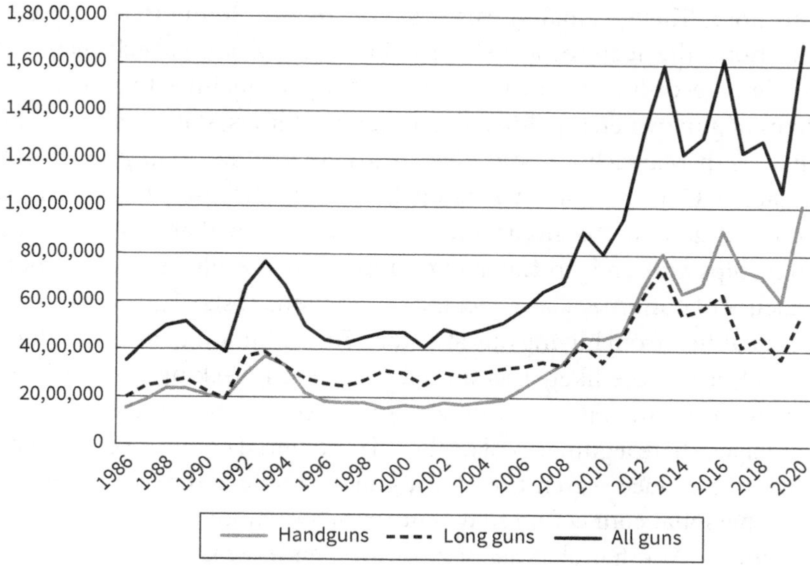


**Figure 3.2** Trends in shipments of new guns, 1980–2020.
*Sources*: Bureau of Alcohol, Tobacco, Firearms and Explosives, *Annual Firearms Manufacturing and Exportation Report (AFMER), 2019* (Martinsburg, WV: Firearms and Explosives Services Division, ATF, January 2021), https://www.atf.gov/resource-center/docs/report/2019-annual-firearms-manufacturers-and-export-report-afmer/download. 2020 data obtained from Bureau of Alcohol, Tobacco, Firearms and Explosives, *Firearms Commerce in the United States* (Washington, DC: U.S. Department of Justice, 2022).

traditions generally. Increasingly, people buy guns not to shoot animals or targets but, rather, to prepare for a time when they might need to shoot or at least threaten another person. Half of gun owners say that self-protection is the reason or primary reason they own a gun, compared with just a quarter of owners who gave that response as recently as 1999.[28]

The retail market for guns is centered on federally licensed gun dealers; approximately 64% of all gun transactions involve a purchase from a dealer.[29] There are currently approximately 64,000 dealers who sell guns from a variety of retail outlets, including stores specializing in firearms and ammunition, sporting goods stores, general department stores, and pawn shops (which need a distinct federal license).[30] The federal license allows dealers to receive interstate shipments of guns, which the rest of us may not do. They are responsible for selling the 15 million or so new guns each year but are also authorized to sell used guns. The remaining transactions include "private sales" at gun shows or in person, as well as gifts and other sorts of transactions. Federal law requires a background check for would-be buyers from a licensed dealer, and a number of states extend that requirement to cover some or all private transactions. The National Firearms Survey of 2015 found that in 78% of all transactions, the acquirer was subjected to a background check against state and federal records to ensure that they were legally qualified to own a gun.[31]

Rates of gun ownership differ widely across regions, states, and localities—from 13% in Massachusetts to 60% in Mississippi, according to one set of estimates.[32] Current gun ownership influences the use of guns in crime directly—a gun in the home increases the chance that violent domestic relationships will end up involving gunplay and result in death.[33] But the prevalence of guns may also affect the transactions costs of guns to those who are disqualified from buying one at a store. In a community in which guns are prevalent, it is more likely that an offender who is seeking a gun will know someone, or know someone who knows someone, who would be willing to lend, sell, or share a gun. It is plausible that potential connections of that sort are likely to reduce search time for a gun—or reduce the money price, because a personal connection may reduce the premium associated with risky transactions. Another channel of guns to offenders may also be sensitive to prevalence of guns: the burglaries and thefts from vehicles are more likely to include a gun as part of the loot.[34] Regardless of the scenario, this line of reasoning suggests that violent crimes in gun-rich communities are more likely to involve guns than in other communities.

## Sources of Guns to Criminal Use

Whereas the vast majority of adults in the United States are entitled to acquire all the guns they want, the federal GCA specifies that certain individuals are disqualified from acquiring or possessing firearms. The list of disqualifications includes felony conviction or under indictment; conviction for domestic violence; dishonorable discharge from military service; illegal alien; and court declaration of mental incompetence for legal purposes. Youths must be at least 18 years old to purchase a handgun. Some states have expanded the list of disqualifications—California, for example, bans those who have a misdemeanor conviction for any violent crime within the previous 10 years. If someone with a disqualifying condition attempts to buy a gun at a licensed dealer, the background check is designed to uncover that fact, and the dealer is then required to refuse to transfer the gun. (The federal and state criminal record databases accessed in the background check have grown over time but are still not comprehensive, so the system is not foolproof.) Denials occur in only approximately 1% of all purchase attempts; most disqualified people who are seeking a gun do not even attempt to buy at a retail outlet.

It is also true that in some states buyers are prescreened by requiring that they obtain a license or permit from a law enforcement agency prior to purchase. North Carolina, for example, has a century-old "permit to purchase" requirement for each handgun, where permits are issued by the local sheriff following a background check.[35] Illinois requires a Firearm Owners ID issued by the state police for any type of gun purchase. Massachusetts requires a license issued by the local police department. Altogether, 15 states have similar requirements.[36]

Most would-be gun owners do not have a disqualifying criminal record or other disqualification, and hence they are eligible to buy and possess legally. For approximately 60% of all transactions,[37] and all purchases of new guns, the seller is a federally licensed retailer with a brick-and-mortar store. Licensed dealers are authorized to receive interstate shipments of guns and presumably offer customers the usual advantages of a legitimate retailer—convenience, quality guarantee, predictable price, and a wide variety of choice. But people who use guns in crime rarely obtain them from a gun store. A government survey of state prison inmates in 2016 confirmed the pattern that has been documented in a number of other surveys of inmates and arrestees: Fewer than 10% of them reported that they obtained their last gun at a retail outlet (Table 3.2). Rather, they obtained their guns from family members, acquaintances, and connections through the underground economy—fences, drug dealers, and other "street" sources. Typically, these guns have changed hands a number of times.

In a sense, this pattern is evidence of success for the system established by the Brady Act and state permit systems. The list of GCA disqualifications does encompass most individuals who commit serious crimes (robbery, assault, and homicide) with guns. Although a disqualified buyer who was determined to buy from a retail outlet could try circumventing the background check by using fake identification or paying a qualified person to buy on their behalf (a "straw purchaser"), those ruses appear quite uncommon. Instead, offenders tend to avoid retail outlets, relying instead on personal connections and the vagaries of the underground market.

A realistic goal for policing the underground market is to reduce the proportion of a typical criminal career in which the offender is in possession of a gun. Criminal careers tend to be quite brief—by one estimate, an average of 5 years for those who begin committing crimes as youths.[38] Interviews with offenders suggest that those who are involved with guns may have several over the course of their career, with some gaps. For example, they may have acquired a gun but then decide to sell it to raise cash, ask a friend to hold it when they are under legal pressure, or lose the gun to confiscation by the police or to theft. The elapsed time between the acquisition of a particular gun and use of that gun in crime is typically a matter of weeks or months. Thus, although guns are highly durable, the high turnover and close link between transactions and use in crime focus attention on transactions (rather than possession) and the underground market in which those transactions take place.

## Availability

Effective policing of the underground market for guns is thus key to reducing the availability of guns to offenders. Of course, there are plenty of skeptics who believe that America has so many guns in circulation (currently estimated at more than 300 million) that it is a lost cause. Anyone—adolescent, gang member, spouse abuser—can surely get access to a gun.[39] Yet based on interviews with offenders, and analysis of crime patterns, that skeptical view is overstated. Inmate and arrestee surveys find that respondents who say they want a gun when they are released differ widely in their assessment of how much time and effort would be required to get one.[40] Direct evidence of gun scarcity derives from actual weapon choice in violent crime: Only approximately 40% of robberies known to police involve a gun, despite the evident advantage to the robber of using a gun rather than a knife or other weapon. (Gun robberies are much more likely to be successful, and are more

**Table 3.2** Sources of Guns to State Prisoners[a]

| Firearm Source | Count | % of All Responses | % of Useful Responses |
|---|---|---|---|
| Gun store, pawn shop | 86 | 9 | 10 |
| Flea market, gun show | 10 | 1 | 1 |
| Friend or family | 270 | 24 | 30 |
| Fence, street, drug dealer | 388 | 36 | 44 |
| Crime scene | 132 | 12 | 15 |
| Unspecified | 68 | 7 | — |
| Non-response | 117 | 11 | — |
| *Total* | 1,071 | 100 | 100 |

[a] The sample is restricted to prisoners aged 18 years or older who were incarcerated in state correctional facilities in the United States in 2016 and who indicated in the survey interview that they had a gun at the time of the offense. The sample is further restricted to those who had not been in prison prior to 2014.

Adapted from Bureau of Justice Statistics, *Survey of Prison Inmates, 2016* (Washington, DC: U.S. Department of Justice, March 2021), https://doi.org/10.3886/ICPSR37692.v2.

lucrative on average, than knife robberies.[41]) Furthermore, the geography of gun use in robbery reveals a close link with the prevalence of gun ownership, suggesting that guns are more readily available to robbers in, for example, Wyoming—where 60% of all households have at least one gun—than Hawaii, Massachusetts, or New Jersey, where gun ownership is only approximately 15%.[42]

To understand what "availability" means in the underground gun market, economics provides a useful construct—"transactions cost." The costs of a transaction can be both financial and in kind. In particular, the transactions cost of buying a gun at a retail outlet is just the money price of the preferred gun, in addition to any fees and time needed to acquire the necessary certification if the state requires a license or permit. On the other hand, the transactions cost of obtaining a gun in the underground or "informal" market may include the time and effort required to make a connection with someone who has a gun available, and the legal and personal risk of the transaction. So we can think of the transactions cost as "hassle plus money." Most every qualified buyer from a retail outlet faces the same hassle, which is usually minimal. But the hassle cost of informal transactions, and the money price for that matter, is highly variable. Search time and risk depend on who you know. For someone whose family, friends, and other social connections have guns or know how to get them, connecting with a gun may take very little time and have minimal legal or personal risk.[43] That would typically be true for a member of a gun-involved gang, whose members are well connected and may even share a stash of guns. But other offenders may not be so "lucky" in making a connection with an acceptable gun.

Here is a sampling of survey results:

- The 1996 and 1997 federal surveys of arrestees in 22 cities found that the typical pattern was diverse. In Chicago, for example, just 20% of respondents had owned a handgun, but one-fourth of the remainder expressed an interest in having a gun. Of those, 61% estimated that it would take them more than a week to make the connection.[44]
- The Chicago Inmate Survey of 221 gun-involved prison inmates from Chicago asked how long it took for them to obtain their most recent gun: 30% of respondents said less than a day, but 40% said it had taken more than a week.[45]
- A survey of 108 high-risk gun-involved adults in Brooklyn and the Bronx were asked how long it would take them to get a gun if needed: 37% of the gang members and 29% of the others said they could obtain a gun the same day, but the others said it would take longer than that.[46]

The police have some of the legal tools that they need to disrupt the transactions that arm violent felons, gang members, and others who are likely to misuse them, but it is challenging in practice. Most of these transactions (with the exception of theft) are consensual and hence have the same problem that law enforcement faces with illicit drugs, prostitution, or dog-fighting rings—there is no direct victim or natural complainant. Building a case generally requires undercover work or informants.

## Tracing and Trafficking

In rare cases, the local police may attempt to trace the chain of transactions involving a gun used in a serious crime in the hope of connecting it to the shooter. Police departments can trace guns through the services of the federal ATF National Tracing Center. Based on the make, model, and serial number of the gun, ATF attempts to follow it from entry into the chain of commerce (manufacture or import) to eventual first retail sale by a licensed dealer.[47] (The tracing process is successful in 75% of cases.) The retail dealer is then contacted to determine when and to whom the gun was first sold, which is information that should be in the dealer's records. ATF sometimes can identify the "last known" purchaser through firearm transfer databases in states that require citizens to report this information and via other secondary market sales information sources. Police investigators may then attempt to locate and interview that identified buyer in order to determine who got it next—and so on, through the chain until it reaches the final possessor. This is a daunting task, especially if the gun changed hands several times; the best bet to tracking down the offender this way is for relatively new guns.

Although only rarely helpful in solving specific crimes, ATF trace data do provide useful intelligence about patterns of activity in the underground market. In Chicago, for example, the Police Department recovers approximately 7,000 guns per year, in most cases from people who are carrying them illegally. From the trace results, we learn that the median age is more than 10 years and that a majority of them were first retailed in another state. Indiana and Wisconsin are especially common source states.[48] That fits a well-established pattern—that interstate movements of guns are closely linked to state regulations.[49] Illinois is an "importer" because it regulates gun transactions more stringently than nearby states. The tightly regulated states of the Northeast end up importing most of the guns that get used in crime from less regulated Southern states along the "iron pipeline," Interstate 95.

Recall that the GCA was intended to protect the states from each other by limiting mail-order shipments of guns to licensed dealers and restricting out-of-state purchasing. A North Carolina resident could buy a rifle or shotgun legally in, for example, Florida but would have to do so in person—and federal law would bar the person from buying a handgun legally outside of North Carolina. In any event, some portion of interstate gun movement is the result of systematic trafficking by people who bypass these restrictions. Most traffickers are small-time operators who supplement their income by occasionally picking up a few guns in a lax-control state and bringing them into New York or other cities in which guns are especially scarce and sell at a premium in the underground market.[50] ATF conducts investigations of interstate trafficking, often in conjunction with local police. A trafficker based in New York would technically be in violation of several federal regulations, such as operating a gun business without a license and knowingly selling to disqualified people. But there is no specific anti-trafficking statute, and prosecutors typically view trafficking cases as too minor to bother with unless a large number of guns are involved.

In addition to trafficking, there are a variety of potential enforcement targets if the goal is to increase transactions costs in the underground gun market. Two that are particularly prominent are straw purchases and theft. A straw purchase of a gun typically occurs when a qualified person acts on behalf of a disqualified person to buy a gun from a licensed retailer. For example, Cook was involved in a study of guns confiscated by the Chicago Police Department and found one indication of the scope of straw purchasing—for crime guns that were less than 2 years old, 15% had been first sold to a female but were recovered from a male.[51] The women in question, unlike the men, were able to buy guns from a licensed dealer because they lacked a serious criminal record and could obtain an Illinois Firearm Owners ID card. If they were buying a gun at the direct request of the man, then they are violating federal law, and in fact buyers sign a statement that among other things testifies that they are buying the gun for themselves:

> Are you the actual transferee/buyer of the firearm(s) listed on this form and any continuation sheet(s) (ATF Form 5300.9A)? Warning: You are not the actual transferee/buyer if you are acquiring the firearm(s) on behalf of another person. If you are not the actual transferee/buyer, the licensee cannot transfer the firearm(s) to you.

In practice, there are few successful criminal cases made against straw purchasers.

Another source of guns to offenders is theft. Various commentators, including scholars and police chiefs, have claimed that theft plays an outsized role with regard to supplying gangs and other violent criminals with guns.[52] The media routinely report gun thefts from dealers and shippers as a threat to public safety.[53] Frank Occhipinti, Deputy Chief of the Firearms Operations Division for the ATF, is quoted: "The impact of gun theft is quite clear. It is devastating our communities."[54] But whether theft is in fact an important conduit for supplying criminal use can be disputed.

That theft is closely linked to gun violence is entirely plausible. There are enough guns stolen every year (approximately 350,000) from homes, vehicles, and retailers to supply every gun robbery, assault, and murder.[55] All that would be required is for each stolen gun to be used in one or two crimes. But is there a direct pipeline by which stolen guns flow into the hands of violent criminals? When offenders are asked where they obtained their guns, fewer than 5% say that they stole them. When a gun used in crime is recovered by the police and checked against police records, it is rare to find that has been reported stolen. What happens to the bulk of stolen guns? Presumably the thieves are in it for the money and will want to sell to the highest bidder. That may turn out to be a violent gang or drug dealer, but it may also be an ordinary person with an eye for a bargain. In particular, it seems plausible that some stolen guns are disposed of through the same channels as stolen electronics or jewelry. Unfortunately, there is little systematic evidence on the extent to which those stolen guns do end up in the hands of violent criminals.

Better evidence on this issue would be helpful in directing law enforcement efforts. A place to start is a reporting requirement for gun theft. All licensees involved in gun commerce are required to report lost or stolen guns to ATF, which amount to approximately 20,000 per year. But the vast majority of gun thefts are from private residences and vehicles, not gun stores. For such thefts, only a dozen states have a reporting requirement. Still, it does appear that upwards of 75% of all gun thefts are reported to the police, no doubt motivated by the victim's hope of recovery or at least an insurance claim. But what happens after the theft? Are there fences or other middlemen who are playing an important role, and if so, how can they be shut down? And bottom line, how many of the guns used in crime have been stolen?

## Possession and Use

When the mob attacked the U.S. Capitol on January 6, 2021, it included members of paramilitary groups that were bent on forcefully stopping

Congress from certifying the presidential election. There is no doubt that members of these groups own guns, a fact that they flaunt in social media posts and in public. But although the insurrectionists at the U.S. Capitol were armed with a variety of makeshift weapons and injuring many officers, few of them actually carried guns that day. That surprising fact surely had the effect of saving many lives. A likely explanation is that gun carrying in the District of Columbia is subject to stringent regulation (with an outright ban on open carry), and the Capitol building and grounds are a gun-free zone. Anyone who had been spotted by law enforcement carrying a gun to the rally and march to the Capitol would have been subject to arrest.[56] It appears that in this case, the District's regulations on gun carrying were effective, and that they forestalled a still greater disaster.

Going back to the days of Dodge City and the wild (heavily armed) west of the 1880s, cities have regulated the place and manner of gun carrying and discharge.[57] Most states adopted stringent regulations on carrying, especially carrying concealed. As recently as the mid-1980s, all but a handful of states either banned concealed carry or required a license that was issued at the discretion of a law enforcement agency. Vermont was the only state that did not regulate gun carrying. But now, the legal landscape has been transformed. The National Rifle Association has been highly effective in getting the great majority of state legislatures to relax their regulations. Most states have now adopted preemption laws (banning local governments from imposing regulations that go beyond the state law) and have eased or erased restrictions on carrying concealed firearms. A parallel effort has been successful in easing restrictions on open carry. Vermont has become more the model than the exception, with 20 states deregulating gun carrying entirely (an idea that is marketed under the term "Constitutional carry") by 2021.[58] On another front, advocates have lobbied, often successfully, for the right to carry guns in public buildings and other areas that were formerly off limits. When a large group of individuals protesting COVID restrictions entered the Michigan legislative building in April 2020, they took advantage of their right to carry assault weapons and other firearms into the gallery overlooking the legislative session. Officers guarding the legislature were allowed by law to screen them for COVID symptoms but were required to ignore the guns.[59]

Thus, the traditional law enforcement goal of keeping private citizens from carrying guns on the street or other public places is now thwarted in many cities. But there are important exceptions—cities such as Washington, DC, New York, Boston, Chicago, and Los Angeles still place stringent limits on carrying, and patrolling against gun carrying in high-crime areas is a legal and productive tactic for gun violence prevention. Of course, gun advocates question these remaining regulations, asserting that armed citizens serve to prevent crime and that the liberalization of carrying laws has generally made the streets safer. The evidence on that issue has been the subject of an extensive debate among experts.[60] In our judgment, the weight of the evidence works against the "safer streets" claim and in support of the reverse—deregulating gun carrying increases violence.

## Disarming People Deemed Dangerous by the Courts

Although most states have relaxed or eliminated carrying restrictions, the trends in other regulatory domains are more mixed. In the 21st century, a number of "blue" states have acted to strengthen regulations on gun transactions, possession, and design. Even Vermont, famous for its laissez-faire approach to gun regulation, acted in 2018 to ban large-capacity magazines, raise the minimum age for gun purchase, and require background checks for all transactions, not just sales by licensed dealers. At the same time, it made provision for the police to seek an Extreme Risk Protection Order (ERPO; a "red flag law") for someone threatening violence to themself or others. In fact, ERPOs have been adopted in recent years in 20 states, including some that are (politically speaking) more red than blue. These laws provide a new tool for law enforcement.

Under the provisions of an ERPO, a judge can be petitioned to issue an emergency ex parte order requiring that an individual give up their guns on a temporary basis. The order may be reviewed and extended at a subsequent hearing in which the individual in question is allowed representation. In a majority of these states, the petition can be brought by family members as well as law enforcement officers. The laws have been touted as a way to forestall mass shootings because the shooters often signal their plans in advance. In practice, the process is more likely to be used to disarm suicidal individuals.[61]

Law enforcement may also take the lead in removing guns from dangerous people by following up on a felony indictment, conviction, or other action by a court that has the effect of disqualifying a gun owner. California leads the way in this respect with a database and enforcement program known as the Armed Prohibited Persons System, managed by the state's Department of Justice.[62] Recordkeeping requirements, and particularly the state requirement that all gun transactions be registered, make this enforcement system feasible. In thousands of cases each year, registered gun owners are disqualified by a criminal conviction, restraining order, or other court ruling. If they do not give up their guns voluntarily, the local police or even state agents may pay a visit to their homes and attempt to locate and confiscate the guns. In states that lack gun registration—which is to say, all but six—the potential scope for this sort of proactive policing effort is more limited.

## Conclusion

Federal regulations on guns place some restrictions on design, transactions, and possession. The goal is to keep guns away from a relatively small slice of the population while allowing the great majority of adults to have all the guns they want. Some states extend federal regulations, but without infringing on the Second Amendment right of the people to keep guns in their home. Those who are prohibited due to their criminal records or other conditions are unlikely to purchase from a licensed retail dealer. Rather, if they are determined to get a gun, they resort to off-the-books transactions with acquaintances or on the "street." Thus, for the most part, the guns used in crime have been diverted from the vast stock of guns kept by private individuals. The amount of time, effort, and expense required for an individual to obtain a gun (i.e., the transactions costs) from such informal sources depends on the individual's connections and, more generally, on the local prevalence of gun ownership. Where these transactions costs are high, assaults and robberies are less likely to involve guns.

Regulation and enforcement are not substitutes; rather, regulations can only be effective to the extent that they are enforced. Local or state agencies are responsible for issuing permits or licenses that are required for legal possession in some states, and the criminal justice system supplies much of the data utilized in conducting background checks. Local police, the federal ATF, and other law enforcement agencies can influence transactions costs through policing the various conduits by which guns are diverted to the underground market—including scofflaw dealers, theft, interstate trafficking, straw purchases, and other illegal exchanges. And increasingly, the police are called on to (temporarily) remove guns already in the possession of people deemed dangerous to themselves or others by petitioning a judge for an ERPO. In practice, the regulatory arena in which local police have been most active is enforcing restrictions on carrying guns on the street and in other public places—although that role has been limited in recent decades by the retreat of state regulation.

In these and other enforcement roles, much more could be done. We discuss programs and tactics in subsequent chapters. Enacting useful regulation is the beginning, not the end, of the process toward preempting gun violence.

# 4

# 21st-Century Policing and Crime Control

4:40 PM—Resident flags down a patrol car to advise officer that there is a body on a picnic table in a small park. The resident is not sure if the man on the table is dead. Police officer leaves patrol car to investigate. The motionless man is lying flat on his back with eyes wide open. His eyes are completely dried out, clothes are filthy, and there is a strong smell of urine, feces, and alcohol. Officer quickly determines that the man is alive but unresponsive; the officer suspects the man is dying from an overdose of fentanyl. Officer then calls EMTs to assist at the scene. A shot of Narcan is given to the man but he remains unresponsive. After a second shot, the man quickly gains consciousness. Officer asks the man basic health questions. Man is initially confused and agitated. He slowly calms down and tells officer that he is homeless and a dope addict. EMTs arrive and begin delivery of further medical assistance. Officer asks and receives additional Narcan from EMTs. Officer comments that he goes through multiple Narcan doses on most shifts.

5:10 PM—Officer responds to dispatched call of an emotionally-disturbed person. Upon arrival, five youth ranging from 9 to 14 years old tell responding officer that an upset teenaged girl was waving a knife in the air and yelling that she was going to kill someone. Three additional officers responded to the call. Officers located the teenaged girl in a park on the same block. From a distance of about ten feet, the officers ask her if she is armed. The teenager responded that she has a knife in her purse. They advise her to slowly place her purse on the ground and step away from the purse. The girl tells them that she needs help and might hurt someone if she doesn't get it. The officers ask if they can transport her to the hospital. She agrees. The officers then tell her that they will place handcuffs on her to ensure their and her safety while bringing her to the hospital. The girl

*Policing Gun Violence*. Anthony A. Braga and Philip J. Cook, Oxford University Press. © Oxford University Press 2023.
DOI: 10.1093/oso/9780199929283.003.0004

agrees to be handcuffed and is placed in the back of another patrol car without further incident.

5:25 PM—Officer responds to a "shots fired" call at a take-out restaurant. Multiple units arrive at the scene. Officer interviews store owner who explains that a delivery person was upset that his order was not ready. The man yelled and left the store. Soon after, there was a loud noise and the front window to the restaurant was smashed. A witness on the street said that there was no gunshot. Rather, the angry delivery man had kicked the window and fled the area.[1]

Policing enjoyed a renaissance beginning in the early 1990s. By that time, the police and the nation had come through the dark ages of high crime rates that had lasted an entire generation and culminated with the unprecedented criminal violence of the crack cocaine era. Police chiefs excused their failure to provide public safety by adopting the view, popular with criminologists of that time, that the police actually had very little influence on crime rates because crime was the product of social conditions. Prominent commentators asserted that serious violence would continue to escalate due to the growing cohorts of "superpredators."[2] Yet as we know, what actually happened, beginning in 1993, was the Great Crime Drop. Homicide and robbery rates in every large city fell dramatically and were about half their former peak level by 2014. Although no one can claim to have a full explanation for this miracle, it does appear that the police get a sizable share of the credit.[3] City councils voted to grow police budgets, augmented by federal grants, and additional resources were put to work in innovative ways for the purpose of controlling crime.

The best known and most influential innovator was William Bratton. As Commissioner of the New York Police Department (NYPD), starting in 1994, he reversed the defeatist narrative, saying that the police should be held accountable for controlling crime—and setting out to implement accountability with his command staff. As chief of the NYPD, then the Los Angeles PD, and again NYPD, he presided over a reduction in crime rates. He developed initiatives that incorporated big ideas about crime coupled with strategic thinking about how best to use the forces at his command. Although the crime reduction impacts of certain initiatives remain unclear, the experimental approach and clear focus on public safety paid dividends. Other departments and chiefs have followed suit.

Although it remains contentious, the claim that the police can and do prevent crime now has a firm foundation. As a general rule, it appears that providing a police department with additional resources will support a reduction in serious crime that is sufficient to more than compensate taxpayers.[4] The most comprehensive evidence derives from analysis of more than 200 cities over the course of 38 years. Expansion in the number of sworn officers is consistently linked to a reduction in serious crime, including, most important, homicide. That result is found whether the variation is due to local budget decisions or federal grants.[5] The value of the lives saved, by the usual measures, exceeds the budgeted cost. Apparently, police chiefs have a pretty good idea of what to do with additional resources if given the chance.

Note that the cost of policing is not limited to budgeted expenditures. Police operations can be experienced as an imposition on the community that has high crime rates and is hence subject to relatively high rates of surveillance and arrest. Most prominently, NYPD efforts to halt offenders from carrying guns illegally, which involved a large volume of contacts that took the form of "stop, question, and frisk," was ultimate discontinued because it did become an unacceptable (and possibly unconstitutional) imposition on the daily activities of those most likely to be targeted—youthful minority males.[6] In any event, it is reassuring that expansion in police employment, while tending to reduce serious crime, does not increase the number of arrests for serious crimes.[7]

The policy goal is to make the police more cost-efficient in controlling crime but also to control serious crime without producing unintended harm or unnecessary imposition on the freedoms of individual citizens. Most important is to curtail excessive use of force by the police. Effective policing does not require harsh tactics.

## The Growth of Police Resources and Employment

The resources going to the police have grown in lockstep with state and local budgets. Year in and year out, the total expenditures, at least since the late 1970s, have been slightly less that 4% of total direct expenditures.[8] That figure is substantially less than for education, welfare, medical care, and transportation but more than for corrections and parks. The substantial growth in state and local budgets has allowed police budgets to grow without displacing other expenditures. The result has been some growth in police employment and in salaries, which has been important in attracting better educated officers.

American policing is provided by thousands of distinct agencies, albeit with somewhat overlapping jurisdictions. In 2016, the most recent year of data available from the U.S. Bureau of Justice Statistics, there were 15,328 general-purpose law enforcement agencies in the United States.[9] This figure includes 12,267 local police departments, 3,102 sheriff's offices, and 49 primary state police departments. Local police departments employed 468,000 full-time sworn officers, and sheriff's offices employed 173,000 full-time sworn officers. Most local police departments are small; three-fourths of them have fewer than 25 full-time officers. Three percent of all local police departments serve populations of 100,000 or more, and they employ approximately half of all full-time sworn police officers.

Have police forces grown or declined in recent decades? The answer is that they have declined relative to population, but increased relative to crime. The number of full-time sworn officers for all state and local law enforcement agencies increased by 26% from 555,000 in 1987 to 701,000 in 2016.[10] General population growth surpassed the increased number of officers, resulting in a nearly 12% *decrease* in the number of officers per capita between 1987 and 2016. However, given an overall decline in Part I index crimes since the mid-1990s, the number of officers per serious crime almost doubled from 41.1 per 1,000 Part 1 crimes in 1987 to 76.5 in 2016.

By any measure, spending on police departments has increased during the past four decades. State and local governments doubled their inflation-adjusted per capita expenditures on police between 1977 and 2018, a year when spending totaled $119 billion—approximately $1,000 per household.[11] As noted above, police expenditures represent only a small share of total state and local government spending, hovering at roughly 4% of total expenditures between 1977 and 2018.

That $1,000 per household supports a wide range of activities. A big city police department has responsibility for responding to citizens' calls and investigating crimes, but it is also responsible for school safety, traffic control, counterterrorism, community outreach, public transit and housing safety, crowd control, protection of dignitaries, and much else. A 2020 *New York Times* analysis of officer time spent on various tasks over the course of a shift in three police departments showed that 60% of the shift was consumed handling noncriminal calls for service, traffic, and medical emergencies (Figure 4.1).[12] Only 4% of the shift involved responding to violent crimes. The remainder of their time involved proactive activities and dealing with property and other kinds of crimes.

Police employment has become more diverse over time, and as of 2016 (the most recent comprehensive data), the representation of Blacks among sworn

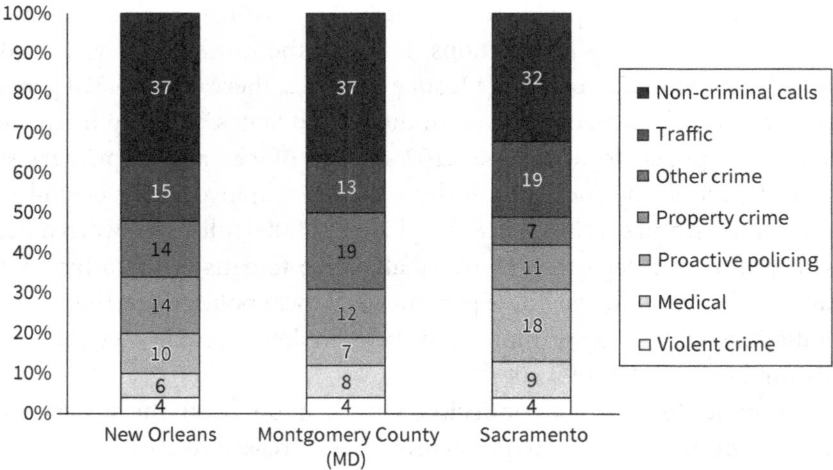


**Figure 4.1** How police time is spent across three U.S. police departments. Incident categories may not be directly comparable due to measurement differences among the three police departments.

*Source*: Adapted from Jeff Asher and Ben Horwitz, "How Do the Police Actually Spend Their Time?" *The New York Times*, June 19, 2020, https://www.nytimes.com/2020/06/19/upshot/unrest-police-time-violent-crime.html.

officers was close to proportional: 12% of officers were Black, compared to 13% of the U.S. population. Both Black and Hispanic employment has grown rapidly during the past few decades. The proportion of officers who are female is also growing, but women still represent a small minority (12%). Minority representation on local police departments differs considerably by geography and agency size; rural areas and smaller departments tend to be composed mostly of White officers. Large urban police departments have much greater shares of minority officers, with some police departments becoming "majority minority." For instance, in 2021, the Los Angeles Police Department reported its 9,799 sworn police officers were 50% Hispanic, 29.5% White, 9.5% Black, 8% Asian, and 3% other races.[13] Big city police departments are now commonly led by minority chiefs.[14] In 2021, 46% of the chiefs leading police departments in the 50 largest U.S. cities were Black and another 16% were Hispanic. Female chiefs are still unusual, leading just 4 of the top 50 departments.

Police officers have also become better educated. Whereas just 3% of officers had a bachelor's degree in 1960, the current figure is approximately one-third.[15] Most others have a 2-year degree.[16] One advantage of hiring college-educated officers is that they tend to have fewer complaints and disciplinary actions against them.[17] Police departments extend their recruits' education by providing academy training, field training programs following academy graduation, and, consistent with state requirements, regular in-service training for officers. Beyond meeting minimum state training requirements, a 2017 Police Foundation survey further revealed that some police departments provide their officers with training on additional topics such as handling mental health crisis situations, ensuring procedurally just encounters with citizens, understanding community policing principles, and avoiding implicit bias in their decision-making.

## Traditional Mechanisms for Crime Prevention

The most prominent mechanism that links policing to crime rates is deterrence through detection, apprehension, and subsequent punishment by the courts. It is an ancient idea that the threat of punishment, if credible, will reduce crime. Faced with the temptation to commit a criminal offense, whether shoplifting or settling an argument by drawing a gun, some individuals will desist for fear of legal consequences. The greater the likelihood, and perceived likelihood, of an arrest, the greater the influence of this threat with potential offenders.

Most of us are not tempted to rob a gas station or join a group of guys in shooting up a rival group's street corner. But for those who are, the calculation of likely legal consequences may be relevant. The perception of whether arrest is a credible outcome may depend on personal experience or knowledge of what happens to other offenders in the neighborhood. Police visibility matters, as does the perception of how capable and concerned the police are in practice. Although most of us have had the experience of making calculations of this sort in deciding whether to drive over the speed limit, or even whether to carry a gun without the necessary permit, we may have trouble projecting ourselves into decisions involving serious criminal violence. But the evidence is clear that many violent offenders are the same as the rest of us in their desire to avoid arrest.

For serious crime, a second crime prevention mechanism may be of great importance—incapacitation. If an arrest is followed by conviction and imprisonment or other restriction on freedom, the offender is physically prevented from committing crimes. Of course, most jail and prison terms lead to release after a few months or years, but for that period at least, the crime rate is lower—assuming the offender is not "replaced" on the street. (Fortunately, criminal violence tends to be a young man's offense, and offenders may age out while incarcerated.) Active shooters are relatively rare, even in the most violent communities, and if well targeted, prison terms can make a substantial difference in rates of gun violence.

Note that there is some confusion about use of the word "prevention" in this context. Incarceration "prevents" subsequent crime, as does the credible possibility of arrest and imprisonment. Especially in public health circles, there is a tendency to degrade arrest and punishment because it is "reactive"—unlike interventions that are intended to attack the basic causes of violence. But the main point of incarceration as a punishment is that it prevents subsequent crime, just as might a summer jobs program. The main question is not whether the intervention is linked to a particular crime or not but whether it results in fewer crimes subsequently.

## Strategic Thinking About Deterring Violent Crime

The key to enhancing public safety through the deterrent effect is to communicate a credible threat of arrest and punishment to those who may be tempted to commit serious crimes. The police have limited resources, and of course they have a variety of responsibilities in addition to combatting crime. The question is how to allocate and direct available resources so as to enhance potential offenders' perception—and the reality—that serious crime will be followed by legal punishment. This strategic issue has spawned a variety of programs that have become familiar in policing circles. In every case, these programs concentrate force. We tell some of the story of these innovations in subsequent chapters, but can summarize it here.

In the prevention of serious violent crime, which is thankfully a rare event, it is possible to concentrate police force against a precursor activity such as gun carrying, at places known to have high concentrations of violence (hot spots), or on individuals and groups known to be at highest risk—practices known as focused deterrence or precision policing.[18] In each case, the police are not simply reacting to 911 calls and investigating crimes but are rather taking the initiative.

Another opportunity to concentrate police resources is in the investigation of crime. The police need to solve a substantial percentage of serious crimes if the threat of arrest is to be credible. The technology of investigating gun violence and other serious crimes has come a long way during the last generation. Big-city investigations of shootings can often garner video evidence (given the increasing ubiquity of video cameras), find links between shootings based on ballistics information from shell casings, scan social media for postings by suspects who may be bragging about their latest shootout, obtain DNA evidence from the crime scene, and so forth.[19] The question here is how much of the police budget to allocate to investigations, as opposed to other activities.

But even in this high-tech era, the police greatly rely on civilians to report crime and provide evidence in investigations. It has long been understood that crime control is co-produced by law enforcement working with the public—much as education is co-produced by schools working with students and their parents. Investigations are facilitated by a trusting relationship with the relevant community, and lack of cooperation may be the greatest obstacle to success, particularly with gun violence, which primarily burdens communities that have a contentious relationship with the police. In part in the hopes of improving that relationship, police chiefs have embraced "community policing" and, more recently, "procedural justice."

We turn next to a brief history of how these ideas developed and have played out over time.

## Evolution of Police Crime Control Strategy

The modern era could be dated to the advent of the professional model of policing. That model was a reform of the deplorable policing practices before the 1930s during the so-called political era. Corruption, widespread abuse of authority, scandals, and a lack of professional standards were pervasive problems. Criminologists such as August Vollmer—the reform-minded chief in Berkeley, California, from 1905 to 1932—and O. W. Wilson—Chicago police chief in the post-World War II period—were pivotal figures in the development of "professional," also known as "reform," policing. The professional model emphasized military discipline and structure, higher education for police officers, adoption of professional standards by police agencies, separation of the police from political influence, and adoption of technological innovations ranging from strategic management techniques to scientific advances such as two-way radios and fingerprinting.

The more rigorous standards and professionalism of the reform model helped establish police work as a respectable profession. During the post-World War II period, the police role as "crime fighter" was solidified.[20] The main strategic elements were preventive patrol, rapid response to crime, and investigation of more serious cases by specialized detective units. All three elements remain in place today.

The success in reforming the police stumbled in the face of escalating crime and civil unrest of the Vietnam War era. High rates of crime lasted an entire generation, culminating in the crack-era epidemic in youth violence.[21] The general consensus among many academics at the beginning of the 1990s was that the police did not matter in crime prevention and control. Respected criminologists Michael Gottfredson and Travis Hirschi reviewed the available research and concluded, "No evidence exists that augmentation of patrol forces or equipment, differential patrol strategies, or differential intensities of surveillance have an effect on crime rates."[22] Police scholar David Bayley more definitively stated,

> The police do not prevent crime. This is one of the best kept secrets of modern life. Experts know it, the police know it, but the public does not know it. Yet the police pretend that they are society's best defense against crime. . . . This is a myth.[23]

Some demoralized police leaders agreed with the view that police could not produce meaningful impacts on crime, and indeed welcomed the chance to duck responsibility.[24] But others did not buy it.

Most famously, former Boston, New York, and Los Angeles Police Commissioner William Bratton, a highly influential police executive who believed that the police could and should play a powerful role in managing crime and disorder problems, accepted responsibility beginning with his first stint in New York. He later summed it up as follows:

> Crime, the theory went, was caused by societal problems that were impervious to police intervention. That was the unchallenged conventional wisdom espoused by academics, sociologists, and criminologists. I intended to prove them wrong. Crime, and as important, attitudes about crime, could be turned around.[25]

Research and practical experience would eventually prove that he was right.

## Police Innovation and Declining Crime Rates

The 1990s became an unprecedented period of police innovation. Police departments experimented with and adopted a wide range of complementary crime prevention strategies, such as problem-oriented policing, focused deterrence, disorder policing, and hot spots policing.[26] New York City served as a high-profile example of what could be accomplished by a police department when properly supported and focused on crime control. In 1994, then NYPD Commissioner Bratton increased the number of police officers in the department to 38,000 and set out to "win the war against crime" by taking five key steps:[27] (a) empowering precinct commanders to develop creative prevention strategies tailored to local crime and disorder problems, (b) holding commanders accountable for local crime rates through ongoing measurement and strategy guidance sessions, (c) addressing disorderly conditions that gave rise to more serious crime problems, (d) analyzing crime patterns to focus police resources on hot spots and high-rate offenders, and (e) maintaining adequate numbers of officers to deal with crime by rewarding them with appropriate wages and recognition for good crime prevention work. These innovations coincided with a remarkable drop in murder and other violence. Murders were down by half by 1996. Over the course of the decade, New York City murders dropped by approximately 70% from 2,245 in 1990 to 673 in 2000. The murder decline continued through the 2000s and 2010s.

Bratton's system for holding his commanders accountable was a management information system called CompStat;[28] it was ultimately adopted in some form by most major police departments in the United States.[29] CompStat is an important administrative innovation that provides mid-level managers the data needed to identify crime trends and problems in the geographic areas (precincts and districts) they command and also a clear way of measuring their performance. In turn, these mid-level managers provide motivation and direction to line-level supervisors and officers working the street.

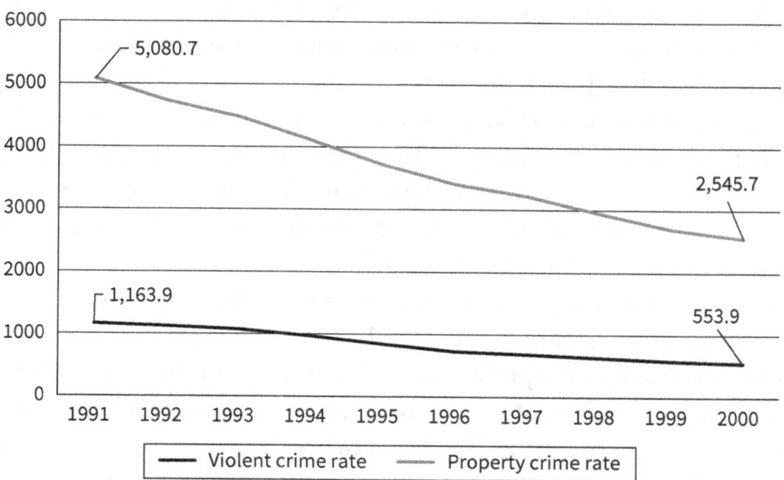


**Figure 4.2** Violent and property crime in New York City, 1991–2000. Crime rates were calculated per 100,000 residents.

*Source*: Uniform Crime Report (UCR) data for 1991–2000 were obtained from annual *Crime in the United States* reports and from the Federal Bureau of Investigation's UCR website at http://www.fbi.gov/about-us/cjis/ucr/ucr (accessed August 12, 2021).

New York City was among many cities that appeared to benefit from improved policing. After decades of increasing crime rates, the United States experienced a surprising crime drop during the 1990s. According to Uniform Crime Report data, violent crime decreased by one-third between 1991 (the decade high point) and 2000, and property crime decreased by a similar proportion (Figure 4.2).[30] Policymakers, academics, and journalists attempted to sort out the various explanations for the crime decrease, such as a strong economy, improved policing, high imprisonment rates, stabilizing crack markets, immigration, new gun policies, and demographic shifts.[31] A careful read of the available scientific evidence suggests that no single factor can be invoked as the cause of the 1990s crime decline. Although it is difficult to specify its exact contribution, improved policing is commonly credited as being among the influential factors in the 1990s crime drop.[32] Increased resources going to the police and innovative policing programs, many of which were developed and popularized during the 1990s, combined to make a difference. Here, we briefly review the available evidence on major police innovations from the 1980s and 1990s.

Community policing was one of the first new approaches to policing to emerge in this period of police innovation. At the outset, community policing did not equate success with crime reduction,[33] but this approach did create a useful mindset, acknowledging the close interdependence of the police with the communities they serve. Any observed crime prevention impacts are more directly associated with specific strategic interventions. For example, analysis of persistent local crime problems may suggest an intervention that would permanently reduce the opportunity for crime in a particular hot spot—better lighting, enforcement of liquor laws, redirecting traffic, or keeping rival gangs separate on school transportation. The possibility here is for the police to cooperate with other community and public institutions to help improve public safety.[34] The problem-oriented policing approach has had some documented success in reducing crime and disorder.[35]

Problem-oriented policing advanced a new mechanism through which police could achieve crime reductions.[36] The approach challenges police officers to identify specific crime problems, analyze their underlying conditions, implement responses to the situations that give rise to crime problems, and assess the impact of these responses. The key idea here is to reduce crime opportunities rather than simply deterring and incapacitating offenders. Several specific police innovations seek to limit the opportunities for crime.

In New York, one of Bratton's big ideas was grounded in a particular notion of how the community environment influenced serious crime, poetically known as "fixing broken windows."[37] A neighborhood with unkempt vacant lots and abandoned houses, with homeless people panhandling and relieving themselves in public, and other indications of neglect and disorder invited more serious criminal activity. In this view, "quality of life" offenses and other misdemeanors contributed to an environment that degraded the neighborhood and ultimately produced violent crime. For a while, the NYPD answer could be characterized as zero tolerance policing, where patrol officers were instructed to make arrests for misdemeanors that they otherwise would have ignored. That particular response to "broken windows" was ultimately discontinued as excessively costly and ineffective. But the basic idea has merit and has become a central element of crime prevention strategies adopted by many American police departments.

Disorder policing strategies can generate crime control gains.[38] Redressing social and physical disorder is foundational to reducing more serious crimes in neighborhoods. However, the types of strategies used by police departments to control disorder matter.[39] Aggressive order maintenance strategies that target individual disorderly behaviors do not seem to generate crime reductions. In contrast, community problem-solving approaches designed to change social and physical disorder conditions at particular places produce significant crime reductions. For example, a remarkable large-scale experiment in Philadelphia demonstrated that clearing and beautifying vacant lots had a measureable effect on local rates of gun violence.[40]

The theme of concentrating deployments has played a major role in modern police strategy. Crime is not evenly distributed across cities; rather, it is concentrated in very small places, known as crime hot spots, that persistently generate a disproportionate share of serious crime.[41] Police have traditionally defined their units of operation in terms of large areas, such as police precincts and beats. In hot spots policing, place refers to a much smaller level of geographic aggregation than has traditionally interested police executives and planners—namely specific buildings, addresses, block faces, or street segments. Police departments can usefully concentrate resources in these small high-crime locations, and a majority of U.S. police departments have adopted this strategy.[42]

Hot spots policing programs generate significant reductions in crime and disorder without simply displacing crime into nearby areas.[43] In fact, the best evidence suggests that hot spots policing programs tend to generate "spillover" crime prevention effects in surrounding areas that do not receive focused police attention. Moreover, problem-oriented policing strategies designed to change underlying conditions at crime hot spots generate stronger crime control gains relative to programs that simply increase traditional police activities, such as patrol, in crime hot spots.[44]

While targeting particular places has become more refined in police work, so have methods for targeting particular individuals and groups who are known to account for a large share of serious crime. The focused deterrence approach, often referred to as "pulling-levers policing," has been particularly prominent and successful.[45] Pioneered in Boston as a problem-oriented policing project to halt serious gang violence during the 1990s,[46] the focused deterrence framework has been applied in many U.S. cities through federally sponsored violence prevention programs such as the Strategic Alternatives to Community Safety Initiative and Project Safe Neighborhoods. Focused deterrence strategies honor core deterrence ideas, such as increasing the likelihood that offenders will be convicted and punished, while finding new and creative ways of deploying innovative methods "market" this change, such as direct "retail" communication with targeted offenders.

In its simplest form, the focused deterrence approach has six components:

selecting a particular crime problem, such as gang homicide;

convening an interagency working group of law enforcement, social service, and community-based practitioners;

conducting research to identify key offenders, groups, and behavior patterns;

framing a response to offenders and groups of offenders that uses a varied menu of sanctions ("pulling levers") to stop them from continuing their violent behavior;

focusing social services and community resources on targeted offenders and groups to match law enforcement prevention efforts; and

directly and repeatedly communicating with offenders to make them understand why they are receiving this special attention.[47]

These strategic approaches have been applied to a range of crime problems, such as outdoor drug markets and individual repeat offenders. The ultimate targets of focused deterrence strategies are to the perceived costs and benefits of criminal activity, as well as the pro-violence norms and dynamics that drive offending and victimization for high-risk individuals. Focused deterrence strategies are associated with significant reductions in targeted crime problems, particularly gang homicide.[48]

Technical advances in policing have contributed to enforcement capacity during the past few decades.[49] New technology has not developed in a vacuum but, rather adopted to the persistent challenges of crime control and police legitimacy. Crime mapping, license plate reader technologies, and body cameras are prominent examples. Other technical advances have improved the capacity of police departments to solve crimes. The impressive list includes DNA testing, automated fingerprint identification systems, mobile phone data analysis, acoustic gunshot detection systems, and ballistic imaging systems. Cameras are pervasive in today's society, and police now commonly use enhanced video capture and analysis to identify and apprehend suspects.

Police departments continued to develop more refined data analysis techniques to guide the concentration of resources. For example, "predictive policing," utilizes algorithms based on combining different types of data to anticipate where and when crime might occur based on patterns identified in past criminal incidents.[50] Although somewhat similar to hot spots policing, predictive policing is generally distinguished by the application of sophisticated analytics to predict likelihood of crime incidence within very specific parameters of space and time and for specific types of crime.[51]

This period of rapid police innovation was also characterized by an increased willingness of police departments to partner with academics to understand crime problems, develop new crime prevention responses, and evaluate these strategies. Many of the police innovations described here flowed from particularly close partnerships between progressive police leaders and academics. Most famously, William Bratton and the late criminologist George Kelling collaborated on developing department-wide commitments to disorder policing to control crime in New York City and then Los Angeles. Wes Skogan, a Northwestern University professor, worked closely with Chicago Police Department leadership to implement community and problem-oriented policing in all city neighborhoods. Academic criminologists Larry Sherman and David Weisburd worked with multiple police chiefs to launch a series of hot spots policing experiments in Minneapolis, Kansas City, Jersey City, and elsewhere. These research–practitioner partnerships not only improved the capacity of individual police departments to control crime but also were essential in developing new knowledge on effective crime prevention practices for the entire police profession.

## Unintended Harms, Legitimacy Crises, and the Move Toward 21st-Century Policing

Surveys of police departments indicate that innovative crime reduction strategies are now common in the United States. For instance, the 2016 Bureau of Justice Statistics Law Enforcement Management and Administrative Statistics survey reported that 87% of local police departments serving 100,000 or more residents had personnel dedicated to community policing programs.[52] A 2012 Police Executive Research Forum survey of 200 police departments, mostly larger and more progressive agencies from its membership, found strong adoption of community policing (94%), problem-oriented policing (89%), hot spots policing (80%), and targeting known offenders (79%). These surveys suggest a meaningful shift in police strategy to control crime.[53]

We do not want to paint too rosy a picture here. Police departments and their officers are often resistant to change. In some cases the change may be more cosmetic than substantive. The routine activities of line officers may change less than suggested by the new program terminology.[54] A department may adopt problem-oriented policing, but actual practice at the street level may remain little changed if there is inadequate supervision and training.[55]

It is also true that the major innovations in policing sometimes conflict with each other. Most notably, William Bratton's embrace of broken windows policing and adoption of stop-and-frisk to get guns off the streets was sometimes at odds with community policing. Ray Kelly's subsequent expansion of stop-and-frisk and zero-tolerance policing was antithetical to community policing and, for a few years, had considerable influence in policing circles.

Other critics noted what seemed to be a slow drift of the police profession away from community problem-solving models of policing popularized during the 1980s and 1990s and toward more aggressive enforcement strategies, such as making large numbers of stops and frisks of citizens and pursuing order maintenance through heightened numbers of misdemeanor arrests. One-dimensional and overly broad police surveillance and enforcement strategies do little to change the underlying dynamics that drive serious urban violence. Indiscriminate police enforcement actions also contribute to racial disparity and mass incarceration problems that harm disadvantaged neighborhoods.[56] This is particularly true when such an approach is coupled with a "crime numbers game" managerial mindset that promotes yearly increases in arrest, summons, and investigatory stop actions as key performance measures (especially in CompStat settings).[57]

Implementing change in police departments has been likened to "bending granite."[58] It is unclear why police departments are so resistant to change. Some innovations, such as CompStat, have been suggested to reinforce traditional police management structures and encourage enforcement actions rather than problem-solving.[59] Police unions have often been identified as obstacles to change.[60] In his work with police departments, Braga can confirm this possibility. For instance, the Boston PD union filed a grievance in response to the adoption of a hot-spots-policing innovation. The innovation required that patrol officers adapt their work hours to shifting crime patterns. Then-Police Commissioner Edward Davis asked Braga to meet with the head of the patrol officers' union to explain the program. After Braga explained the rationale, the union head said, "Hey professor, I get what you're saying . . . and I understand how this can reduce crime . . . but this is an opportunity to get the bosses to the bargaining table and get more perks for my membership." The hot spots policing officers had to wait until this "change of work conditions" issue was settled before being allowed to pursue a commonsense adjustment to keep the community safe.

Although the on-the-ground evidence suggests that the implementation of crime reduction innovations in many police departments leaves much to be desired, the unprecedented period of innovation in the 1990s produced a meaningful shift in at least three areas: (a) Police now take responsibility for crime control, (b) data analyses are commonly used to inform strategy, and (c) community needs are taken more seriously by police leaders. Certainly, there is ample room for improvement as the past decade has painfully illustrated.

## Heightened Tensions with Minority Communities

Long-simmering police–minority community tensions were exacerbated in the early 2010s by a string of police killings of unarmed Black men in cities such as Ferguson, Missouri; Baltimore, Maryland; North Charleston, South Carolina; and New York City. The Black Lives Matter political and social movement emerged in 2013 and gained further attention after the 2020 death of George Floyd at the hands of Minneapolis Police Department officers. Reminiscent of the conflicts between minority communities and the police in the 1960s, a wave of very large, and sometimes violent, Black Lives Matter protests decried unfair police treatment and persistent police violence. Protestors demanded various police reforms, including more lawful policing, expanding body-worn camera programs, and "defunding" police budgets to move funds away from the police and toward alternative approaches to crime prevention.

It is against this backdrop of renewed police–community tensions that procedural justice policing came into prominence in the United States.[61] Like community policing, this approach did not emerge as an innovation focused primarily on crime control. Rather, it is a response to a crisis in the relationship of the police to the public. But the reasoning behind, procedural justice policing does offer hope that it can enhance crime control. Indeed, some of its advocates have argued that it will in the long term yield stronger crime prevention gains than more traditional innovations that focus directly on crime control.[62] It is worth noting that the crime control effects of procedural justice have not yet been well established.[63] However, a randomized experiment with 120 hot spots in three cities found promising results from training officers in procedural justice methods. The "treated" hot spots had a 14% reduction in crime incidents and a large reduction in arrests.[64]

This approach, like community policing, is in part motivated by the belief that the police cannot succeed in their efforts to control crime without the support of the public. Procedural justice policing is concerned with how the police interact with citizens in everyday encounters,[65] but it does not seek to define new strategic tactics of crime control. It does, however, seek to alter the relationships between the police and the public. In this policing model, changes in how police behave in encounters with citizens have the potential to alter not only the perceptions of the police of those directly affected but also, through them, the community's perceptions of police legitimacy. With a change in such perceptions, they expect that individuals will be more willing to comply with police authority and that they will cooperate more with the police by reporting crime and collaborating with the police in crime prevention. This police innovation, although a product more of recent crises between the police and the public, also responds directly to the crisis of police legitimacy that helped spur police innovation four decades ago.

In 2014, former President Barack Obama established the Task Force on 21st Century Policing and charged the task force with identifying best practices and offering recommendations on how policing practices can promote effective crime reduction while building public trust. In its 2015 report, the task force made a series of recommendations, each with action items, that were organized around six main topic areas or "pillars": building trust and legitimacy, policy and oversight, technology and social media, community policing and crime reduction, officer training and education, and officer safety and wellness.[66]

As suggested by the Task Force, police strategies that violate civil rights, compromise police legitimacy, or undermine trust are counterproductive. This belief is precisely why they recommended that law enforcement agencies develop and adopt policies and strategies that reinforce the importance of community engagement in managing public safety. Developing close relationships with community members would help the police gather information about crime and disorder problems, understand the nature of these problems, and solve specific crimes. Community members can also help with key components of strategies tailored to specific problems by making improvements to the physical environment and through informal social control of high-risk people.

Community engagement in developing appropriately focused strategies would help safeguard against indiscriminate and overly aggressive enforcement tactics and other inappropriate policing activities, which in turn erode the community's trust and confidence in the police and inhibit cooperation. Collaborative partnerships between police and community members improve the transparency of law enforcement actions and provide residents with a much-needed voice in crime prevention work. Ongoing conversations with the community can ensure that day-to-day police–citizen interactions are conducted in a procedurally just manner that enhances community trust and compliance with the law.

## Conclusion

Policing has evolved during the past few decades in a variety of ways. The police have become less corrupt, better educated, more professional, better paid, and far more diverse with respect to race and sex. They have by and large become more respectful of citizen rights, due to exclusionary rules, felony review, citizen review boards, consent decrees, and other accountability measures. Excessive use of force remains a real problem, but the reality of greater restraint clashes with the vast increase in visibility due to the ease of video recording.

What remains true today is that police have a unique role in crime prevention, and the prevention of gun violence in particular. The traditional role of investigating gun crime, arresting suspects, and building cases that will hold up in court is sometimes dismissed as "reactive," although its main purpose (and effect) is to prevent future crime. The relevant mechanisms include deterrence and incapacitation, but also interruption of retaliatory cycles. The police also engage in proactive efforts to gather intelligence on gangs and dangerous criminals, communicate the threat of legal consequences as effectively as possible, and disrupt what might be thought of as "precursor" activities—for example, stopping a stolen vehicle with armed gang members on the way to a drive-by shooting or breaking up a street corner drug-dealing operation. Much of the proactive work is not focused specifically on gun crime but includes a general effort to reduce crime and violence through helping solve neighborhood problems that generate "hot spots" of crime.

There is every reason to think that the police are more effective in crime control than they were even a generation ago due to improved technology, greater resources, and better strategies. But there remain some generic challenges:

1. Crime control is a co-production process, and civilian cooperation in reporting crimes and providing evidence is vital. Distrust of police by the communities most affected by gun violence, together with the "no snitching" culture and fear of retaliation, impairs investigations. Police work would benefit from improved community relations, but it is not clear how to achieve that. "Community policing" and "procedural justice" provide some guidance in that respect.
2. There are instances of conflicting values that must be resolved. Potentially effective proactive police tactics may be experienced as an imposition on individual freedom of movement and action. Chapter 5 tells the story of stop, question, and frisk in New York City.
3. The police are "street-level bureaucrats" who need motivation and direction. CompStat was an effort to focus the police on crime control, but motivation remains a continuing challenge, which is made more difficult by union restrictions.
4. Police work has benefitted and been transformed by technological change. The modern police department is fully engaged with social media. Cameras are everywhere. Acoustic gunshot detection and ballistics imaging systems facilitate investigation of gun violence. These innovations are complementary to improved education and training. But there is more to be done to figure out how to make these inputs as effective as possible.

# 5

# Targeted Patrol and Problem-Solving in Hot Spots

Bullets fly all over New York City—cops count a 92% increase in shootings this year—and in the worst-hit area of all, Marvada Barthelemy raises the son of one of the dead and wonders why no one can stop the carnage. "There is nothing we can do," said Barthelemy, 40, an Amazon warehouse worker who lives in the Howard Houses in Brooklyn, scene of four shooting murders so far this year, more than any other city housing project. Barthelemy's boyfriend, Jamal Windley, 47, was shot June 22 in one of the East New York project's courtyards. The shooting and the shooter were captured on video—but so far, cops have not made any arrests.

Howard Houses has 10 tall red-brick buildings set among grass lawns and trees typical of New York City Housing Authority projects of its era. When it opened in 1955, a Daily News writer hailed Howard Houses as one of three NYCHA projects "rising out of what was once the worst slum area in Brooklyn," which had been dominated by the infamous Italian and Jewish "Murder Inc." gangsters.

Gang violence reigns again in the old neighborhood. "It's public housing at its worst," a veteran NYPD Housing Bureau officer said of the Howard Houses. "There are remnants of drug use in the hallways and stairwells—blood splatter, needles, broken glass," said the officer, who asked that his name not be used. Howard Houses is thick with members of the Bloods gang, the veteran cop said. It's not easy for the officers to keep up with the shootings. "Every day, it seems like the FIOs (Field Intelligence Officers) are handing out wanted posters for new shootings to cops who are demoralized and burnt out, and expecting them to run out and catch these guys," said the officer. Howard Houses' four homicides lead NYCHA projects in the city, NYPD data shows (*New York Daily News*, October 25, 2020).[1]

*Policing Gun Violence*. Anthony A. Braga and Philip J. Cook, Oxford University Press. © Oxford University Press 2023.
DOI: 10.1093/oso/9780199929283.003.0005

Gun violence is not evenly spread throughout cities. Particular neighborhoods experience elevated levels of shootings, and specific public places within those neighborhoods, such as the Howard Houses, can be persistent and very dangerous gun violence "hot spots." These repeated shootings are often generated by a small number of well-known offenders, such as the Bloods gang, that appears to dominate violence in the Howard Houses. The gunfire, while common, is concentrated on weekend nights. Given these more-or-less stable hot spots, it makes sense to concentrate patrol activities in specific times and places. But what should officers actually do there? Their visible presence may serve as a deterrent. But proactive measures may also be warranted. One approach is to curtail illicit gun carrying by engaging with dangerous people in these locations. Another approach involves analyzing violent situations in these hot spots, identifying ways to reduce risky situations, and implementing community problem-solving responses to improve public safety.

A traditional police goal has been to get guns off the street, particularly in areas with high rates of gun violence. Enforcing laws controlling the illegal possession, carrying, and use of guns is a traditional, well-accepted part of police work. There is little reason to expect that officers would balk if directed to do more of it or to do it more systematically.[2] Not surprisingly, most police efforts to prevent gun crime have engaged this approach. Some cities, such as Chicago, have a very long tradition of trying to get guns off the street. This traditional police strategy can be advanced by being much more targeted at risky places, times, and people. The controversy over enforcement stems in part from the concern that police, if sufficiently motivated, may conduct illegal searches in the effort to get guns off the street. Proactive enforcement of gun laws can also be a burden on young minority males who may be targeted even if law-abiding. Gun violence is costly, and so is enforcement. The enforcement costs can only be justified by the good that police are doing. To the extent that enforcement operations can be well targeted, these efforts may minimize cost while preserving benefit.

Police innovation during the past four decades has yielded another very promising approach to controlling gun violence hot spots. Problem-oriented policing can be applied to analyze the underlying conditions and dynamics that cause a "spot" to be "hot." Armed with detailed knowledge on the opportunities for violence in specific places, police officers can help design and implement tailored responses to enhance public safety. The key prevention idea here is that by reducing violence more generally in these very risky places, the opportunities for guns to be deployed during violent transactions will also be reduced. And, by engaging community members in identifying and changing problem conditions, the approach can help improve police relationships with the public they serve.

## Gun Violence Is Highly Concentrated in Small Public Places

Serious gun violence, like other crime types, is highly concentrated in very small locations known as hot spots. The police of course knows that homicides are concentrated in particular neighborhoods. Often these are low-income, predominantly minority areas, where the violence may be linked to gangs and drugs.[3] However, within these larger neighborhood contexts, gun violence further concentrates at specific addresses, buildings, and blocks. For example, the disadvantaged mostly Black neighborhoods of Roxbury, Dorchester, and Mattapan suffer from disputes emanating from gang turfs and drug market settings and generate roughly three-fourths of the yearly total number of fatal and nonfatal shootings in Boston.[4] Within these distressed neighborhoods, gun violence hot spots are further concentrated at particular locations. As shown in Figure 5.1, gun violence hot spots covered only 5% of Boston's 48.4 square miles, generated nearly 53% of the city's fatal and nonfatal shootings in 2006, and were predominately located in these three distressed neighborhoods.[5]

Many cities show similarly skewed spatial distributions of gun violence. For instance, in Irvington, New Jersey, a small city adjacent to Newark with a population of 65,000 residents and a murder rate of 38.7 per 100,000 in 2008 (compared to the U.S. murder rate of 4.9 that same year),[6] the top 10% of the riskiest 100 foot by 100 foot places experienced 40% of the shootings in the 6-month period following their initial identification. These risky places were characterized by home addresses of known gang members, drug arrests, and particular kinds of business establishment locations (e.g., bars, liquor stores, strip clubs, fast-food restaurants, pawn shops, and check-cashing stores). In nearby Newark, long known to suffer from persistent drug and gang violence problems, a spatial analysis of the city's street network found that gun violence disproportionately clustered within 25 feet of liquor stores, grocery stores, bus stops, and foreclosed residences.[7]

Once a place has experienced a shooting, it is much more likely to suffer recurring shootings. The shooting location and its immediate surroundings experience repeat and near-repeat shootings after the original event. An analysis of spatial and temporal patterns of shootings in Philadelphia between August 2003 and September 2005 found that the risk of a shooting occurring

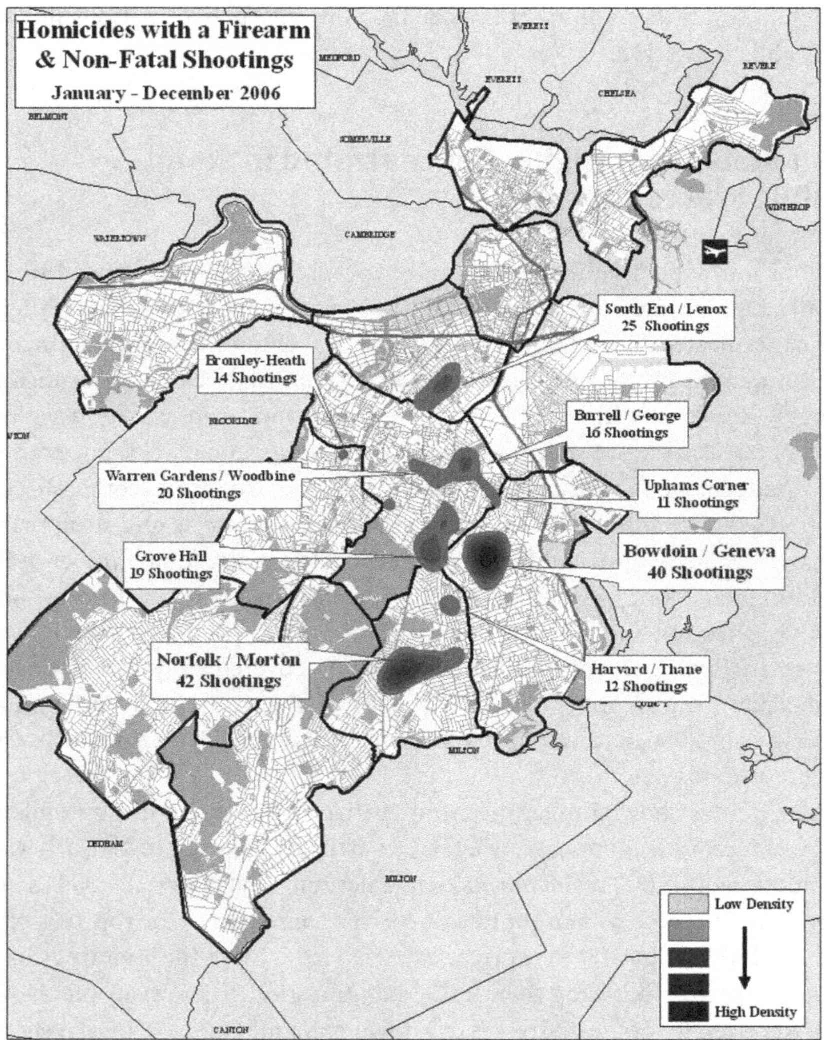


**Figure 5.1** Firearm homicides and nonfatal shootings in Boston, January—December 2006.

*Source*: Anthony A. Braga, David M. Hureau, and Christopher Winship, "Losing Faith? Police, Black Churches, and the Resurgence of Youth Violence in Boston," *Ohio State Journal of Criminal Law* 6, no. 1 (2008): 151.

within one city block of the original shooting increased by 33% in the 2 weeks following the original event.[8] A replication in Houston, Texas, found similar results. Once a location experienced a shooting, the chance of a second shooting taking place within 1 to 400 feet and within the next 14 days was

35% greater than if there was no discernible pattern.[9] It seems clear that police programs to prevent retaliatory shootings should be focused on these small high-risk places immediately after a shooting takes places rather than taking an unfocused approach that simply targets areas with the highest volume of shootings.

City-level gun violence trends may best be understood by the analyses of trends at a very small number of micro places, such as street segments and intersections, rather than analyses of trends at larger areal units such as neighborhoods or arbitrarily defined policing districts. A longitudinal analysis led by Braga found that slightly more than 88% of Boston street segments and intersections did not experience a single shooting incident between 1980 and 2008.[10] Boston gun violence trends were largely generated by repeated incidents at less than 5% of the city's street segments and intersections that accounted for 74% of total shootings between 1980 and 2008. The most violent 65 street segments and intersections accounted for roughly 1,000 shootings during the study period. The persistence of gun violence at small places over extended time periods suggests they are good targets for focused police intervention. Simply stated, gun violence does not move around very much within so-called violent neighborhoods.

Figure 5.2 shows how the late 1980s and early 1990s gun violence epidemic in Boston and the city's sudden downturn in the mid-1990s were almost completely driven by trends at a very small number of places. The darkest-shaded portion of the graph represents the yearly number of gun assault incidents generated by a volatile group of street segments and intersections characterized by unstable counts of multiple shootings over time (i.e., steep annual increases and decreases): Roughly 3% of all street segments and intersections were in this group that experienced 53% of all shootings during the study period. The lightest-shaded portion of the graph represents the yearly number of gun assault incidents generated by a group of street segments and intersections characterized by stable numbers of multiple shootings over time: Almost 2% of all street segments and intersections were in this group that experienced 21% of shootings during the study period. The other portion of the graph represents the yearly number of shootings generated by a group of street segments and intersections with only one gun assault incident each during the entire study time period: Nearly 7% of all street segments were in this group that collectively accounted for the remaining 26% of shootings between 1980 and 2008.

This striking spatial concentration of gun violence faces an important statistical challenge—to some extent, such a concentration may be an artifact of natural clustering of a small number of incidents among a large geographic space. You could imagine having 250 golf balls (roughly the annual number

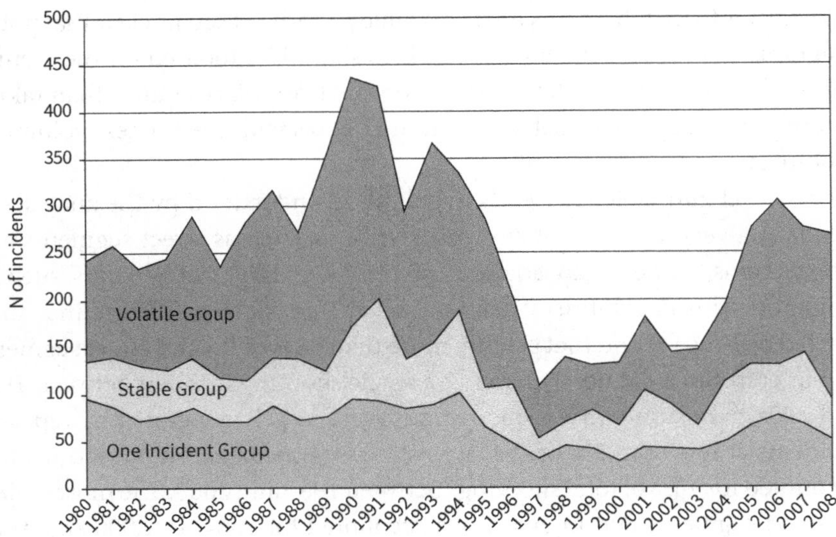


**Figure 5.2** Group yearly counts of shootings in Boston, 1980—2008.
*Source*: Anthony A. Braga, Andrew V. Papachristos, and David M. Hureau, "The Concentration and Stability of Gun Violence at Micro Places in Boston, 1980–2008, *Journal of Quantitative Criminology* 26, no. 1 (2010): 47; Springer Nature.

of shootings in Boston) to throw into a grid made up of approximately 28,500 coffee mugs (roughly the total number of street segments and intersections in Boston). After throwing the golf balls into the grid of mugs, you would naturally observe all golf balls in a small number of mugs. If all 250 golf balls landed in separate coffee mugs, less than 1% of the mugs would have captured the population of golf balls thrown. And if the golf-ball toss were repeated, the cups that caught the ball in the first round would be no more likely than all the others to catch one in the second round.

There are statistical tests to determine whether observed distributions of crime events across spatial units of analysis are greater than what would be observed by chance.[11] To address this issue in the Boston analysis, Braga and colleagues constructed a negative binomial distribution of the expected number of street segments that would have between zero and "5 or more" incidents for each 5-year period in the data.[12] Then, they conducted a simple chi-square goodness of fit test to assess the extent to which the observed concentration significantly differs from the randomly generated negative binomial distributions. The results clearly demonstrate that in each time period there was significantly more clustering in the observed distribution than in the expected distribution; this was especially true among the "5 or more" category. This supplemental analysis provided considerable support for the fact that the observed distribution of shootings across street segments and intersections in Boston over time was not merely an artifact of natural clustering.

It is also important to note that shootings are rare events and very difficult to anticipate even within hot spot locations. Any given block is very unlikely to have a shooting regardless of what the police do or do not do at that location. And having a shooting on a specific block in a given year does not guarantee that a shooting will occur on that block in the following year. For instance, simple analyses of publicly available data suggests a considerable drop off in shootings at hot spots across 1-year periods. In Baltimore, approximately 4% of block groups accounted for 29% of 2015 shootings, but these same block groups accounted for only 15% of 2016 shootings. In Philadelphia, just over 3% of block groups generated almost 27% of shootings in 2017, but these same block groups accounted for only 14% in 2018.

As this book was being completed, the Washington, DC, mayor announced a 2021 summer gun violence reduction initiate that focused police resources on 151 street blocks that accounted for roughly 40% of the gun violence in 2020.[13] Given the short period of time that was used to define these hot spots, the city might be disappointed with the results of its efforts. The Boston analyses showed that shootings were limited to only 12% of the city's street geography, and 5% of street segments and intersections generated the bulk of the shootings over a 29-year period. However, nearly half of the gun violence hot spots were characterized as volatile concentrations, with some experiencing zero shootings in a specific year.

## Targeted Patrol to Reduce Illegal Gun Carrying and Use in Hot Spots

James Q. Wilson, a preeminent criminal justice scholar, argued that, "the *most* effective way to reduce illegal gun-carrying is to encourage the police to take guns away from people who carry them without a permit."[14] It is worth noting that Wilson made this observation prior to adoption of permitless carry laws in many states (as discussed in Chapter 3). Nevertheless, in his view, this meant encouraging the police to make street frisks. Stop and frisk encounters are grounded in constitutional laws that allow police officers to briefly detain citizens based on "reasonable suspicion"—rather than the higher standard of probable cause—that they have committed, are in the process of committing, or are about to commit a crime.[15] If officers reasonably suspect that stopped citizens may be armed and possibly dangerous, they may frisk citizens for weapons. These proactive encounters are generally called *Terry* stops, named after the 1968 U.S. Supreme Court case *Terry v. Ohio* affirming the practice. Drawing on deterrence theory,[16] gun violence can be reduced when prospective offenders perceive the risks of illegally carrying guns in public places to exceed any rewards of doing so when police are frisking suspicious persons for guns. If guns are not being illegally carried in public places, they are less likely to be deployed in assaults and robberies of others. More refined policy proposals during the 1990s suggested that increased law enforcement efforts against guns could be effective in preventing homicides if they were targeted at gun carrying in high gun crime areas.[17]

The influential Kansas City Gun Project examined the gun violence prevention effects of proactive patrol and intensive enforcement of firearms laws, under the direction of criminologist Lawrence Sherman. Enforcement efforts included safety frisks during traffic stops, plain view searches and seizures, and searches incident to arrests on other charges.[18] The goal was to reduce gun crimes in the targeted location. The Gun Project intervention was limited to one target patrol beat that was matched to a comparison beat with nearly identical numbers of drive-by shootings in 1991. Simple computer analyses of call and incident data were used to focus police interventions at hot spot locations within the targeted beat. A pair of two-officer cars, working overtime from 7 p.m. to 1 a.m. 7 days a week and not required to answer citizen calls for service, provided extra patrol in the targeted beat. The officers initiated a high volume of contact with the street population. During 29 weeks in 1992–1993, the directed patrols resulted in 1,090 traffic citations, 948 car checks, 532 pedestrian checks, 170 state or federal arrests, and 446 city arrests.[19] The comparison beat's numbers were routine, and much lower.

In comparison with the comparison beat, the "treatment" beat had 29 additional guns seized (a 65% increase) and 83 fewer gun crimes (a 49% reduction) (Figure 5.3).[20] The evaluation also examined whether gun crimes were displaced into seven beats contiguous to the target beat. None of the contiguous beats showed significant increases in gun crime, and two of the contiguous beats reported significant decreases in gun crimes.

At first blush, compared to an estimated stockpile of 100,000 guns in Kansas City, seizing an additional 29 guns over a 29-week period does not seem like a substantive change in the number of guns potentially carried on the streets. There seemed to be three mechanisms through which hot spots patrol may have reduced gun crime in the targeted beat: Guns seized in high gun crime areas may have been at significantly higher risk of imminent use in crime; the illegal gun carriers who were arrested may have been more frequent gun users; and the visibility of the intensive patrols coupled with increased

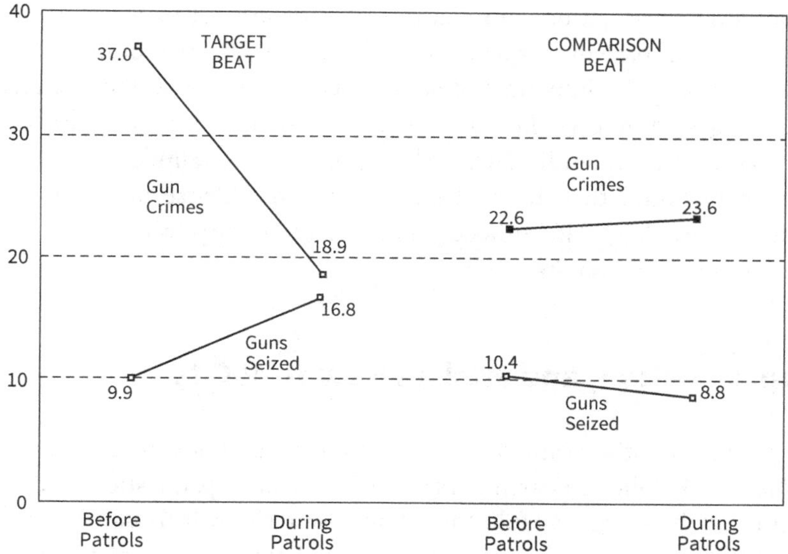


**Figure 5.3** Firearm offenses and guns seized per 1,000 persons, first and second half of 1992.

*Source*: Lawrence W. Sherman and Dennis P. Rogan, "Effects of Gun Seizures on Gun Violence," *Justice Quarterly* 12, no. 4 (1995): 684.

contacts with citizens may have generally deterred gun carrying by those who were not checked by the police.[21]

A separate study examined community reaction to the Kansas City intervention and, through surveys of randomly selected residents in the treatment and control areas, found that the community strongly supported the intensive patrols and perceived an improvement in the quality of life in the treatment neighborhood.[22] In contrast to broader concerns about the effects of proactive policing programs on police–community relations, the Kansas City hot spots patrol program apparently did not increase community tensions. The research did not, however, attempt to measure the views of persons stopped by police patrolling in the hot spot areas. The study did reveal that two-thirds of all persons arrested for illegally carrying concealed weapons in the target area in 1992 did not live in the target area. Most offenders in the study gun hot spot areas seemed to be outsiders who came to these places looking for trouble and, as such, the street population who were stopped and checked by the police may have held very different views on the strategy from the residents of that area.

The results of the Kansas City Gun Project promising, but based on the experience in just one beat of one city. But the results were generally supported in subsequent replications in Indianapolis, Pittsburgh, and St. Louis.[23] These studies offered some more nuanced views on how officers should be deployed when searching for guns in hot spot areas. For instance, the Indianapolis study suggested officers should focus their gun enforcement efforts on suspicious activities and individuals in hot spot locations. Similarly, the St. Louis experiment found that directed patrols in gun violence hot spots needed to be supported by self-initiated enforcement activity in order to generate reductions in gun assaults.

## Stop, Question, and Frisk in New York City

The most influential example of this approach—and how it can go awry—is the New York Police Department's (NYPD) use of stop, question, and frisk to get guns off the street. The full story of how New York City became safe during the 1990s[24] and the ongoing criminological debate over what factors mattered in the steep crime drop[25] has been fully aired out in other forums and is not repeated here. However, there are two elements of that story that are relevant to our discussion. The first is the establishment of the CompStat management and accountability model that sought to focus police departments on specific crime reduction goals and encouraged geographic analysis of crime to focus on hot spots as one of its innovations.[26] In the words of then NYPD Deputy Commissioner Jack Maple, "The main principle of deployment can be expressed in one sentence: 'Map the crime and put the cops where the dots are.' Or, more succinctly: 'Put cops on dots.' "[27]

The second element involves the increasing use of *Terry* stops as a crime control strategy rather than an officer safety tactic. Beginning in 1994, then Commissioner William Bratton had the NYPD's plainclothes Street Crime Unit aggressively target high gun violence areas for proactive stops of citizens to seize illegal guns. Between 1994 and 1997, the NYPD made 46,198 gun arrests and confiscated 56,081 firearms. Shootings declined by 62% between 1993 and 1997. There is a strong case to be made that the NYPD's stop-and-frisk program gets part of the credit for this remarkable improvement in public safety[28] and for large crime reductions overall.[29] The U.S. Department of Justice recognized NYPD efforts to get guns off the streets of New York City during the 1990s as a promising strategy to reduce gun violence.[30]

NYPD enjoyed some well-deserved positive attention for its role in reversing the crime epidemic in America's largest city. However, the aggressive policing tactics of the NYPD were increasingly criticized as generating larger numbers of citizen complaints about police misconduct and abuse of force.[31] There were also growing concerns that many of the searches were not justified by the officers' safety, and in fact violated Fourth Amendment protections against illegal searches and seizures. The program also produced racial disparities in who was stopped.[32] Instead of reining in the stops, the NYPD doubled down on the approach during the 2000s and launched programs such as Operation Impact that deployed extra officers to 20 high-crime "Impact Zones" throughout New York City, and Operation Trident that further concentrated police enforcement efforts in hot spots in three separate areas of Brooklyn's very violent 75th Precinct.[33] At the time, Mayor Michael Bloomberg and NYPD Commissioner Raymond Kelly claimed that increased use of stop, question, and frisk practices (now known simply as "stop reports") was the primary driver of a citywide 37% reduction in violent and property index crimes between 2000 and 2010.[34] As Figure 5.4 reveals, the number of stop reports increased dramatically from 97,296 in 2002 to a peak of 685,724 in 2011.

Some observers suggest that the Kelly-era CompStat process led to a "crime numbers game" managerial mindset[35] that promoted yearly increases in arrests, summonses, and investigatory stops as key performance measures. When being held accountable for exceeding the previous year's enforcement activity numbers, NYPD managers seemed to become more concerned with increasing their outputs rather than considering how crime problems were being addressed. This constant pressure to "increase the numbers" seemed to

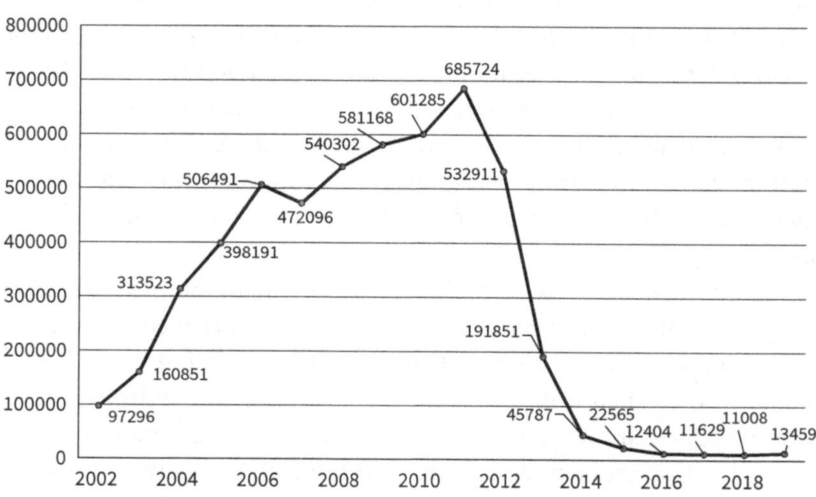


**Figure 5.4** Annual number of NYPD stop reports, 2002–2019.

*Source*: New York Civil Liberties Union, "Stop-and-Frisk Data," https://www.nyclu.org/en/Stop-and-Frisk-data. Accessed July 8, 2020.

diffuse NYPD enforcement efforts from very specific hot spot locations into the broader neighborhoods. Indeed, former NYPD captain John A. Eterno lamented,

> My take is that this has become more like a "throw a wide net and see what you can find" kind of thing. I don't see it as targeted enforcement, especially when you see numbers that we are talking about.[36]

A study of eight blocks of Brownsville, Brooklyn, found the NYPD made nearly 52,000 stops between January 2006 and March 2010,[37] or roughly 12,000 stops per year in this very small area. To put that number in perspective, the NYPD reported only 13,459 stops *for the entire city* in 2019.

The relationship between increased stop reports and crime reductions in New York City is somewhat unclear, with more rigorous studies suggesting small crime reductions associated with increased stops of citizens.[38] It is important to note that the studies reporting crime reductions frame their evaluations as tests of hot spots policing strategies where the effects of increased stops were measured at small units of space and time.[39] An evaluation of the effects of the NYPD's Operation Impact found that the program significantly reduced crime in the targeted areas relative to high-crime comparison areas.[40] The study also found that Impact Zones were significantly associated with increases in investigative stops for suspected crimes; however, only increases in stops made based on probable cause indicators of criminal behaviors were associated with crime reductions. Unfortunately, the largest increase in investigative stops in Impact Zones was based on indicators of suspicious behavior that had no measurable connection to crime. The study concluded that saturating high-crime blocks with police helped reduce crime in New York City but that the bulk of the investigative stops did not play an important role in the crime reductions.[41] The findings indicated that crime reduction could have been achieved with a much smaller number of more focused investigative stops.

As the number of stops skyrocketed over the course of the 2000s, community members, civil liberties activists, and others argued that Black and Hispanic residents were being explicitly targeted by NYPD stop practices in violation of the Equal Protection Clause of the 14th Amendment.[42] Studies have also suggested that repeated NYPD stops of young minority men were associated with increased mental health trauma and anxiety symptoms,[43] as well as reduced school performance.[44] In response to these concerns over glaring racial disparities in NYPD stops, Mayor Bloomberg said in 2015 that crime had declined in the city "because we put all the cops in minority neighborhoods. Why do we do it? Because that's where all the crime is," "and the way you get the guns out of the kids' hands is to throw them up against the wall and frisk them."[45]

The Center for Constitutional Rights filed a federal class action lawsuit, known as *Floyd, et al. v. City of New York, et al.* (959 F. Supp. 2d 540), that alleged the NYPD's use of stop, question, and frisk was unconstitutional. While making their case, the plaintiffs highlighted a series of statistical analyses that suggested that a substantial share of justifications for stops did not meet reasonable suspicion standards and that unwarranted racial disparities were being generated by NYPD stop activities, as evidenced by the fact that the racial composition of census tracts and precincts were significant predictors of the stop rate net of police deployment patterns, arrest and crime rates in previous periods, neighborhood characteristics, and other factors.[46] In 2013, the federal judge hearing the lawsuit ruled that the NYPD was liable for a pattern and practice of unconstitutional stops of citizens that violated the 4th and 14th Amendments. Soon thereafter, the newly elected Mayor Bill de Blasio administration halted an ongoing appeal of the decision and agreed to participate in the court-ordered joint remedial process. To ensure that officer stops of citizens conformed with federal and New York state law, the federal court ordered modifications to NYPD policies, training, and auditing; the handling of civilian complaints and officer discipline; and the measurement and evaluation of organizational performance objectives. The court also mandated that the NYPD establish and evaluate a pilot body-worn camera program. An independent monitor was appointed by the federal court to oversee the execution of the settlement reforms.

The number of stop reports filed by NYPD officers started to decline between 2011 and 2012 before the settlement was reached. However, as Figure 5.4 reveals, the number of NYPD stop reports plummeted by nearly 98% in the years following the 2013 settlement—from 532,911 in 2012 to 11,008 in 2018. Based on a rigorous analysis of stop reports between 2012 and 2015, the post-*Floyd et al.* reforms to NYPD stop practices seem to have been effective in reducing racial disparities in their stop patterns.[47] After the settlement, the racial composition of census tracts was no longer a significant predictor of the stop rate after controlling for other factors, and differences in stop outcomes and contraband "hit rates" between Blacks and Hispanics and similarly situated others diminished substantially. However, minority citizens still make up the bulk of people stopped by the NYPD.

The NYPD now pursues an approach it calls "precision policing," based on the idea, as put forward by William Bratton in 2018 during his second stint as NYPD Commissioner, that police should pay careful attention to the relatively few individuals who make communities unsafe.[48] "We know that there are very few people involved in the violence and crime in New York City," said Bratton's successor, Commissioner James O'Neill,[49] an understanding now routinely heard in policing. An evaluation of precision policing gang "takedowns" in New York City housing projects found that gun violence in and around public housing communities fell by approximately one-third in the first year after the enforcement action was launched.[50] Although nowhere near prior levels, the NYPD is still making stops of citizens as a key part of its crime control strategy. The NYPD seems to be much more economical and focused when making stops, however.

Serious violence in the city remained low after the NYPD shifted away from its indiscriminate use of stops. However, as illustrated by this chapter's opening story of gun violence in the Howard Houses, New York City experienced a massive spike in shootings in 2020, even larger than for the nation as a whole. In 2020, the NYPD disbanded its Street Crime Unit because it had been involved in some the city's most infamous police-involved shootings.[51] The number of shootings by civilians soared 97% from 777 in 2019 to 1,531 in 2020 and murders jumped by 44% from 319 to 462 in 2020.[52] Some observers suggest that the increase in gun violence in New York City and elsewhere in the United States might be linked to a general pullback from proactive policing in the wake of federal consent decrees, racial justice protests, and associated anti-police activism.[53]

We believe the police need to be proactive to control serious gun violence in cities. The research reviewed here as well as other policing studies, such as tests of foot patrol in Philadelphia violent crime hot spots,[54] have established a strong link between increased pedestrian stops and reduced violence. In the Philadelphia studies, these were called field interrogations and often included frisks. No matter what the name, the available research evidence seems clear that proactive stops of suspicious persons and vehicles help police departments get guns off the street. However, these strategies need to be very carefully implemented because they risk undermining police legitimacy in the communities they serve if stops are done excessively and unlawfully.

## Problem-Solving to Change the Underlying Conditions and Dynamics of Violent Places

Police departments should balance their efforts to get guns off the street with systematic efforts to identify and address recurring violent crime problems, of which gun violence is one part. Randomized experiments have shown that problem-oriented policing is an effective method to control violent crime hot spots.[55] In Jersey City, New Jersey, a problem-oriented policing strategy significantly reduced violence in targeted hot spots by dealing with disorderly conditions emanating from street drug markets, poorly managed taverns, and abandoned buildings, as well as taking "target hardening" steps to make stores, gas stations, public transport less attractive targets for robbery.[56]

## Safe Street Teams in Boston

The city of Boston experienced an increase in violent crime beginning in 2003 and continuing through 2006.[57] The violent crime wave was primarily driven by increases in street robberies throughout the city and a resurgence of gang-involved gun violence that was largely concentrated in Boston's disadvantaged and mostly minority neighborhoods of Roxbury, Dorchester, and Mattapan. Former Boston Police Commissioner Edward F. Davis was a firm believer that police departments could reduce citywide crime trends if they applied community problem-solving techniques to address the small number of people and places that generated the bulk of urban crime problems. Soon after his appointment in December 2006, Davis started working with members of his newly appointed command staff to implement a new Safe Street Teams (SST) hot spots policing initiative to manage violent places and, as will be described further in Chapter 6, reconstitute the well-known Operation Ceasefire gang violence reduction strategy that had been discontinued in 2000.

Participating in the development of the SST hot spots policing program was the first major task that Davis asked Braga to perform in his role as Chief Policy Advisor. In designing the SST program with the Boston Police Department (BPD) command staff, Davis and Braga drew upon their previous experiences with implementing a hot spots policing program in Lowell, Massachusetts, when Davis was the police chief in that city.[58] Davis also reflected on his experiences in reforming the Lowell Police Department from a traditional police department to an organization that embraced community policing as its core operational strategy. During these discussions, Braga presented the available evidence on hot spots policing for the BPD command staff to inform their deliberations on the design of the hot spots initiative.

A particularly important moment in the design of the Boston SST program occurred when Braga reviewed the Kansas City, Indianapolis, and Pittsburgh studies discussed above. The BPD command staff firmly rejected the development of a one-dimensional hot spots intervention that called for a dramatic increase in *Terry* searches for guns in hot spots located in Boston's disadvantaged minority neighborhoods. Many of the BPD commanders were street officers when the BPD experienced strong community backlash against a wholesale stop-and-frisk policy aimed at young Black men in Roxbury, Dorchester, and Mattapan to control gun violence during the early 1990s. Noting mounting public concerns about the NYPD's overuse of stop-and-frisk tactics in nearby New York City, Davis and the command staff decided to develop a hot spots policing strategy designed to change underlying conditions and dynamics at violent places rather than implement a program that risked generating racial disparities in who was being stopped that would further distance the BPD from communities it was trying to serve.

The BPD command staff decided to dedicate teams of officers to work assigned hot spots on a permanent basis to facilitate the development of strong community connections in these places. As a result, not all identified violent crime hot spots in Boston received a team of community problem-solvers. That was fortunate from a program evaluation perspective because untreated hot spots areas could serve as counterfactuals. The BPD only had enough patrol personnel to staff 13 SSTs. Braga worked with the BPD Boston Regional Intelligence Center (BRIC) to identify violent crime hot spot areas to receive the SST program based on spatial analyses of 2006 violent index crimes. The selection of the treatment areas proceeded based on BPD command staff perceptions of need. The 13 SST hot spots covered 6% of Boston's street geography and experienced 23% of Boston's robberies and aggravated assaults in 2006.

The BPD's head of the patrol division during SST program development immediately raised a concern about permanently assigning officers to specific places. He noted that gun violence tended to follow sudden outbursts at particular locations throughout the city and, at their weekly deployment meetings, it felt like they were playing "whack a mole" with place-based assignments of their patrol resources. He questioned whether the permanent assignments would undermine their ability to respond to gun violence outbursts as they occurred. Other BPD commanders in the meetings were similarly concerned that violent crime spatial concentrations might not be stable over time. Long-term investments of scarce police resources in violent crime hot spots would make little sense if the location of these hot spots shifted year to year irrespective of police activities.

As the program was implemented in early 2007, the BPD wanted to make certain that the SST areas were indeed centered on some of the most persistently violent places in Boston. Davis assigned two BRIC programmers to work with Braga and some of his colleagues to analyze the concentration and stability of violent crime in specific hot spot locations over time in Boston.

The BPD did not want to make investments of scarce police officer resources at locations that represented short-term or temporary problems. As described earlier, these longitudinal analyses found that only 5% of street segments and intersections experienced 74% of the gun violence from 1980 to 2008. The analysis also uncovered remarkable stability in robbery trends at these small places. Approximately 1% of street segments and 8% of intersections were responsible for nearly 50% of all commercial robberies and 66% of all street robberies between 1980 and 2008.

The analyses confirmed that the SST violent crime hot spots were located at some of the most dangerous places in Boston. As these analyses were being completed, Braga presented initial findings to the BPD command staff. He commented that the results showed that patrol was playing "whack a mole" in only a very small portion of the city and, by taking a longer view on the locations where shootings repeatedly occurred, weekly deployments obscured the stability of gun violence at specific hot spots. The BPD patrol superintendent then commented that he should have known that it was not a good idea to act like firefighters when dealing with shootings in the city (prompting laughter in the room at the expense of their civil service rivals); he was now convinced that the use of long-standing assignments at very specific places was a better way to deal with shootings and robberies in the city.

A deputy superintendent was assigned to oversee the SST initiative, and in each violent crime hot spot, a team of one sergeant and six patrol officers was assigned to implement the program in the targeted 13 violent crime hot spots.[59] The SST officers applied problem-oriented policing to identify recurring violent crime problems in their assigned hot spot area, analyze the underlying conditions that caused these problems to persist, and develop an appropriate response. SST officers were required to engage community members and local merchants in defining and responding to identified problems in the hot spot areas. Unless there was an emergency that required additional support outside their defined areas, SST officers were required to stay in their assigned hot spot, and not even allowed to ride around in patrol cars; rather, they patrolled target hot spot areas on foot or on bicycles. SST teams were required to attend quarterly CompStat-like meetings with command staff members in which violence trends and patterns in their assigned hot spots were reviewed and their strategies to control recurring violence were discussed and assessed.

The identified problems and their underlying causes were highly varied across the 13 targeted hot spot locations. For instance, the Downtown Crossing and Tremont/Stuart SST officers faced street violence problems tied to three very different disorder-based problems. First, these two teams bordered the Boston Common area, which has a large and transient homeless population. Although many homeless individuals posed no threat, a small number of mentally disordered and criminally active individuals engaged in street fights to settle disputes and committed robberies of other homeless people, shoppers, and workers in the area. Second, large groups of high school students congregated around Boston Common during the afternoons after school release. Most of the students did not cause problems; however, gang members blended into this crowd, sold drugs to homeless individuals and others, and sometimes fired guns when in dispute with rival gang members. Third, during the late-night hours, the many clubs and pubs in the Common area attracted young adults who tended to drink too much alcohol and get into fights inside the bars and out on the streets. Other SST areas, such as Codman Square in Dorchester, had high rates of street robbery and other violence. Local hoodlums preyed on commuters, rival youth gangs did battle, local bars overserved clients, and drug dealing engendered robbery.

The number of problem-oriented interventions implemented at the target locations differed for various reasons, including the SST sergeant's commitment to this approach. In the SST areas deemed to be not properly implementing community and problem-oriented policing interventions, the BPD command staff required additional training and closer supervision to ensure that all targeted hot spots received adequate crime control and prevention attention. Fortunately, innovative problem-solving was occurring in many SST areas.

For instance, in the Orchard Park SST area, high school youth using public transportation were repeatedly robbed and often assaulted by other local youth when commuting between the train station and their high school. The offenders usually robbed the students of their Apple iPods, Apple iPhones, and other technology when they walked in secluded areas and were not paying attention to their surroundings. In addition to increasing their presence and making robbery arrests in the area, SST officers made the place less attractive to youth robbers by collaborating with public works to fence a vacant lot and trim overgrown bushes and other vegetation that helped conceal robbers from their victims. The officers then collaborated with the local high school to raise awareness among the students that they should be aware of their surroundings and refrain from using smartphones and other items that were attractive to robbers when commuting in the risky area. The officers also sponsored a contest for students to design robbery awareness fliers and posters that used slogans and lingo that would appeal to youth. The fliers were distributed to all students, and posters were displayed on school grounds, in the train station, and in the windows of stores on the route between the train station and the school.

An evaluation compared violent crime trends at the 13 SST hot spots relative to violent crime trends at matched untreated hot spot locations elsewhere in Boston.[60] The study found that the SST problem-oriented policing program reduced robbery incidents by 19% and aggravated assault incidents by 15%. A subsequent analysis of two-block buffer zones surrounding the SST program and comparison areas revealed no evidence of significant violent crime displacement. Violent crime did not simply move around the corner due to focused police attention in the hot spot areas. Equally important, the number of fatal and nonfatal shootings in the SST violent crime hot spots declined by almost 12% relative to fatal and nonfatal shootings in the comparison violent crime hot spots. As these problem places experienced fewer violent events, the opportunities for guns to be deployed in violence also decreased.

## Greening Vacant Lots in Philadelphia

A randomized field experiment in Philadelphia further documents the preventive impacts of changing the underlying conditions and dynamics of places that generate gun violence hot spots.[61] As suggested by the Boston case study, problem-oriented police should pay attention to environmental factors associated with repeated shootings in specific places. While the police were not involved in the Philadelphia program, the experience highlights the strong potential for environmental approaches to reduce gun violence.

In many U.S. cities, vacant and blighted land tends to concentrate in neighborhoods suffering from high levels of gun violence.[62] Thirty percent of fatal and nonfatal shootings in Philadelphia between 2011 and 2015 were concentrated in only 6% of street blocks. Furthermore, 1 in 13 street blocks in Philadelphia were at least half vacant. In collaboration with city officials, University of Pennsylvania researchers randomly assigned 110 geographically contiguous clusters of vacant lots to receive (a) a greening intervention, (b) a less-intensive mowing and trash cleanup intervention, or (c) no intervention. The vacant lots assigned to the greening intervention had trash and debris removed, the land graded, new grass and trees planted to create a park-like setting, wooden perimeter fences installed, and routine maintenance. Vacant lots were randomly assigned to these conditions between April and June 2013 and included in the experiment through March 2015.

The experimental analyses found that relative to the no intervention comparison vacant lots, the greening intervention reduced shootings by almost

7% and the mowing and trash cleanup intervention reduced shooting by 9% at the treated vacant lots.[63] Shootings were not displaced into surrounding areas as a result of the greening and mowing interventions. The evaluators speculated that vacant lot remediation encouraged residents to use these public spaces for recreation and socializing while discouraging illegal activities such as drug dealing and disorderly behavior. In turn, the increased guardianship of public spaces generated by the residents reduced opportunities for altercations that resulted in shootings. The transformation of public spaces from blighted violent environments to safe orderly places is consistent with the basic premises of problem-oriented policing.[64] And the basic lesson for police from the Philadelphia vacant lot experiment is that changing places can be an effective approach to reducing gun violence.

## Conclusion

The research and experiential evidence reviewed in this chapter suggests that the police, if strategically deployed in high gun violence places, can prevent gun violence. The key to effective prevention seems to rest on the ability of the police to focus on the places, times, and people who pose the highest risks for gun violence. Getting guns off the street through lawful stops and frisks is an important activity to deter prospective offenders from illegally carrying their guns in public places. Some observers question the fairness and intrusiveness of aggressive law enforcement approaches and caution that street searches, especially of young men and minorities, constitute police harassment.[65] We believe that it is critically important for police departments pursuing these activities to focus their actions on high-risk offenders in gun hot spots. This focus will require additional intelligence gathering and analysis as well as making an effort to get to know area residents and people who routinely use these public spaces. Such steps are necessary to avoid indiscriminate and unfocused enforcement efforts that will undermine the legitimacy of the police in eyes of citizens who desperately need their help.

Residents of communities suffering from high rates of gun violence seem to welcome intensive police efforts against guns.[66] The police managers involved in the Kansas City and Indianapolis hot spots projects secured community support before and during the interventions through a series of meetings with community members. The police departments also stressed to their officers that they needed to treat citizens with respect and explain the reasons for the stop. Effective police management (leadership, supervision, and maintaining positive relationships with the community) seems to be the crucial factor in securing community support for proactive but respectful policing. Both up-front and ongoing training of officers involved in proactive policing efforts are also required to ensure that encounters in hot spot locations are conducted lawfully and in a procedurally just manner.

Problem-oriented policing strategies have great promise to address the underlying situations and dynamics that engender recurrent violence. Problem-oriented approaches often provide important opportunities to engage communities in strategy development and implementation. Employing these approaches also economizes on the use of costly enforcement actions that could produce unintended harms. Safer public spaces will result in diminished opportunities for guns to be deployed during violent encounters. Relative to repeated arrests and gun seizures, efforts to modify place characteristics and conditions are better positioned to create lasting changes that do not dissipate as soon as officers are deployed to other assignments. Because this strategy is not exclusively focused on seizing guns, we believe that such an approach will not be affected by current gun legislation trends that encourage gun carrying in public spaces. This approach clearly belongs in police gun-violence-prevention portfolios.

# 6
# Retail Deterrence of Very High-Risk Groups

> On a brisk October day in 2014, "Greg," a 24 year old black male member of the G-Shine Bloods, and "Tony," a 23 year old black male non-gang associate, were standing in front of a carwash near Spencer Street and Alexander Street in the Vailsburg neighborhood of Newark, New Jersey. A blue BMW with tinted windows containing members of the 793 Bloods, rivals of the G-Shines, cruised down Spencer Street and pulled over not far from where Greg and Tony where standing. At least one member of the 793 Bloods leaned through the window and opened fire with a .40 caliber handgun on Greg and Tony, wounding both men non-fatally in their legs. While the exact motive of the shooting is unclear, police believe it was related to an ongoing drug turf-related dispute between the G-Shines and 793 Bloods.[1]

Not everyone is at equal risk of being the victim of a violent gun attack. As the grim statistics presented in Chapter 2 document, young Black males are at highest risk of being killed with a gun. Their elevated risk of violent gun victimization originates in the United States' depressing history of excluding Black citizens from equal access to well-functioning schools; good health care; and labor, housing, consumer, and credit markets.[2] However, within communities of color, there are social networks that are at extreme risk of suffering fatal and nonfatal gun injuries.[3] In U.S. cities, most shootings are highly concentrated among groups of criminally active individuals who use guns to settle disputes emanating from personal clashes, drug market business, ongoing gang rivalries, and other conflicts.[4] These elevated shooting risks extend to third parties and bystanders, such as "Tony" in the opening example, who

*Policing Gun Violence.* Anthony A. Braga and Philip J. Cook, Oxford University Press. © Oxford University Press 2023.
DOI: 10.1093/oso/9780199929283.003.0006

have social connections to gang members and high-risk individuals but are not involved in emergent and ongoing disputes in these high-risk networks.[5]

Cities can diminish their overall gun violence problems by reducing violent victimization in these high-risk social networks through the strategic application of "carrots and sticks" or, more formally, incentives and disincentives. "Focused deterrence" programs designed to change offender behavior through a credible threat of law enforcement are effective in controlling crime if well designed and faithfully implemented.[6] Anecdotal evidence, and some formal research, suggests that these programs gain legitimacy if coupled with an offer of support in making a transition from gang life to a successful "straight" life, and can help improve police–community relationships in disadvantaged minority communities.[7] Contrary to much conventional wisdom, the credible threat of criminal sanction does deter members of gangs, drug crews, and other criminally active groups from shooting rivals.

Groups of offenders receive focused attention based on their ongoing involvement in gun violence. Simply stated, groups are not targeted because they fit a particular profile or some stereotype; rather, the intervention is triggered by intelligence indicating that they are responsible for shooting injuries and deaths. Although some offenders will be arrested for their involvement in shootings and other ongoing criminal behavior, the goal of the intervention is not the wholesale removal of criminally active groups from their communities. The goal of the focused deterrence is to reduce gun violence by targeted groups.

## Most Gun Violence Is Driven by Gangs and Groups of Co-Offenders

Youth gun violence is usually concentrated among groups of serious offenders, and conflicts between youth street gangs have long been noted to fuel much of the serious street violence in major cities.[8] Moreover, relative to non-gang delinquent youth offending patterns, youth involvement in gangs leads to elevated levels of criminal behavior, especially violent offending.[9] In some cities, such as Baltimore, the violent street scene is characterized by various criminal groups ranging from small informal networks of drug sellers and street robbery crews to more formal gangs and larger drug trafficking organizations.[10] Dealing with group-related violence is a challenge for most U.S. police departments. City-level studies have found gang-related motives in more than one-third of homicides in Chicago,[11] half of the homicides in Los Angeles' Boyle Heights area,[12] and nearly two-thirds of Oakland homicides.[13]

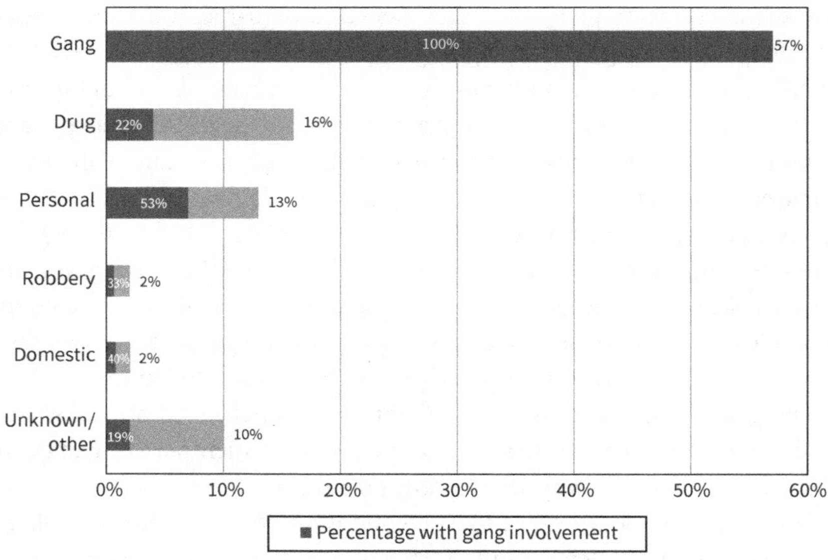


**Figure 6.1** 2010 Boston shootings: Motives and gang member involvement (*N* = 264).
Adapted from Anthony A. Braga, David M. Hureau, and Leigh S. Grossman, *Managing the Group Violence Intervention: Using Shooting Scorecards to Track Group Violence* (Washington, DC: U.S. Department of Justice, Office of Community Oriented Policing Services, 2014), 19.

A study of more than 20 cities generally found that, on average, less than 1% of a city's population were involved in gangs, drug crews, and other criminally active groups but were connected to more than 50% of a city's shootings and homicides.[14]

Figure 6.1 summarizes the motives and gang involvement for fatal and non-fatal shootings in Boston in 2010.[15] Gang-related violence, mostly involving cycles of retaliatory violence between two groups, accounted for 57% of Boston shootings in that year. Drug-related motives, such as drug market disputes and drug robberies, accounted for 16% of shootings, whereas personal disputes, emanating from ongoing conflicts or sudden arguments between individuals, represented 13%. Beyond generating a high level of shootings from gang-related disputes, gang members are also disproportionately involved in gun violence related to other motives. Gang members were heavily involved as victims, offenders, or both in shootings that were drug motivated (22%), personal disputes (53%), street robberies (33%), domestic violence (40%), and self-inflicted shooting victimizations (40%).[16]

Even in cities in which gang conflict is less prominent, high-risk co-offending networks are central to gun violence problems. In Newark, New Jersey, an analysis of homicide data for 2009–2012 found that although only

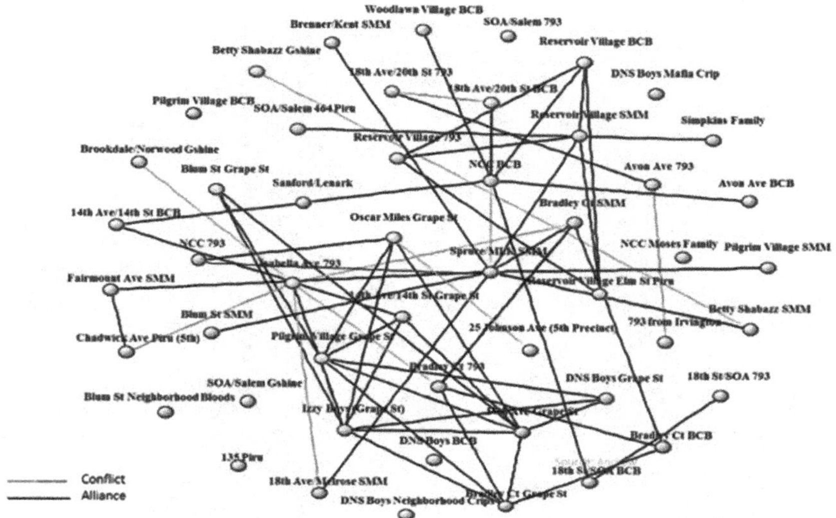


**Figure 6.2** Gangs and criminally active groups in the 4th Precinct, Newark, New Jersey, 2014.

Adapted from National Network for Safe Communities, *Newark Violence Reduction Intervention: Strategic Law Enforcement* (New York, NY: National Network for Safe Communities, 2014).

16% were the result of disputes between gangs, most homicides (60%) involved gang members.[17] Newark's 4th Precinct, which includes the Vailsburg neighborhood discussed in the opening example, was home to 47 sets of gangs and criminally active groups that represented less than 2% of the area population but were involved in 69% of the murders in that area. Figure 6.2 presents the conflicts and alliances among these groups. Nearly one-third of all shootings in Newark occur in a co-offending network that contains less than 4% of the city's total population (Figure 6.3). Being a gang member in this risky social network increased an individual's risk of being shot by 344% (e.g., Greg in the example), and being a non-gang member who is socially connected to a gang member increased an individual's risk of being shot by 94% (e.g., Tony in the example).

Rates of nonfatal and fatal shootings within such co-offending networks are considerably higher than both city-level rates and rates in high-crime communities in those cities. In Chicago, for example, 70% of all fatal and nonfatal gunshot injuries occurred in identifiable networks composed of individuals arrested in previous years that comprised less than 6% of the city's total population; the rate of gun homicide in the network was more than nine times higher than that for the city as a whole.[18] In Boston, conflicts amongst Cape Verdean gangs were a prominent feature of a resurgence of gang violence in

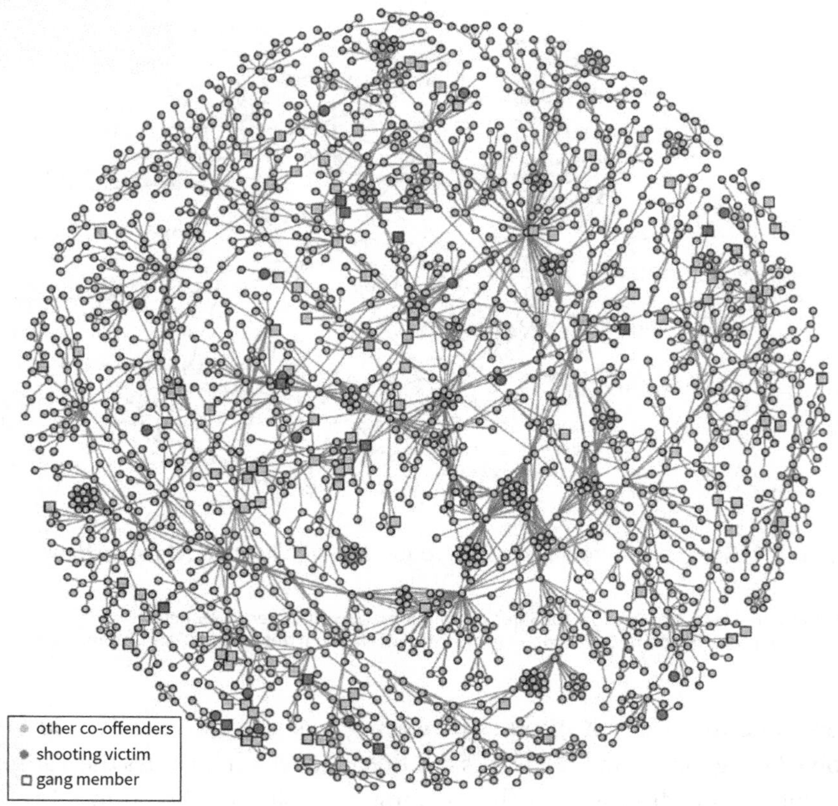


**Figure 6.3** High-risk co-offending network in Newark, New Jersey, 2009–2012.
Republished with permission of John Wiley & Sons–Books, from Andrew V. Papachristos, Anthony A. Braga, Eric L. Piza, and Leigh S. Grossman, "The Company You Keep? The Spillover Effects of Gang Membership on Individual Gunshot Victimization in a Co-Offending Network," *Criminology* 53, no. 4 (2015): 640. Permission conveyed through Copyright Clearance Center, Inc.

the mid-2000s.[19] Social network analysis revealed that 85% of total shootings in a Cape Verdean neighborhood were concentrated among a co-offending network of 763 individuals connected to 10 gangs who represented less than 3% of the resident population of that neighborhood; in addition, each "handshake" an individual was closer to a gunshot victim in the network increased their personal risk of gunshot injury by 25%.[20]

The small populations at great risk for violent gun victimization are socially connected, and these identifiable co-offending networks provide an important opportunity for strategic intervention.[21] Mapping out rivalries and alliances among criminally active groups can inform decisions to mobilize resources to disrupt retaliatory cycles. Interventions may also be justified for high-risk individuals, such as recently released prisoners with a criminal history of gun violence.

Chronic and serious violent offenders engage in a wide range of offending and other risky behaviors, including other crimes, drug and alcohol use, traffic offenses, and the like—behaviors that also put them at high risk of victimization.[22] "Cafeteria-style offending" is a central aspect of gangs and gang dynamics.[23] For instance, a study of 2016–2017 Oakland homicides found that in 72% of these cases, gang members were involved as offenders, victims, or both.[24] Three out of 4 victims and suspects were previously known to the criminal justice system. These "criminal justice known" individuals had, on average, 12 prior arrests for a wide variety of armed and unarmed violent crimes, drug offenses, property crimes, and disorder offenses. More than two-thirds were previously convicted felons, more than one-third were on active probation supervision at the time of the homicide event, and more than two-thirds had spent time incarcerated before the homicide occurred.

Given that a high percentage of likely shooters are involved with the criminal justice system, they are quite likely to have warrants against them or are in violation of probation or parole conditions. They face a credible threat of being arrested and sanctioned, should the authorities decide that it is worthwhile to do so.

## Focused Deterrence to Reduce Gun Violence

Focused deterrence strategies, sometimes called "pulling levers" policing programs, are often framed as problem-oriented exercises in which specific recurring crime problems are analyzed and responses are highly customized to local conditions and operational capacities.[25] These strategies seek to change offender behavior by understanding underlying violence-producing dynamics and conditions that sustain recurring violence problems and implementing a blended set of law enforcement, informal social control, and social service actions. Focused deterrence operations have tended to follow this basic framework:

- Selection of a particular crime problem, such as serious gun violence
- Pulling together an interagency enforcement group, typically including police, probation, parole, state and federal prosecutors, and sometimes federal enforcement agencies
- Conducting research, usually relying heavily on the field experience of frontline police officers, to identify key offenders—and also groups of

offenders, such as street gangs, drug crews, and the like—and the context of their behavior
- Framing a special enforcement operation directed at those offenders and groups of offenders and designed to substantially influence that context, for example, by using any and all legal tools (or levers) to sanction groups such as drug-selling crews whose members commit serious violence
- Matching those enforcement operations with parallel efforts to direct services and the moral voices of affected communities to those same offenders and groups
- Communicating directly and repeatedly with offenders and groups to let them know that they are under particular scrutiny, what acts (e.g., shootings) will get special attention, when that has in fact happened to particular offenders and groups, and what they can do to avoid enforcement action.[26]

This list provides a clear sense of the steps involved in a particular focused deterrence operation. For instance, putting together a working group of representatives from relevant criminal justice, social service, and community-based organizations who can bring varied incentives and disincentives to influence targeted offender behavior is a key early operational step.

## Controlling Gang-Related Gun Violence in Boston

Many American cities experienced a sudden and large increase in gun violence soon after the crack cocaine epidemic emerged during the late 1980s and early 1990s.[27] In Boston, the crack epidemic started in early 1986, and soon after, Boston youth gangs became engaged in the highly profitable crack trade, which led to increased acquisition of firearms.[28] As Figure 6.4 reveals, Boston experienced approximately 28 homicides of youth aged 24 years or younger per year between 1980 and 1988. Youth homicides then suddenly increased to a 1990 peak of 73 victims. The yearly number of Boston youth homicides decreased after that peak but did not return to pre-crack epidemic levels and remained historically high. Boston averaged roughly 45 youth homicide victims per year between 1991 and 1995.

The Boston Police Department (BPD) and Harvard University researchers collaborated on a U.S. Department of Justice–sponsored problem-oriented policing exercise, known as the Boston Gun Project, to develop an innovative response to the city's persistent youth homicide problem.[29] David Kennedy and Anne Piehl at Harvard's Kennedy School of Government hired Anthony

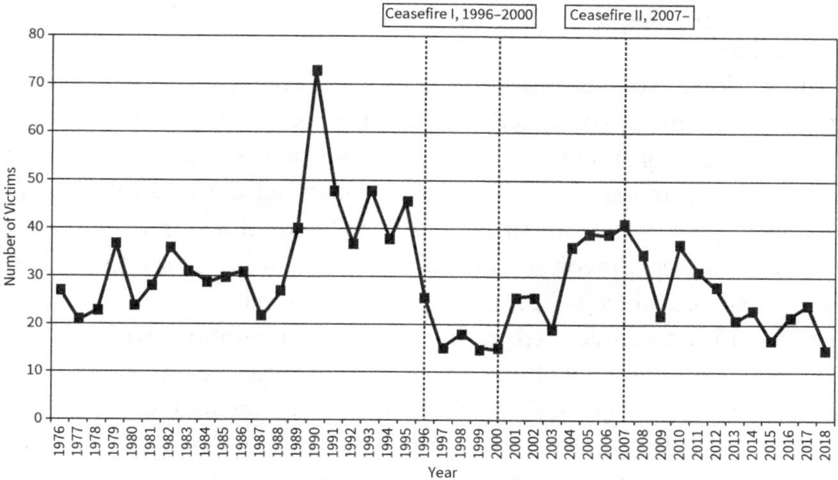


**Figure 6.4** Youth homicides in Boston, 1976–2018 (victims aged 24 years or younger).
*Source*: Anthony A. Braga and David M. Kennedy, *A Framework for Addressing Violence and Serious Crime* (New York, NY: Cambridge University Press, 2020), 16.

Braga to help with data collection and analysis to understand persistent youth gun violence in Boston. Together, they helped develop a strategic response to the underlying dynamics driving homicides and shootings, and then they evaluated the resulting program. At the time, Braga was a doctoral student at the Rutgers School of Criminal Justice and in the end stages of completing his dissertation on a randomized field experiment that tested the impacts of problem-oriented policing on controlling violent places in Jersey City, New Jersey.[30] He was born in Boston and excited to return home to work on an applied research project intended to help the city deal with a seemingly intractable problem that was gripping cities throughout the country.

The Boston Gun Project was led by an interagency working group consisting of criminal justice, academic, social service, and community-based partners. The Harvard research team completed a problem analysis that revealed the bulk of youth homicide was generated by a very small number of youths who were involved in ongoing gang violence. Youth homicide offenders and youth homicide victims were well known to the criminal justice system, involved in a variety of different crimes, and often on probation or under some other kind of criminal justice system control. Most youth homicides and shootings were highly concentrated in the disadvantaged and mostly minority neighborhoods of Roxbury, Dorchester, and Mattapan. The research showed that gun violence had become "decoupled" from the crack trade. It remained highly concentrated among members of drug-selling gangs, but it was associated strongly with group and individual vendettas, or "beefs"; group and individual retaliation; disputes over respect; issues around romantic partners; and the like.[31]

The working group considered the problem analysis research findings in light of policy insights on effective applications of deterrence theory to reduce criminal offending and their past experiences using alternative approaches to quell outbreaks of gang violence.[32] This process led to the development and implementation of the Operation Ceasefire "focused deterrence" strategy in May 1996. Ceasefire involved direct communications to gangs through group call-ins and customized street conversations. The message was that gun violence would not be tolerated. Law enforcement operations were tailored to criminal justice vulnerabilities of targeted gangs, and they were coupled with powerful expressions of anti-violence community norms and offers of social services and employment opportunities to gang members who wanted to change their lives. The Ceasefire strategy was supported by a strong "network of capacity" of criminal justice, social service, and community-based organizations that enabled the working group to launch a robust response to gang violence through coordinated efforts that magnified their separate effects.[33] This program eventually included a partnership with the Ten Point Coalition, consisting of a group of activist Black clergy, who helped strengthen the legitimacy of the Ceasefire strategy and enlisted the political support of Boston's minority communities.[34]

A key element of the newly developed Ceasefire strategy involved the direct communication of a deterrent message to Boston gang members.[35] First, the interagency Ceasefire working group thought it was important to communicate to all gang members in Boston so they were aware of the new "don't shoot" rule and understood how to avoid getting in trouble. Second, when a gang broke the rules, the working group wanted the gang to understand that its violent behavior had drawn the focused attention of the working group and that the gang would remain "under the microscope" until the shooting stopped. These communications were made through informal meetings with gang members on the street and via planned "forums" that involved a gang being called into a public place, such as a courthouse or community center. There, the broad capacity and partnership represented by the working group were showcased and the anti-violence message was delivered face-to-face. It is important to note that the message delivered was not a deal that the authorities would not enforce the law as long as gangs were not shooting at each other.[36] If gangs were involved in other crimes, there was a baseline risk that they would be investigated and held accountable for their transgressions. Rather, it was promised that gun homicides would bring a swift and certain response.

The first gang that drew the attention of the Ceasefire working group was the Intervale Posse, an infamous crack-selling gang with a long history of murder and intimidation in its Roxbury neighborhood.[37] The gang had taken over a wooded vacant lot, created a hangout space with couches and televisions powered by stolen electricity from nearby abandoned homes, and even set up a firing range to practice shooting their guns. The lot was well known for an "Adidas Tree" that was adorned with dozens of sneakers taken from people who the Intervale gang regarded as trespassers in their turf. The Ceasefire working group sent the message, primarily through conversations with the gang's leader and other influential members, that the gang's homicidal behavior needed to stop immediately. The Intervale Posse was not interested in taking advantage of social services offered by streetworkers and clergy, nor was it impressed by promises of enforcement if it continued shooting at its rivals. The BPD then collaborated with the Drug Enforcement Administration (DEA) on a slow-moving but highly focused investigation of the Intervale gang's crack sales.

As the Intervale investigation unfolded, a very violent dispute emerged within the Vamp Hill Kings, a gang that claimed turf on Dorchester's Bowdoin Street.[38] Two warring factions of the gang repeatedly fired shots at each other that resulted in three "King on King" homicides. This violent outbreak prompted an immediate response that included a heavy BPD presence on Bowdoin Street that generated 10 arrests and shut down the gang's street-level drug sales, 38 home visits by probation officers that resulted in 10 surrenders, several surrenders of Kings who were under the supervision of the Department of Youth Services (DYS; juvenile corrections), and the mobilization of streetworkers to offer social services and job opportunities to Kings who wanted help. Gun violence immediately stopped.

The working group then held its first Ceasefire call-in with the Vamp Hill Kings at the Dorchester courthouse on May 15, 1996.[39] Roughly a dozen Vamp Hill Kings were in attendance, encouraged to be present through their strong relationships with street outreach workers and Bowdoin Street community members or via a mandatory requirement imposed by their probation supervision. DYS brought several other surrendered Kings in restraints from their secured facilities. The members of the Ceasefire working group sat at the front of the room with posters detailing the enforcement actions taken to halt the violence on Bowdoin Street. Billy Stewart, then an assistant chief probation officer in the Dorchester court, served as the emcee and started the conversation by telling the audience,

> "Thanks for coming. . . . This isn't a sting, everybody's going to be home for dinner, we just wanted you to know a few things. And this is nothing personal, either; this is

> how we're going to be dealing with violence in the future, and you just happened to be first. So go home and tell your friends about what you hear today.[40]

Each Ceasefire working group member then described the capacities of their agency and what specifically they were doing to reduce violence on Bowdoin Street. The repeated message to the Kings was that they and their activities were known to the authorities and that serious gun violence would no longer be tolerated. Early during the call-in, many of the Vamp Hill Kings present smiled and scoffed. They stopped smiling when Assistant U.S. Attorney Ted Heinrich told them,

> This kind of street crime used to be a local matter. Not anymore. [The] Attorney General cares more about youth violence than almost anything else. My boss works for [the Attorney General], so that's what he cares about more than anything else. Right now, the youth violence in Boston is happening in your neighborhood, which means that the U.S. Department of Justice cares about *you.* We can bring in the DEA, we can bring in the FBI, we can bring in the ATF; we can prosecute you federally, which means you go to Lompoc, not stateside, and there's no parole in the Federal system any more: You serve your time. We don't want to do that, and we won't if we don't have to, but it's violence that will get that kind of attention.[41]

The message was intended to draw cause (gun homicide) and effect (swift and certain law enforcement action) in the minds of the Vamp Hill Kings. As then Commander of the BPD Youth Violence Strike Force (YVSF, informally known as the gang unit) Lt. Det. Gary French stated when discussing the federal prosecution of a King who was picked up on a felon-in-possession gun charge, "We are *not* putting up with this stuff anymore."[42] The tough talk with the Vamp Hill Kings was balanced with offers of services and opportunities. Tracy Lithcutt, then director of the Boston Community Centers' Streetworker program, made an impassioned speech to the Kings:

> We know you're all caught up in something you can't control. We know it's dangerous out there. And we'll help, any way we can. If you need protection from your enemies, if you want a job, if your mom needs treatment, if you want back into school, tell us; here's my phone number. . . . If you don't hear what's being said to you today, it's on your heads. Take what we're offering. I've been to over 100 funerals, and I'm not going to any more. The violence stops *now*.[43]

The Ceasefire working group continued its work over the course of the summer of 1996 by addressing violent gang outbreaks as they occurred in the city. The Intervale Posse, however, continued shooting at its rivals and did not respond to Vamp Hill King–style street enforcement work, social service offers, and ongoing street conversations to halt its violent behavior. The covert DEA investigation also continued. On August 29, 1996, an early morning sweep resulted in the arrest of 15 key members of the Intervale Posse on federal drug charges and arrests of 8 more on state charges. The gang leader's first question to the arresting officers was "State or federal?" When the answer was federal, he hung his head and made no reply.[44] The city of Boston cleaned up the gang's lot and cut down the intimidating Adidas Tree. It is important to note that the harshness of this specific operation was unusual. Most Boston gangs subjected to Ceasefire responded to swift and certain street enforcement work. When that failed to make an impression on the Intervale Posse and the gang continued its shooting spree, it became necessary to launch a more punitive response to maintain the credibility of the deterrent message.

The Interval Posse operation received extensive media coverage. However, the Ceasefire working group wanted to ensure that Boston's gang population and the broader community understood what happened. As such, they held a series of call-ins with rival and allied gangs at local courthouses, made presentations to juvenile inmates held in secure DYS facilities and in local middle and high schools serving students from the Intervale neighborhood, had numerous street conversations with gang members and neighborhood youth, and handed out fliers that described the Ceasefire approach. The working group delivered the following message:

> We warned them; they didn't listen. The papers say this was a drug operation, and it was, but it really happened because of the violence, and it's violence that will draw anything similar in the future. We have BPD, we have DEA, we have ATF, we have probation, we have parole, we have DYS, we have the U.S. Attorney, we have the county District Attorney, we have everybody. If we focus on you, you can't win, so don't make us [act].[45]

These ongoing discussions served to clarify the risks of punishment driven by Ceasefire action. In one tense conversation, a seasoned streetworker asked, "Is everybody who might sell drugs on the street facing these huge federal penalties? My son, God forbid, might choose to do a little of that; is he going to be exposed?"[46] Donald Stern, then U.S. Attorney for the District of Massachusetts, replied, "No. This is about *violence*. Only the key players in the most violent groups have to worry, and they'll get fair warning, just like Intervale did."[47] The streetworker said, "Ah, in that case, the crew I work with in Mattapan asked me to send you guys a message. The message is, *we* got it, we're not doing anything, leave us alone."[48]

Immediately following the mid-1996 launch of the Ceasefire focused deterrence strategy, Boston youth homicides decreased dramatically (see Figure 6.4). Throughout the project, Braga spent much of his time doing ride-alongs with the BPD YVSF to develop a better understanding of Boston's gang violence problem and, after Ceasefire was launched, to monitor the implementation of the intervention. While riding with Lt. Det. French in an unmarked car in late August 1996, Braga learned that French was stunned Ceasefire actually seemed to be working. French shared that he initially thought that his beeper might not be working properly because he usually received a constant stream of messages on shootings during the late summer. The beeper was working fine. He observed that gangs were just not shooting at each other as frequently—an observation that was supported by data. The impact evaluation found that Ceasefire was associated with a 63% reduction in youth homicide in Boston. That abrupt drop was unique to Boston and not found in most large U.S. and New England cities.[49] Partly due to the involvement of Black ministers in the strategy, this surprising large reduction in youth homicide was called "the Boston Miracle" by the national media.

After several years of sustained reductions in youth homicides, the BPD halted the Ceasefire program in January 2000.[50] At that time, the BPD implemented a wider set of violence reduction programs, including a reentry initiative to assist violent offenders to transition from jail back to their communities, a strategy to coordinate service delivery to high-risk families that generated and experienced repeat serious violence across generations, and an effort to improve unsolved shooting investigations. Regrettably, the broader slate of programs seemed to dilute the capacity of the BPD and its partners to halt outbreaks of serious gang violence in Boston. Youth homicides soon started to increase. As Figure 6.4 shows, the yearly number of youths killed in Boston steadily increased from 15 victims in 2000 to 41 victims in 2007. During this time period, the BPD did not engage in strategic analyses of its increasing youth homicide problem. Furthermore, there was substantial internal dysfunction in both the BPD and the influential Ten Point Coalition that precluded the implementation of strategic response.[51]

Braga remained involved in research partnerships with the BPD during this time period and regularly attended its unsolved shootings meetings. It seemed obvious to the detectives, YVSF officers, civilian crime analysts, and state and federal prosecutors attending these meetings that the resurgence in gun violence was driven by gang violence. Unfortunately, this common knowledge did not seem to influence decisions on violence reduction policy at the upper echelons of the department. The BPD also did not use existing information resources to unravel yearly homicide trends in a way that would have detected the steady increase in gang-related homicides. Indeed, in April 2006, then Commissioner Kathleen O'Toole blamed the growing gang violence problem on an increasing juvenile population and prisoner reentry issues.[52]

As described previously in this book, Ed Davis was appointed as the BPD Commissioner at the end of 2006 and immediately started laying the groundwork for a "risky people, risky places" approach to deal with gun violence in Boston. Davis asked Braga to work with the YVSF, homicide unit, and Boston Regional Intelligence Center on a fresh analysis of gun violence trends in Boston and the implementation of focused deterrence. With the start of 2007, a revitalized Ceasefire focused deterrence strategy was launched.[53] The newly completed problem analysis revealed, once again, that Boston's youth homicide problem was largely driven by surging gang violence concentrated in the disadvantaged, mostly minority Roxbury, Dorchester, and Mattapan neighborhoods of Boston.[54] The yearly count of youth homicides with gang motives increased sevenfold between 1999 and 2006—indeed, two-thirds of youth homicides had gang motives and 70% of nonfatal shootings involved gang members in 2006. The problem analysis further revealed that fatal and nonfatal shootings were largely carried out by 65 active street gangs representing roughly 1% of Boston's youth population between the ages of 15 and 24 years. One-third of all shootings in 2006 were generated by only 10 street gangs.

The Lucerne Street Doggz, a loosely organized street gang with roughly 50 members and active conflicts with eight rival gangs, was the first group selected for the post-2007 implementation of the Ceasefire.[55] The Doggz were involved in almost 10% of Boston's 377 total shootings in 2006—they were suspected offenders in 30 shootings and victims in 7 shootings. Through the end of May 2007, the Lucerne Street Doggz was suspected of committing another 21 shootings and suffered an additional 6 shootings of its members. The reconstituted Ceasefire working group realized it was critical to mount a strong response to the persistent gun violence generated by the Doggz in order to reestablish the credibility of its anti-violence message to other street gangs.

The formal planning for the Lucerne Street Doggz operation started in January 2007 with the convening of the BPD drug control unit and district personnel, Suffolk County District Attorney's Office, U.S. Attorney's Office, Drug Enforcement Administration, and Bureau of Alcohol, Tobacco, Firearms and Explosives. An interagency investigation resulted in the arrests of 25 members of the Lucerne Street Doggz on federal and state drug and gun offense charges on May 24, 2007. The Ceasefire working group used a series of group call-ins and individual notifications to deliver the anti-violence message that continued shootings would provoke an immediate law enforcement response to the remaining Lucerne Street gang members and their eight rival gangs. The targeted gangs were also informed that the community supported criminal justice actions to reduce gun violence by Ten Point Coalition ministers, Boston city youth outreach workers, and local neighborhood groups. These community-based partners also advised the targeted gang members to enroll in the social services and opportunities offered by Youth Opportunity Unlimited, Boston Centers for Youth and Families, and other nonprofit agencies.

The revitalized Ceasefire strategy resulted in a sudden large decrease in shootings by and against the Lucerne Street Doggz (Figure 6.5). In 2006 and 2007, the Doggz averaged almost 34 total shootings per year. The yearly number of shootings involving the Doggz decreased by roughly 88% to approximately 4 per year between 2008 and 2010. The Ceasefire working group subsequently marketed the highly effective Lucerne Street operation to other Boston street gangs as credible evidence that outbreaks of gun violence would be met with a swift and certain law enforcement response. Between 2007 and 2010, the Ceasefire working group engaged with 19 Boston gangs through the reconstituted strategy. A rigorous evaluation of the post-2007 Ceasefire

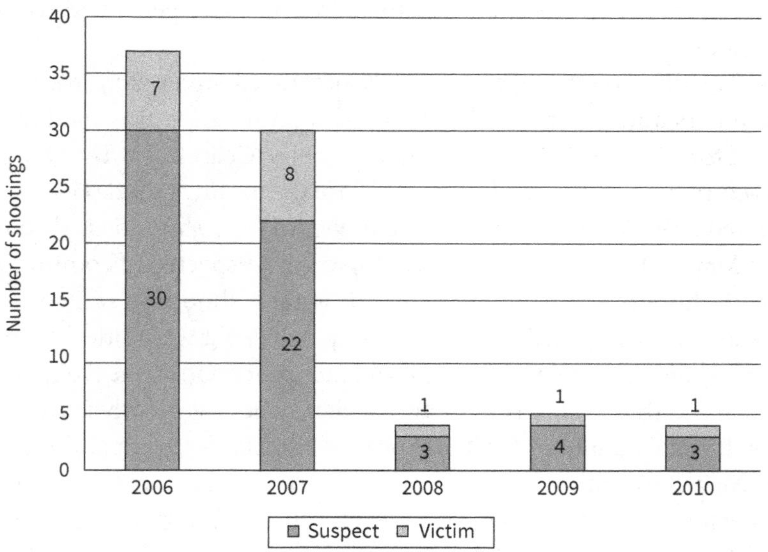


**Figure 6.5** Total shootings involving Lucerne Street Doggz, 2006–2010.
Adapted from Anthony A. Braga, David M. Hureau, and Andrew V. Papachristos, "Deterring Gang-Involved Gun Violence: Measuring the Impact of Boston's Operation Ceasefire on Street Gang Behavior," *Journal of Quantitative Criminology* 30, no. 1 (2014): 133; Springer Nature.

implementation found that total shootings involving treated Boston gangs decreased by 31% relative to total shootings involving matched untreated Boston gangs.[56] Citywide youth homicides in Boston also decreased by almost two-thirds from 41 victims in 2007 to 15 victims in 2018 (Figure 6.4).

A companion analysis examined whether the Ceasefire focused deterrence violence reduction impacts spilled over to untreated gangs that were socially connected to treated gangs through rivalries and alliances.[57] Figure 6.6 illustrates the social connections among directly treated and "vicariously treated" gangs in a clique centered on the Heath Street gang. Academy Homes, Annunciation Road, Egleston Square, H-Block, and Walnut Park gangs had active rivalries with the Heath Street gang. The Bragdon Street and Lenox Street gangs had alliances with Heath Street. H-Block, Orchard Park, Annunciation Road, and Heath Street gangs were targeted by the Ceasefire program during the 2006–2010 evaluation period. Although they did not directly experience the Ceasefire program, the Academy Homes, Bragdon Street, Egleston Square, Lenox Street, and Walnut Park gangs may have altered their violent behaviors based on knowledge of what happened to their rivals and allies.

The main evaluation excluded these untreated groups from the analysis because of treatment contamination concerns. However, the companion analysis focused on the shooting behaviors of these gangs to determine whether

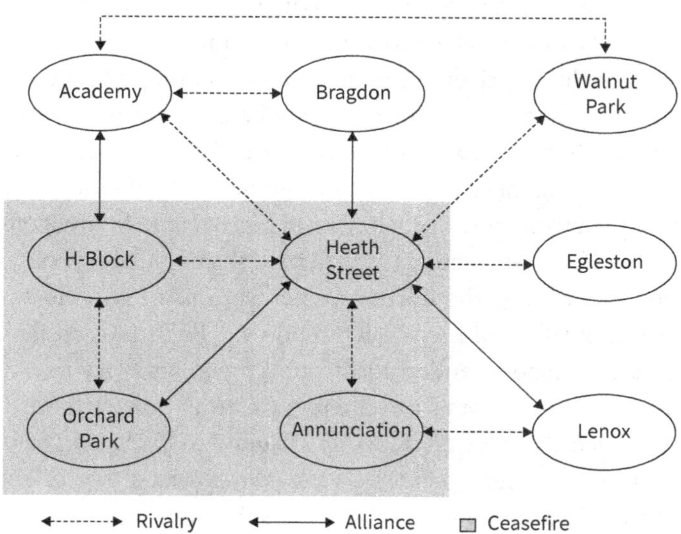


**Figure 6.6** Heath Street gang clique of rivals and allies.

*Source*: Anthony A. Braga, Robert Apel, and Brandon C. Welsh, "The Spillover Effects of Focused Deterrence on Gang Violence," *Evaluation Review* 37, no. 3–4 (2013): 325.

Ceasefire generated any spillover deterrent effects among these vicariously treated groups relative to comparison gangs that did not receive direct treatment and were not socially connected to targeted gangs. This study found that total shootings involving these vicariously treated gangs were reduced by 24% relative to total shootings involving matched comparison gangs.

## Prisoner Reentry and the Prevention of Gun Violence in Chicago

The Chicago Project Safe Neighborhoods (PSN) experience represents an innovative application of focused deterrence principles. The immediate goal was to reduce violent recidivism by individuals with prior gun offenses who were released from correctional settings into the community. The PSN taskforce started meeting on a monthly basis in May 2002 to design gun violence reduction strategies in two adjacent Chicago Police Department (CPD) districts suffering from very high levels of serious gun violence.[58] The PSN taskforce included representatives from the U.S. Attorney's Office for the Northern District of Illinois, CPD, Illinois Department of Correction, Cook County Department of Probation, Cook County State's Attorney's Office, City of Chicago Corporation Counsel, and more than 12 community-based organizations. Although multiple PSN initiatives were launched, four key components were directly focused on reducing gun violence in the targeted policing districts in the near term: offender notification meetings, federal prosecutions, federal prison sentences, and multiagency gun recoveries. The offender notification meetings provided a community intervention; the other components reflected coordinated law enforcement actions. Taken together, these components represent the basic elements of a focused deterrence strategy designed to change the behavior of high-risk individual offenders.

Offender notification meetings represented the key activity launched by the PSN taskforce to change the normative perceptions of gun violence held by the targeted population of high-risk offenders.[59] Beginning in January 2003, the PSN taskforce held offender notification meetings twice per month with randomly selected offenders from the two treatment districts who had prior gun violence records and were recently assigned to probation or parole. The 1-hour notification meetings stressed the *consequences* that offenders faced if they continued to use guns and the *choices* they needed to make to prevent further re-offending. Three distinct segments of the meeting reinforced this message: (a) Law enforcement officials emphasized their enhanced efforts to reduce gun violence in the targeted communities and informed offenders of their vulnerability as felons to federal firearms laws with stiff mandatory minimum sentences, (b) ex-offenders from the community who worked with social intervention programs described how they managed to turn away from violence and change their life trajectories, and (c) a series of speakers from community-based groups discussed the choices the offender could make to enroll or participate in specific social service and opportunity provision programs. These programs included substance abuse assistance, temporary shelter, job training, mentorship and union training, education and GED courses, and behavior counseling.

Federal prosecutions of gun offenders and increased law enforcement efforts to recover illegal guns represented the on-the-ground enhanced risks of apprehension faced by former offenders being released under community supervision to the target areas.[60] Multiagency PSN gun teams staffed by federal, county, and local law enforcement representatives concentrated their resources on gun crime in the two treatment districts. The gun teams investigated illegal gun sales and use, conducted gun seizures, and served warrants on pending firearm cases. On a biweekly basis, the broader PSN taskforce reviewed every gun case generated by the gun teams to determine whether a federal or state prosecution would lead to the longest prison sentences.

A rigorous quasi-experimental program evaluation assessed the impact of the various PSN programs on neighborhood-level homicide rates in Chicago.[61] The two adjacent PSN police districts were statistically matched to two other police districts selected as near-equivalent controls. The research team analyzed the overall effects of the PSN program as well as the four interventions that comprised it: (a) increased federal prosecutions for convicted felons carrying or using guns, (b) the length of sentences associated with federal prosecutions, (c) gun recoveries by the gun teams, and (d) social marketing of deterrence and social norms messages through offender notification meetings. The research team found that the PSN treatment was associated with a statistically significant 37% reduction in the number of homicides in the treatment district relative to the control districts (Figure 6.7). The overall PSN treatment was also associated with statistically significant decreases in gun homicide incidents and aggravated assault incidents.

The PSN component that generated the largest effect on decreased homicide in the treatment districts relative to control districts was the offender notification forums. In short, the greater the proportion of offenders who attended the forums, the greater the decline in treatment district levels of homicide. A supplemental assessment focused on the offending behaviors of individuals after they attended a PSN offender notification meeting.[62] Analyses suggested that notification meeting participants had 30% lower risk for committing new

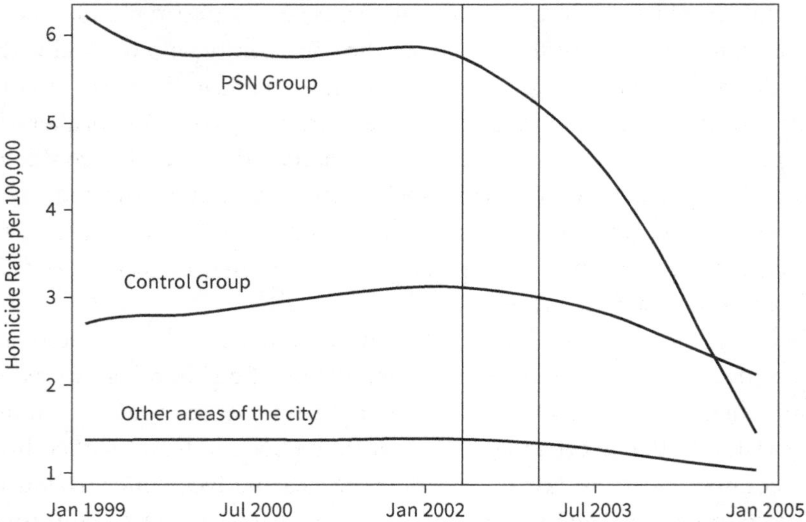


**Figure 6.7** Smoothed quarterly homicide rates in Chicago by PSN group assignment, 1999–2004.

*Source*: Andrew V. Papachristos, Tracey L. Meares, and Jeffrey Fagan, "Attention Felons: Evaluating Project Safe Neighborhoods in Chicago," *Journal of Empirical Legal Studies* 4, no. 2 (2007): 256.

offenses compared to similar offenders in no-treatment comparison groups. And more recently, a social network analysis was used to evaluate the direct and spillover effects of the Chicago PSN intervention on gunshot victimization of program participants and their untreated socially connected peers.[63] The analysis found that participation in the PSN program reduced gunshot victimization for both groups over a 2-year post-treatment period.

The evaluation also found that increased federal prosecutions and the number of guns recovered by the gun teams were associated with modest but statistically significant declines in homicides in the treatment districts relative to the control districts.[64] Getting more guns off the street and prosecuting more offenders federally for gun crimes were associated with small but meaningful homicide decreases. The length of sentences associated with federal prosecutions, however, was not associated with the observed homicide decreases.

## Drug Market Intervention in High Point, North Carolina

Guns are often used to settle drug market disputes. As such, developing effective interventions to manage violence stemming from disorderly drug market conditions can be an important part of an overall police-led gun violence reduction strategy. In 2003, the then newly appointed High Point Police Department (HPPD) chief decided to apply the focused deterrence approach to deal with violence and disorder emanating from overt street-level drug markets with surprising success.[65] Like many urban police departments, the HPPD struggled to develop effective working relationships with African American residents of disadvantaged areas that were suffering from serious violence and street-level drug selling problems. The generally poor relationship between the HPPD and the city's Black communities was rooted in a problematic history of overly aggressive and disrespectful policing.[66] The development and implementation of the drug market intervention (DMI) was aided by a new narrative on police–community relations led by the HPPD chief. The engagement approach was brutally honest about the harms imposed on disadvantaged Black communities by past policing regimes and attempted to reconcile with residents by promising carefully constructed community crime prevention strategies.[67]

These frank conversations about race, drugs, and policing positioned the HPPD to partner with West End neighborhood residents to launch a focused deterrence strategy to address violence and disorder emanating from a highly active street drug market. The DMI proceeded by first conducting careful data analyses and intelligence gathering on key participants in the targeted drug market.[68] Undercover drug buys were then made from all identified dealers in the West End drug market. When this operation was completed, the violent dealers were immediately arrested. The nonviolent dealers were brought to a "call-in" where they faced a roomful of law enforcement officers, social service providers, community figures, ex-offenders, and "influentials"—parents, relatives, and others with close, important relationships with particular dealers.

During the call-in session, the nonviolent drug dealers were told that (a) they were valuable to the community and (b) the dealing must stop.[69] Community members and influentials sent a norm-changing message to the participants by describing the harm that drug dealing was doing to the neighborhood and voiced support of the targeted offenders' capacity to change these behaviors. Social services and opportunities were offered to the dealers. Ex-offenders explained how they successfully made the transition from drug selling to employment. Law enforcement officials then informed the dealers that they faced pending drug charges and showed videos of the undercover buys from each of the call-in participants.[70] The officials stated that these cases were being temporarily suspended (or "banked"). The dealers were told that the cases would be activated if they continued to sell drugs. The West End call-in was supported by the continued delivery of resources and an increased police presence in the neighborhood to reinforce the message that drug selling would no longer be tolerated in the area.

The High Point DMI was implemented on a rolling basis across neighborhoods suffering from overt drug market problems.[71] In each site, data analyses and investigation of key drug market offenders lasted between 1 and 3 months. These upfront activities ensured that enforcement was limited to a select few individuals who were directly involved in the street drug trade. For instance, four call-in meetings were held with offenders from four different neighborhoods between 2004 and 2007. As described above, key offenders with prior violent felony convictions were arrested, whereas nonviolent offenders were selected to participate in the call-ins. In total, 83 dealers were identified across the four intervention locations; 20 were arrested and 63 were selected to participate in a call-in.[72] At all call-ins, the message communicated to participants consisted of deterrence, social services and opportunity, and changing norms.

A series of evaluations suggest the High Point DMI produced significant reductions in crime. For instance, a quasi-experimental evaluation reported modest 12–18% reductions in violent crime in four treated areas relative to control areas located elsewhere in the city.[73] Using a different methodology and a fifth treated neighborhood, RAND Corporation researchers found that the High Point DMI program generated a 21% reduction in general crime rates in treated areas with little evidence of spatial crime displacement.[74]

## Growing Evidence on Focused Deterrence Violence Reduction Impacts

An ongoing systematic review of the program evaluation evidence has been highly influential in documenting the positive impacts of focused deterrence on serious violence. The most recent iteration of the review identified 24 quasi-experimental evaluations of focused deterrence programs.[75] These studies evaluated focused deterrence programs implemented in small, medium, and large cities. With the exception of an evaluation of a focused deterrence program implemented in Glasgow, Scotland, all included studies were conducted in the United States. Twelve evaluations tested the violence impacts of gang and group intervention programs, 9 evaluations considered the effects of focused deterrence on crime problems connected to street-level drug markets, and 3 evaluations appraised crime reductions generated by focused deterrence programs targeting individual repeat offenders. The evaluation evidence on the effects of focused deterrence on crime is relatively new, with all 24 evaluations completed after 2000 and half released after 2013.

Nineteen of the 24 focused deterrence evaluations (79%) included in the review reported at least one noteworthy crime control impact.[76] A meta-analysis of the program impacts found a statistically significant moderate reduction in targeted crime problems associated with focused deterrence programs, with the largest impacts produced by the gang and group violence reduction programs followed by individual repeat offender programs. The meta-analysis suggested smaller crime control effects were generated by the DMI programs. However, several of these DMI programs had noteworthy implementation problems.

None of the studies that examined possible crime displacement effects noted significant movement of offending from targeted areas into surrounding areas or increased violence by untreated gangs socially connected to targeted gangs.[77] In fact, the review suggested focused deterrence programs created unanticipated crime control benefits in untreated areas and spillover effects to untreated groups. For instance, the City of Los Angeles replicated the Boston Ceasefire program to deal with persistent gang violence problems in the early 2000s. The Los Angeles Ceasefire evaluation reported that violent crime had decreased by 34%, gang crime decreased by 28%, and gun crime decreased by 26% in targeted areas following the start of the intervention.[78] In immediately proximate areas, violent crime had also decreased by 33%, gang crime decreased by 44%, and gun crime decreased by 28% after the Ceasefire program commenced in the targeted areas.

The Los Angeles Ceasefire evaluation also explored whether the intervention generated displacement and diffusion impacts on the violent behavior of socially connected gangs.[79] The Ceasefire program targeted two rival gangs located in the Hollenbeck area of Boyle Heights. The program substantially reduced violent crimes, gang-involved crimes, and gun crimes among the two gangs over a 6-month period. The evaluation further noted that there were slightly larger reductions in these crimes among four rival gangs located in surrounding areas that were not specifically targeted by the Ceasefire program during the same 6-month period. The evaluators suggested that the observed diffusion effects were driven by social ties between the targeted and nontargeted gangs and that as the targeted gangs committed less violence, active feuds with nontargeted gangs diminished over time.

The rigorous program evaluation evidence on the impacts of focused deterrence on targeted crime problems continues to grow. Completed after the latest version of the systematic review, quasi-experimental evaluations of focused deterrence in two very challenging urban environments—Oakland[80] and Philadelphia[81]—reported statistically significant reductions in shootings in areas with targeted gangs relative to matched comparison areas with untreated gangs. The Oakland evaluation also examined the main and spillover focused deterrence impacts on total shootings involving treated gangs and vicariously treated gangs connected to targeted gangs through rivalries and alliances relative to total shootings by matched comparison gangs. The Oakland study reported that total shootings were reduced by more than 25% for both directly treated and vicariously treated gangs relative to matched comparison gangs.[82]

The available program evaluation evidence of focused deterrence has been previously characterized as limited by an absence of randomized experiments.[83] Recently, the first randomized controlled trial was completed that tested an individual-offender-focused deterrence program centered on reducing subsequent recidivism by high-risk probationers and parolees in St. Louis.[84] Probationers and parolees were randomly assigned to a treatment group that was invited to attend a focused deterrence notification meeting and a control group that was not invited to attend a notification meeting. Using an intention-to-treat approach, the randomized experiment found that the parolees and probationers who were invited to attend the focused deterrence notification meeting were less likely to be arrested over the following 17 months relative to those who did not attend the meeting. These findings aligned with those of prior evaluations of individual-level focused deterrence initiatives that suggest the notification meeting, the crux of focused deterrence, reduces future criminal behavior.[85]

While there is a continued need for strong program evaluations, an emerging policy consensus on the crime control value of these strategies has also been shaped by other systematic assessments of the growing body of evaluation evidence on the crime reduction impacts of focused deterrence programs. For instance, a U.S. Agency for International Development meta-review of 43 systematic reviews that considered more than 1,400 studies of community violence prevention programs concluded that focused deterrence had the largest direct impact on violence of all the interventions reviewed in the report.[86] Likewise, Public Safety Canada, which is the country's Department of Public Safety and Domestic Preparedness, published a systematic review and meta-analysis of street gang violence control strategies that concluded focused deterrence programs were the most consistently effective solution to gang-related delinquency.[87]

## Optimizing Deterrence and Other Violence Prevention Mechanisms

Even serial offenders fear going to prison. The lesson of the focused deterrence programs is that gang members can be persuaded to reduce involvement in gun violence by a credible threat that it will result in a serious sanction. When the authorities increase the priority for arresting and prosecuting shooters, and communicate that new regime effectively to gang members, the result is that gun violence is prevented.

Deterrent impacts are ultimately determined by offender perceptions of sanction risk and certainty.[88] Focused deterrence strategies are explicitly designed to prevent crime through the advertising of sanctions and the personalized application of deterrence messages through direct meetings with identified individuals. The effective communication of punishments to relevant audiences is an important step in generating deterrent impacts.[89] The approach directly confronts offenders via group notification meetings (i.e., call-ins and forums) and customized individual notifications provided by criminal justice officials, community partners, and service providers which inform offenders that continued offending will not be tolerated and explain how the system will respond to violations of these new behavior standards. Direct communications, coupled with swift and certain sanctions for violating established behavioral norms, influence offender perceptions of apprehension risk. Face-to-face meetings with offenders are an important first step in altering their perceptions about sanction risk.[90] Direct communications and affirmative follow-up responses are the types of new information that may cause offenders to reassess the risks of continuing their criminal behavior (in this case, shooting at rivals).[91]

Group-based focused deterrence strategies, such as Boston Ceasefire, do not attempt to eliminate gangs and violent groups from cities. Although specific gang members were removed from the street as a direct response to serious violence, the ultimate goal was to reduce shooting by modifying group perceptions of risks that informed their decisions to shoot. Concerns about replaceability, largely driven by drug enforcement experience that deterred and incapacitated members of drug-selling groups can be easily replaced by a pool of people willing to make money meeting a seemingly never-ending demand for drugs, do not undermine the potential efficacy of focused deterrence. No Boston gang "disappeared" as a result of focused Ceasefire attention. Boston had gangs before, during, and after the implementation of Ceasefire. Their willingness to use serious gun violence to settle disputes, however, did change.

Another plausible reason for gang members to stop shooting is that many do not like the violence and are looking for an "honorable exit"—a way to step back from the violence without losing face to their peers.[92] Most do not want to kill other people who are just like them, and they are not at all interested in being locked up by the police for a very long time if they are caught. However, given the pressures to retaliate and maintain status within their groups, and the harm they may experience if they do not conform, gang members and drug dealers are not able to have a conversation with their peers that shooting people is a bad idea. In the words of one Boston gang member during the 1990s, "The police is very definite about what the rules is. . . . It helps because we say to each other now, 'Don't shoot that boy because we're going to have problems with the police.'"[93]

Focused deterrence strategies represent a new approach to generating deterrent impacts as it attempts to make the prospect of sanctions more legitimate by bringing in individual norms, values, and informal social control.[94] Punishments that are excessive, poorly motivated, and not well aligned with individual and community norms can be viewed as illegitimate.[95] The application of sanctions should be viewed as consistent with community and individual norms rather than threats wielded by external and possibly hostile authorities. Focused deterrence builds upon concepts of police legitimacy and procedural justice when communicating with offenders and engaging community partners (as described in Chapter 4). Offender notification meetings are administered according to the two key elements of procedural justice.[96] First, establishing quality decision-making, the identification of the group for the focused intervention is justified to the offenders in the room. It is important for the attending offenders to understand that they were selected for intervention because their behavior (e.g., serious gun violence that traumatizes their community) rather than their status (i.e., drug-selling gang members who live in a disadvantaged neighborhood with very limited economic opportunities). Second, promoting quality of treatment, the partnership expresses concern for the well-being of the community and of the offenders and offers offenders a clear choice in a respectful and business-like manner. Law enforcement officials promote accountability by spelling out the group consequences for continued offending by its members while community members and service providers promise support and assistance.

Community-based organizations and resident groups can be potent crime prevention partners for law enforcement agencies.[97] Focused deterrence programs seek to stimulate informal social control crime prevention mechanisms to reduce both offending rates and punishment rates. These programs customarily include relevant community-based organizations in the larger crime reduction partnership to participate in operational decision-making and deliver key intervention actions. For instance, in the Oakland and Boston Ceasefire programs, activist Black clergy helped police by mobilizing local communities to act against violence through peace walks and other public events, sharing information on the underlying nature of ongoing disputes between rival gangs with law enforcement agencies, communicating the anti-violence message during call-ins and throughout the city, and appealing to gang youth and their families to take advantage of services and opportunities rather than persisting in high-risk activities.[98]

Focused deterrence programs also provide "outreach and support"—social services and various kinds of facilitative interventions—to the identified high-risk populations. The role of outreach and support in focused deterrence is complex.[99] There is hope that support services can reduce individual offending. Unfortunately, the actual outcomes of these traditional social service and opportunity provision strategies in the focused deterrence framework have not been encouraging. In most cities that have tried the approach, very few targeted offenders took advantage of such traditional services, and the outcomes associated with such services have been generally poor.[100] In Cincinnati, an evaluation found no association between violence reduction outcomes and the number of people who received services through their focused deterrence program.[101] Anecdotal evidence suggests that the provision of social services and various types of facilitative interventions to identified high-risk populations through "outreach and support" efforts seems to be an important step toward improving the perceived legitimacy and procedural fairness of the focused deterrence approach.[102] As such, including service and opportunity provision components in the strategy is an important way to secure community buy-in for the approach.

## Implementation Challenges

Focused deterrence programs are composed of multifaceted intervention activities and a complex interagency structure that presents multiple opportunities for implementation problems and program integrity threats. The systematic review of focused deterrence programs found that nearly one-third of the 24 included evaluations reported implementation challenges.[103] As described above, the original Boston Ceasefire program was discontinued despite several years of noteworthy success in reducing gang violence. Key challenges in sustaining the Boston Ceasefire intervention stemmed from a lack of ongoing analysis of evolving gun violence problems, inadequate governance structures that did not support continued implementation after key working group members moved on to other positions, and political infighting in lead partnering agencies. Other focused deterrence programs also experienced very concerning program management challenges during implementation. Moreover, replication programs in Baltimore, Minneapolis, and San Francisco unraveled rapidly due to serious political problems and a lack of true interagency partnership after some encouraging initial crime control success.[104]

As more cities have included focused deterrence as a central element of their broader approach to reduce crime, systematic efforts have been launched to ensure the proper program implementation. Most prominently, the National Network for Safe Communities (NNSC) at John Jay College of Criminal Justice of the City University of New York has developed a range of practitioner-friendly guides to structure program activities and promote the integrity of focused deterrence strategies. We highly encourage interested readers to consult the various resources available through the NNSC that aid local jurisdictions in maintaining and ensuring treatment integrity from the outset of implementation.[105] The gang and criminally active group focused deterrence strategy in particular has reached a stage such that detailed and sophisticated routine assessments have been designed and implemented.

In addition to these resources on specific programmatic activities and strategic orientation, cities need to develop the following three capabilities to facilitate the successful implementation of focused deterrence:

- *Create a network of capacity.* Focused deterrence strategies strive to launch "relationship-intensive" interventions rooted in trust, mutual accountability, and the capacity of a diverse set of individuals to work together toward a common goal. Delivering a robust response to complicated violence problems, such as gang shootings, requires effective collaborations. Unfortunately, the fact that such collaborations are needed does not guarantee that they inevitably rise or, once developed, are sustained. There are many significant obstacles to their development and maintenance, such as giving up control over scarce resources that could compromise agencies' traditional missions, aligning agencies' individual work efforts into a functional enterprise, and developing a collective leadership among a group of individuals aligned with the needs of their individual organizations.[106] Prior to program launch, jurisdictions need to identify and address these obstacles, or the resulting focused deterrence intervention will not be implemented properly.

- *Develop accountability structures and sustainability plans.* Jurisdictions need to establish a governing structure that extends beyond the working group and creates a performance maintenance system for intelligence gathering and analysis as well as continually keeps partners engaged in the project.[107] For instance, the Cincinnati Initiative to Reduce Violence (CIRV) developed a comprehensive approach to remedy sustainability concerns by the establishment of a formal multilevel governance structure. Prior to the start of the program, CIRV staff recruited local business executives and social science researchers to contribute to the planning process by providing policy advice intended to enhance long-term viability of the intervention. Other jurisdictions have also developed systematic efforts to guide the implementation of focused deterrence. For instance, the Oakland Mayor's Office institutionalized its Ceasefire program by establishing a directive designating that the initiative would be managed through weekly shooting reviews, biweekly coordination meetings, and bimonthly performance appraisals.[108]
- *Conduct upfront and ongoing problem analyses.* Simply adopting particular tactics implemented in other cities, such as call-ins or partnerships with clergy, will not result in a successful implementation of focused deterrence. Partnering agencies in specific jurisdictions need to follow the process, which begins with an upfront analysis of the targeted gun problem. Problem analysis involves conducting in-depth, systematic analysis and assessment of gun violence problems. The role of problem analysis in focused deterrence, and problem-oriented policing more generally, is crucial because it requires the careful examination of underlying factors that lead to crime and disorder problems. Following the completion of the initial analysis, key elements of the focused deterrence framework can be customized to local crime conditions and the operational capacities of partnering agencies.

## Conclusion

Serious gun violence in U.S. cities is driven by a small number of chronic offenders who use guns to settle personal quarrels, gang rivalries, drug market disputes, and other problems. Focused deterrence better positions law enforcement agencies and their community-based and social service partners to manage ongoing disputes between gangs and criminally active groups and deal with individual violent behavior. This strategy includes a number of innovative tactics, such as publicizing rather than hiding police enforcement actions; holding the targeted group responsible and directing punishments toward all group members, not just the one or two involved in the shooting that triggered intervention; and the "Al Capone" punishment approach (Capone was put in prison for tax evasion) of being willing to punish the targeted group for any crime rather than just the shooting that made it the targeted group. A growing number of program evaluations have revealed that focused deterrence reduces gun violence in cities—including some very challenging urban environments such as Chicago, Philadelphia, and Oakland. When properly implemented, these strategies seem to avoid unintended harms associated with indiscriminate and unfocused enforcement efforts while improving police legitimacy in the eyes of the communities they serve. Although police departments need to customize the focused deterrence framework to local conditions, this strategy should be a core component of a portfolio of gun violence reduction implemented in every jurisdiction.

# 7

# Strengthening the Investigation of Shootings

At 9:30 p.m. on a Wednesday night, the Boston Police Department (BPD) received multiple calls for shots fired at a residential location. BPD district officers and detectives responded to the scene within 3 minutes of the initial dispatch and found a 15-year-old Hispanic male on the front stoop of his house who was shot in the thigh. Eleven officers and detectives interviewed 15 individuals at the scene. Several witnesses reported that a young Hispanic male wearing a white t-shirt and blue jeans pulled up to the house on a bicycle and fired shots at the victim. The victim's brother chased the shooter but was not successful in stopping him. The family answered the detectives' questions and expressed concern that the victim had recently started associating with a local gang. Unfortunately, no witnesses were able to make a positive identification of the shooter. The victim was transported to Boston Medical Center and was not cooperative with the police when interviewed at the hospital. Two crime scene response unit officers processed the crime scene and recovered three .22 shell casings.

The victim was eventually released from the hospital and re-interviewed by district detectives approximately 10 days after the initial shooting. The victim was much more cooperative and reported that he did not know the actual identity of the shooter. He just knew the shooter as "JT." The district detectives contacted the BPD Youth Violence Strike Force (YVSF) and asked whether officers knew a gang member who used the nickname "JT," but no luck. The detectives and YVSF officers then worked with the Boston Regional Intelligence Center to establish the identity of "JT" via analyses of intelligence information and social media resources. After JT's identity was confirmed, the detectives applied for a search warrant for his home. The execution of the search warrant led to the recovery of a .22 semiautomatic pistol.

*Policing Gun Violence*. Anthony A. Braga and Philip J. Cook, Oxford University Press. © Oxford University Press 2023.
DOI: 10.1093/oso/9780199929283.003.0007

> The suspect, an 18-year-old Hispanic male, was initially charged with illegal possession of a firearm. After the BPD Ballistics Unit confirmed that the .22 semiautomatic pistol did fire the shell casings recovered at the crime scene, the suspect was charged with "assault and battery with deadly weapon—firearm." The arrest occurred about 4 months after the shooting.[1]

Fans of the television shows *CSI* and *Law & Order* may believe that this sort of resource-intensive, sustained investigation is routine when someone is shot. Unfortunately, that is not the case. Indeed, fewer than half of gun homicides are "cleared" by an arrest, and the clearance rate for nonfatal shootings is lower still. Data from the Chicago Police Department indicate that between 2013 and 2020, there was an arrest in 30% of the fatal shootings and 11% of the nonfatal shootings.[2] Only about half of the homicide arrests result in conviction. Many other violence-plagued cities have similar track records, and it is fair to say that the police are failing either to satisfactorily protect or to serve their community. Fortunately, there is much that can be done to improve investigative performance.

Low clearance rates for fatal and nonfatal shootings are a deadly problem in U.S. cities. Most important, the failure to arrest and convict undermines the deterrent effect of the law, as discussed in previous chapters. Furthermore, unsolved shootings contribute to cycles of urban gun violence. Violent career criminals, gang members and others, remain free and can continue as a deadly threat. Gunshot wound survivors and the associates and families of gun homicide victims may take the law into their own hands to get justice. And trust in the police erodes, which in turn undermines the willingness of community members to share information on suspected shooters. In minority neighborhoods, the routine failure on the part of the police to arrest the shooters can only fuel suspicions that the police do not care about Black and Brown victims of gun violence. As a long-time resident of such a Baltimore neighborhood lamented, "Mind your own business, and stay alive. . . . The police aren't going to do nothing about it anyway, so why should I say anything?"[3]

The probability of arrest for homicides has been declining since the 1960s.[4] Jill Leovy, who for many years served as a crime reporter for the *Los Angeles Times*, has distilled her first-hand knowledge into an illuminating book called *Ghettoside*:

> This is a book about a very simple idea: Where the criminal justice system fails to respond vigorously to violent injury and death, homicide becomes endemic. African Americans have suffered from just such a lack of effective criminal justice, and this, more than anything, is the reason for the nation's long-standing plague of Black homicides."[5]

In a commentary in *The Atlantic* in 2021, Conor Friedersdorf suggests that the slogan "Defund the Police" has been a disaster in the face of mushrooming rates of gun violence.[6] Here is his suggestion for a progressive slogan on police reform: "Solve All Murders." He observes that "Precisely because Black lives matter, people who take Black lives shouldn't get away with it." That is true, he suggests, whether the criminal perpetrator is cop or a civilian.

## Solvability

The first step to improving police performance in solving serious crimes is to understand the challenges. Some shootings essentially solve themselves, as with a domestic shooting in which the contrite husband calls the police from the scene and confesses to the responding officer that he shot his wife. At the other end of the spectrum may be something like the Washington Beltway sniper attacks by John Allen Muhammed and Lee Boyd Malvo in 2002, in which 13 randomly selected people were picked off over the course of 3 weeks, terrorizing the metro area and triggering a massive investigation by local, state, and three federal agencies. Somewhere in between on the "solvability" spectrum are the routine (unfortunately) cases of community gun violence—drive-by shootings, shootings in the course of robberies, and arguments that escalated to gunplay. Whether there is an arrest in such cases may depend on happenstance combined with detective work and possibly a technological assist—the shooting is captured on video by a security camera, the shooter brags about it on social media, or shell casings at the scene can be matched to a gun recovered in a traffic stop. Ultimately, the case is unlikely to result in an arrest and conviction without one or more willing witnesses who can support the circumstantial evidence.

The clearance rate (percentage of cases resolved through arrest or exceptional circumstances) is often put forward as an indicator of the performance of a police department. But given the diversity of cases with respect to solvability, this performance measure has obvious limitations. A high clearance rate in a city in which most homicides result from domestic disputes or barroom brawls (with many witnesses) is good but not that impressive. There is an obvious analogy here to a team's won–lost record as a measure of its performance: We want to know the strength of the competition. The same is true in comparing clearance rates over time or among cities. Indeed, it may be that it is the changing mix of cases, rather than a decline in the quality of detective work, that explains the secular decline in homicide clearance rates nationwide. And it should also be noted that "arrest" as an endpoint is problematic; what we want from the police is not just an arrest but a lawful investigation and a case that will hold up in court. Evidentiary standards for making an arrest can differ among jurisdictions and change over time.

Detectives have long enjoyed an outsized reputation as being effective crime fighters in books, movies, and television. A series of research studies in the 1970s and early 1980s largely debunked this image.[7] The most influential of these studies was the landmark RAND Corporation study that directly observed detective operations in 25 police agencies and surveyed detective practices in an additional 156 police departments.[8] Among the findings were the following: Crimes of violence are solved by the responding patrol officer through information obtained from the victim or victims rather than leads developed by investigators; in more than half of the cases solved, the suspect's identity is known or easily determined at the time the crime is reported to police; an investigator's time is largely consumed reviewing reports, documenting files, and attempting to locate and interview victims on cases that experience has shown are unlikely to be solved; and many investigations are conducted without any hope of developing leads but simply to satisfy victims' expectations.[9] But other studies, especially in recent years, have provided a much more positive assessment of both the practice and the potential of detective work for serious crime.[10]

There have been noteworthy improvements in specific investigative practices in the United States, such as the development of more effective and just ways of interviewing victims, witnesses, and suspects; the implementation of proper methods of conducting perpetrator lineups; and the handling of physical evidence. Forensic technology available to investigators has vastly improved their ability to make links between crimes and offenders. For instance, a National Institute of Justice–sponsored experiment using DNA to solve property crime found that the collection and analysis of physical evidence at crime scenes improves the ability of investigators to identify, arrest, and prosecute criminal offenders.[11] Although improved investigative techniques and technology have arguably improved the likelihood that the "right" people are being arrested for their crimes, these advances have not translated into an increased probability of arrest for offenders, as evidenced by stagnant clearance rates for volume crimes, such as burglary, larceny, assault, and robbery.[12] There may well be countervailing trends—such as a decline in community cooperation—although these dynamics have not been sorted out in any systematic study.

As in all other challenging endeavors, the success of police investigations depends on resources, organization, and skill.[13] Homicide investigations in particular are often complex, with several detectives supported by patrol and other departmental units, technicians, and often, state and federal agencies. Almost uniquely to homicides, the investigation may stretch out for months. After securing and documenting the crime scene, there is the laborious work of tracking down and interviewing witnesses; accessing digital evidence from any cameras, telephones, social media, and other sources; and seeking lab tests on DNA evidence and shell casings. Translating a successful investigation into an arrest, prosecution, and conviction requires coordination with the prosecutors.

What can be done to improve investigative performance in homicide and other cases of serious violence? An obvious answer is to try harder, and in particular allocate more of the department's resources to shooting investigations. But making that argument requires demonstrating that more investigation resources would actually matter. If the case does not "solve itself" and the police do not get lucky, then what can they do? The answer, we have found, is to stay with the case, conduct more interviews, take full advantage of evidence from video and ballistics, and keep checking gang intelligence sources and social media. The typical department can only afford that approach for the highest priority cases, but gun violence—nonfatal shootings as well as murders—should be the top of the list.

## Lessons Learned from Comparing Nonfatal and Fatal Shootings

The strongest evidence that resources matter in the investigation of gun crime derives from a surprising source: a comparison of arrest rates in fatal with nonfatal shootings. Whether the victim survives a shooting attack appears to be largely a matter of chance—whether the bullet happens to strike a vital organ.[14] In any one time and place, the distribution of victim characteristics and circumstances in nonfatal cases is very similar to that for fatal cases (murders). Yet arrest rates for fatal cases tend to be substantially higher than for nonfatal cases. Why? A principal reason is that police departments give higher priority to homicide investigations than to investigations of gunshot assaults. Resources matter.

Actually, Cook first heard this explanation for the "arrest gap" from detectives with the Durham, North Carolina, Police Department (DPD). In Durham, as in many larger cities, homicide detectives have a relatively light caseload, but detectives assigned nonfatal shooting cases are also responsible for other major crimes and may be handling scores of cases at any one time. Furthermore, the homicide detectives have greater access to other resources in the department. It is fair to say that the DPD, like any department, is under much greater pressure to solve homicide cases than nonfatal shootings, despite their similarity of circumstance and intent. Cook's assistant, Sara Shilling, interviewed 17 DPD investigators and asked them about the fatal–nonfatal disparity in arrest rates. Most respondents mentioned that homicide investigators have a far lighter caseload, and more resources generally, compared with the investigators for nonfatal cases. As a result, the homicide investigators can spend more time working a case, tracking down evidence, and creating a relationship with potential witnesses.[15] The other common answer, incidentally, was that witnesses were more likely to cooperate with homicide investigations than with investigations of nonfatal shootings.

Cook and Braga teamed up for a larger and more systematic study of Boston shooting cases. In particular, we analyzed the 204 shooting cases that included at least one homicide (2010–2014), as well as a representative sample of all shooting cases in which no one died ($n = 231$).[16] Detailed data were collected from police investigation files, forensic evidence databases, and interviews with detectives. Data items included information on the circumstances and medical outcome of the shooting, characteristics of the victim, measures of the amount of evidence collected during the investigation by the BPD, and detective reports of the key reasons for the success or failure of the investigation. The quasi-experimental analysis of these data resulted in a series of findings relevant to the research and policy.

The two groups of cases, fatal and nonfatal, were statistically indistinguishable with respect to the circumstances of the shooting, with the sole exception of whether the shooting was indoors or outdoors. (Indoor shootings were more lethal.) The clearance-by-arrest rate for gun homicide cases was more than twice as high as the corresponding rate for gunshot assault cases (43% and 19%, respectively). That difference could possibly have been still larger except for the fact that homicide arrests (but not assault cases) were subject to prior review for probable cause by the district attorney. For both fatal and nonfatal cases, the likelihood of arrest was higher for cases involving personal disputes or domestic violence than for cases arising from gang- and drug-related disputes. But regardless of circumstance, fatal cases had a higher clearance rate compared with nonfatal cases.

**Table 7.1** Time to Clearance in Fatal and Nonfatal Shooting Cases in Boston, 2010–2014

| | One or More Gun Homicides | | Nonfatal Only | |
|---|---|---|---|---|
| Clearance Time | *N* | Cum. % | *N* | Cum. % |
| Scene, leaving scene | 12 | (6.0%) | 13 | (5.7%) |
| Not scene, same day | 5 | (8.5%) | 6 | (8.3%) |
| 1–2 days | 5 | (11.0%) | 6 | (11.0%) |
| >2–7 days | 1 | (11.5%) | 5 | (13.2%) |
| >1 week–1 month | 10 | (16.5%) | 3 | (14.5%) |
| >1–6 months | 30 | (31.5%) | 6 | (17.1%) |
| >6 months–1 year | 11 | (37.0%) | 3 | (18.4%) |
| >1 year | 13 | (43.5%) | 1 | (18.9%) |
| Open investigation | 113 | (100.0%) | 185 | (100.0%) |
| *Total* | 200 | | 228 | |

Republished with permission of John Wiley & Sons–Books, from Philip J. Cook, Anthony A. Braga, Brandon Turchan, and Lisa M. Barao, "Why Do Gun Murders Have a Higher Clearance Rate than Gunshot Assaults?" *Criminology & Public Policy* 18, no. 3 (2019): 536. Permission conveyed through Copyright Clearance Center, Inc.

Interestingly, when we narrowed the focus to just the first 2 days of the investigation, the arrest rates for fatal and nonfatal cases were identical—11% (Table 7.1). The fatal–nonfatal difference in arrest rates emerged later; few nonfatal shooting cases were solved after the first few days, but homicide arrests continued to be made even months after the shooting. The relatively easy cases, both fatal and nonfatal, were solved quickly and without the need for the extra resources deployed in homicide investigations.[17] Given the similarity in fatal and nonfatal case mixes, it makes sense that the prevalence of easy cases is about the same in homicides as in nonfatal cases.

As in other cities, BPD's homicide unit has lighter caseloads and priority access to the crime lab and other units of the police force. Based on a variety of indicators, the initial crime scene investigations yielded more evidence of various sorts. The commitment of additional resources to homicide cases was also evident from comparing the amount of evidence collected outside of the crime scene. Most successful investigations had as one key source of evidence the information provided by a cooperating eyewitness. Excluding exceptional clearances, that source was named as the key in solving the case for 28% of all homicide investigations (67% of arrests) compared with just 14% of all nonfatal investigations (77% of arrests). The direct connection with effort is clear for collecting other types of evidence, such as ballistic and video evidence, latent prints, and analysis of phone calls. One or more of those were mentioned as the key to success more than 100 times in homicide cases but only 24 times in nonfatal cases.

In summary, the comparison of these similar groups of cases, distinguished by the random event of whether a gunshot wound proves fatal, allowed us to identify the effect of investigation effort as opposed to solvability. The fatal cases engendered increasingly more sustained effort and ultimately a much higher arrest rate. It is reasonable to interpret the result as follows: The BPD only allocated the resources required to make an arrest in the easiest of the nonfatal cases, whereas for homicide cases resources were available to solve many of the more challenging cases.

The Boston study was the first to consider the role of the large differential in investigation resources in accounting for why gun homicide cases have a higher clearance rate compared to nonfatal gunshot cases. This clearance rate gap is apparently ubiquitous, but it has only been established systematically for a handful of jurisdictions: For example, from 2006 to 2016 in Milwaukee, clearance rates ranged between 56% and 78% for homicides and between 13% and 31% for nonfatal shootings; for any given year during this period, clearance rates were 29–65 percentage points lower for nonfatal shootings than for homicides.[18] A comparable but less pronounced discrepancy was observed in Chicago between 2010 and 2016 when annual clearance rates for homicide ranged from 26% to 46% and from 5% to 11% for nonfatal shootings, with a yearly disparity of 21–35 percentage points.[19] In Durham in 2015, half of all gun homicides resulted in an arrest, but an arrest was made in just 10% of the 145 nonfatal shootings that occurred.[20]

The first lesson from the Durham and Boston studies, then, is that resources matter in investigations of gun violence. The difficult-to-solve homicide cases are more likely to be successful than the difficult-to-solve nonfatal shootings. The suggestion here is that a police department could increase its clearance rate of nonfatal shootings by giving them the same priority as homicide cases. The more generic point is that in shooting investigations, resources matter, and that applies to both fatal and nonfatal cases.

It is understandable why police chiefs would prioritize homicides. They are bound to be under more pressure from the community if the victim dies. But a moment's thought suggests that from the standpoint of preventing future violence, it is almost as important to arrest shooters who wound their victims as shooters who kill them. Because the circumstances and intentions are very similar, so, presumably, are the preventive effects of arrest in terms of incapacitating shooters and putting a price on shooting. Still, the police chief has scarce resources, and nonfatal shootings are approximately five times as common as fatal shootings. Furthermore, an increase in priority may have to overcome the investigators' natural inclination to back off if the victim is uncooperative—as is usually the case in nonfatal shootings.[21] As one BPD district detective relayed to Braga during an interview,

> So I ask this gang member to tell me who is responsible for shooting him in the hand . . . and he tells me to fuck off. And then his mom tells me to stop harassing her son and get the fuck out of the hospital room. It doesn't take a study to tell you this investigation is going nowhere.

That problem does not arise so directly in homicide cases. But ultimately the purpose of police investigations is to serve the public, not the victim.

The BPD developed plans to test whether nonfatal shooting clearances were improved by the establishment of a specialized shooting investigations unit that was resourced like the homicide unit. Unfortunately, these plans were never implemented. Other cities, however, have established similar units with very promising results. For instance, the Denver Police Department created a special unit to investigate nonfatal shootings with the same level of effort as homicides. In the first 7 months of 2020, the unit solved 65% of the city's nonfatal shootings, a dramatic improvement over its 39% nonfatal shooting rate the previous year.[22] In Buffalo, New York, however, the establishment of a shootings investigations unit did not improve shooting clearance rates.[23] Unfortunately, the unit was not structured and resourced in a way that mimicked the intensity of homicide investigations. The bottom line here is that investigative resources matter.

## Raising Clearance Rates in Boston

Providing investigators with a lighter caseload and better access to the crime lab and other departmental resources can help solve more cases. But such generalizations are just a start. A department determined to do better can benefit from a comprehensive approach including systematic analysis and input from all the relevant groups. The BPD under Commissioner Ed Davis provides one successful model.

Around the turn of the century, the BPD was regularly criticized by community activists and the local press for low homicide clearance rates.[24] Between 2004 and 2011, the BPD Homicide Unit cleared, on average, approximately 44% of the homicides investigated compared with the national clearance rate of 63%. When he was appointed BPD Commissioner in late 2006, Davis pledged to reduce serious violence, among other things by improving clearance rates. But they remained stubbornly low for his first 5 years, at which point he tasked Braga with securing a federal grant and helping guide a comprehensive effort to turn things around.

The BPD homicide clearance project was led by sworn and civilian staff. Braga collaborated with this team to conduct a problem analysis of current BPD homicide investigation policies and practices. A key product of this work was a statistical analysis of 314 total homicide victimizations between January 1, 2007, and December 31, 2011. Drawing on homicide case file information and interviews with homicide detectives, this analysis examined the influence of homicide case characteristics and BPD investigative practices (response time, actions of first responders securing the scene, number of detectives assigned to a case, use of computerized databases in the investigation, forensic testing, etc.) on the likelihood that homicide cases were cleared. The development of the homicide clearance intervention then drew upon the insights of BPD investigators and the best practices in other jurisdictions, most notably from the United Kingdom. The BPD hired a UK investigative consultant to review and make recommendations on the proposed reforms to the BPD's homicide investigation policies and practices.

Based on these research and development activities, a series of recommendations to increase the size of the Homicide Unit, enhance the training of detectives, and adopt new practices and policies were made to the BPD Commissioner. The BPD homicide clearance intervention implementation started in January 2012 with the expansion of the homicide unit from 28 to 38—including additional detectives and a civilian crime analyst. The BPD also added a second Victim–Witness Resource Officer and strengthened its connections to victim assistance organizations in an effort to improve relationships between detectives and homicide victims' families and witnesses.

The Homicide Unit and other relevant staff received extensive additional training in cutting-edge investigative techniques over the course of the intervention implementation. The BPD also sent two deputy superintendents to the UK National Policing Improvement Agency's Senior Investigative Officer Training, which detailed its investigative business model and covered important concepts such as peer review of homicide investigations.

A key issue identified during the problem analysis phase of the project was lack of a standardized approach focused on best practice. The project developed protocols to guide work activities across the different stages of homicide investigation. Among the new protocols were the following:

- The formal designation of a crime scene entry log scribe
- Techniques for identifying and managing witnesses

- Deployment of Forensics Group technicians to homicide scenes
- The collection and transfer of evidence to the Forensic Group for storage and testing
- Processes for working with homicide prosecutors to prepare cases for grand juries

The protocols provided guidance for supervisors and line-staff working in each investigative area and required participants to complete checklist forms. These documents were reviewed by command staff to ensure standardization was achieved.

The BPD Homicide Unit convened monthly peer review sessions for all open homicide investigations. These meetings were intended to ensure that all possible avenues were being pursued. Investigating detectives presented key aspects of the case to their peers and supervisors and solicited their suggestions. A similar process was put in place to manage the processing and testing of physical evidence by the Forensics Group. Over the course of the intervention period, new forensic technology was also acquired and used by the BPD, such as three-dimensional shooting incident reconstruction technology to more accurately identify bullet trajectory flight paths at homicide scenes.

So what was the effect of the additional resources and reform of investigative practices?[25] The homicide clearance rate increased sharply. As Figure 7.1 shows, the BPD Homicide Unit cleared 47% of homicide victimizations during the 2007–2011 pre-intervention time period and 66% of homicide victimizations during the 2012–2014 intervention time period. The "solvability" of Boston's homicide cases did not change during that period—almost the entire increase was due to more resources and better practice.[26] And a more detailed look at the data found that the reforms were successful in improving investigations for all kinds of homicides, regardless of weapon type, victim characteristics, or gang involvement. (Historically, gun homicides tend to have lower arrest rates, as do those with minority victims and those with gang involvement.) The success of these reforms brought a greater measure of justice to the survivors of marginalized victims and ultimately helped prevent subsequent violence.

## Challenges and Opportunities

It is vital that real police performance in solving crimes of serious violence be improved. We have learned that better resourced, smarter investigations will have better results and that a local problem-solving approach can pay major

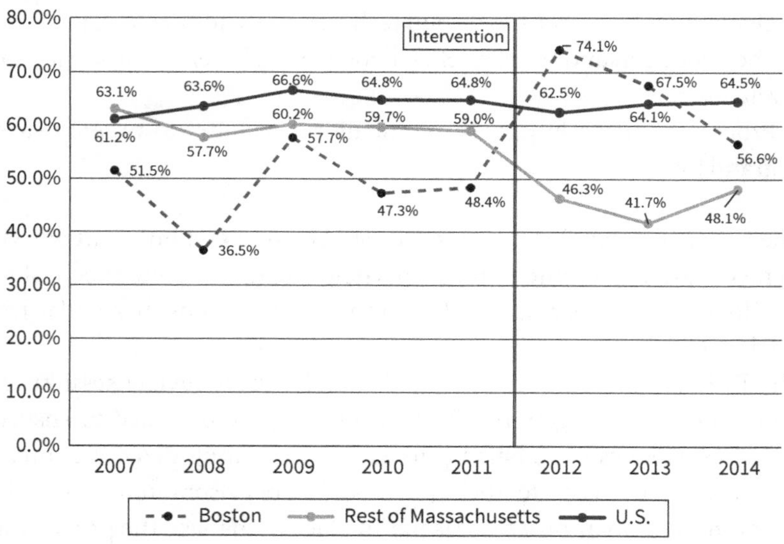


**Figure 7.1.** U.S., Massachusetts, and Boston homicide clearance rates, 2007–2014.
*Source*: Anthony A. Braga and Desiree Dusseault, "Can Homicide Detectives Improve Homicide Clearance Rates?" *Crime & Delinquency* 64, no. 3 (2018): 293.

dividends. But it is also useful to step back and consider the generic challenges and opportunities to improving investigations.

Detectives attempting to solve gun assaults and homicides have more tools at their disposal compared to their predecessors from a few decades ago. DNA analysis provides more accurate evidence than fingerprints ever did. Ballistics imaging technology creates the possibility of reliably associating bullet fragments and shell casings with a particular pistol. Cell phones create a record of location and contacts that can provide helpful evidence on a suspect's movements and communications (if a subpoena can be obtained to download these data). Social media have become a vehicle for gang members to taunt their rivals and brag about their violent engagements and are fair game for investigators. Perhaps most important has been that surveillance cameras are now ubiquitous, providing the potential of capturing digital images of perpetrators, victims, and witnesses. These and other technological assists require a well-developed technical capacity and training, but in a larger department confronting a high volume of gun violence, such investments are surely worth considering.[27]

Despite these new tools, clearance rates, as we have seen, are dismally low in many cities. The great challenge arises from this fact: Building a strong case against a particular shooter almost always requires human witnesses. But witnesses are typically reluctant to cooperate or downright refuse. In part, that is a reflection of the community's low esteem for the police. The Gallup Poll in July 2021 found that less than half of respondents expressed confidence in the police—a 30-year low. The Black–White gap with respect to the police is larger than for other institutions: Just 19% of Black respondents expressed confidence in the police.[28] Lack of confidence or trust is not conducive to willing cooperation, and it is compounded by other reasons for noncooperation, including fear of retaliation and the real possibility that the witness may themself be in trouble with the law for some reason.

A survey of Chicago residents in Illinois prisons, conducted by Cook and colleagues, provided a sense of the potential value of cooperation and the reason why it is so scarce. Half of the prisoners reported they had been shot before. (For such nonfatal shootings, the willing cooperation of the victim is particularly important in developing probable cause and ultimately gaining a conviction.) Very few of the respondents had cooperated with police investigations of these shootings, although at least half of them could have provided useful information about the identity of the shooter. Respondents explained their choice not to cooperate by reference to "street codes" against snitching, mistrust of the police, and the desire to retaliate against the shooter personally.[29]

It is particularly difficult to get young men who are involved in gangs and the illegal drug trade to provide information on shootings to the authorities. A study of 50 young Black men from the Bronx and Brooklyn, many of whom were gang members and had been involved in gun violence, found that 92% of the respondents preferred self-help in the form of retaliatory violence over cooperating with the police after shootings.[30] One respondent commented, "Hell no, I would never talk to cops." Another explained, "That's not me, I don't talk to the police . . . I don't even like the police." While yet another subject commented, "I would never talk to the police, period. . . . They not here to help me. They just want to take someone down, put someone away." Finally, one respondent explained his preference for street vengeance over police intervention:

> If I go and tell the [cops and] this nigga fuck around and beat the case . . . this nigga still out here smoking blunts, doing everything while my [friend] dead, you feel me . . . that's why I don't understand that snitching to the cops shit . . . this nigga shot my [friend] . . . a real nigga would just go out and kill that nigga.

The lack of confidence and hostility toward the police are only exacerbated when arrest and conviction rates are low. Rightly or wrongly, if there are no legal consequences for most shootings, that will be viewed as further evidence that the police simply do not care. So another vicious cycle emerges—noncooperation contributes to low arrest rates, which then reinforce attitudes that engender noncooperation. But there is also hope. When vicious cycles are reversed, the gains become self-reinforcing.

With effort and skill, witnesses can be "converted." The detectives need time to track down elusive witnesses, to get to know them and their families, and gather intelligence. A hostile attitude from a gunshot victim does not need to be the end, because ultimately it is not the victim but, rather, the community that is being served by a successful investigation. Training, a clear sense of departmental priority, and lighter caseloads can make the difference, as well as resources to protect the safety of witnesses who do cooperate.

At the systemic level, it may help over the long term if the police can find ways to improve their relationship with the community. That project begins with curtailing unnecessary use of force, a topic for Chapter 8.

## Conclusion

The main purpose of solving shootings is to reduce subsequent shootings. Denigrating detective work as "reactive" ignores the preventive value of holding shooters accountable for their crimes. If the mission of the police is to protect and to serve, then both purposes are accomplished by arresting perpetrators of crimes that result in serious injury or death and degrade the quality of life in the community. Success in this basic task of policing is important for building trust and interrupting the cycle of violence. Many police forces do not focus their resources on improving shooting investigations, and resulting low arrest rates undermine their efforts to deter prospective shooters.

There is much that police departments can do to improve the arrest rate. We believe there is a strong case for assigning the same priority to nonfatal shootings as fatal shootings. If the investigators have a lighter caseload and better access to other resources, some of the less solvable cases will be solved. More generally, there are a variety of steps that police departments can take to expand their investigative prowess. That begins with a local decision to give higher priority to reducing gun violence and serving marginalized communities.

# 8

# Reducing Shootings by the Police

On August 9, 2014, Michael Brown and a friend were walking in the middle of Canfield Drive, a two-lane street in the St. Louis suburb of Ferguson, Missouri, when a police officer drove by and told them to use the sidewalk. After words were exchanged, the white officer confronted the 18-year-old Brown, who was black. The situation escalated, with the officer and Brown scuffling. The officer shot and killed Brown, who was unarmed.

August 15, 2014: Police identify the officer who shot Brown as Darren Wilson, who had been with the department since 2011. They also release surveillance video that shows Brown grabbing large amounts of cigarillos from behind the counter of the Ferguson Market and pushing a worker who confronts him as he leaves the convenience store. Police say Brown took almost $50 worth of cigarillos.

November 24, 2014: St. Louis County prosecutor Bob McCulloch announces that the grand jury has decided not to indict Wilson.[1]

January 6, 2021: [Ashli Babbitt was] at the front of an angry mob trying to get through to the "Speaker's Lobby," where members of Congress and staff are holed up. She's screaming at the police, apparently demanding entry.

The crowd is surging. It's at the doors. "F— the blue!" can be heard. People are bashing at the glass panels on the doors with sticks and flagpoles. Several police officers are doing their best to hold back an entire crowd, but it seems like a losing battle. "Break it down," yells the crowd.

Members of Congress can be seen on the other side of the door. Also on the other side of the door is a police lieutenant holding a gun, pointing it at the mob, an unmistakable warning to stay back.

But Babbitt decides instead—although it's a little hard to see on the video—to climb through the shattered glass window into the

*Policing Gun Violence*. Anthony A. Braga and Philip J. Cook, Oxford University Press. © Oxford University Press 2023.
DOI: 10.1093/oso/9780199929283.003.0008

> Speaker's Lobby, past the police barricade, toward the pointed gun. If she is allowed through, it seems inevitable that the mob will follow.
>
> As she climbs through, a single shot is fired and she drops to the floor.
>
> . . . The U.S. Capitol Police declared the shooting lawful, and said it would not pursue disciplinary charges against the lieutenant who killed Babbitt. That follows April's decision by the Department of Justice not to bring criminal charges against the officer.[2]

For approximately 1,000 gun homicides each year, the shooter is a law enforcement officer acting in the line of duty. An additional 200 or so homicides by the police are committed with other types of force. Police killings typically occur in the context of fraught encounters with people carrying guns or other weapons, who in many cases are intoxicated or impaired due to mental illness, and who pose an imminent threat to the officer or others. But police shootings can also arise from "extralegal violence," which involves the deliberate use of excessive force by officers, and from "unnecessary violence," which may involve well-meaning officers who lack the skill or patience to resolve a dangerous situation by other means.[3] In a legal sense, most police shootings are justifiable, but in a larger sense, they are problematic and preventable.[4]

One in four of the victims are African American, and some of those cases have done great damage to police–community relations, fueling the Black Lives Matter movement and inspiring widespread outrage. A prominent case was the 2014 shooting death of Michael Brown in Ferguson, Missouri, by an officer who was attempting to take him into custody. In 2020, the response to the George Floyd killing by a Minneapolis officer (who was later convicted of murder) led to street demonstrations in cities throughout the nation and even abroad. The public response to these and other police killings has been intensified in recent years by the widespread use of smart phones that allow bystanders to video record events and post the result on social media. Although most suspects killed by the police are not Black, it is reasonable to suggest that the response is more explosive for Black victims because it galvanizes the belief that police are indifferent or hostile to the Black community. Still, there is no reason to think that the police have become more prone to excessive violence—quite the contrary. But without a doubt police behavior has become much better documented. The damage done by police shootings thus goes far beyond the loss suffered by the immediate victims. The distrust of the police and the police withdrawal from proactive crime control activities in response to their public vilification are very real concerns.

The damage to police relations with the Black community is "the problem within the problem" of lethal police violence.[5] The overall problem is that the police are killing so many people of all races and ethnicities. We believe that there are ways to greatly reduce the police use of lethal violence without substantially impairing their ability to control serious crime or increase the risk that they will be injured. The solution begins with a commitment on the part of police agencies to reduce use of excessive and unnecessary force through adoption of clear rules of engagement, appropriate training, and accountability for noncompliant officers.

## Defining the Problem

One constructive consequence of the Ferguson shooting was to inspire private media organizations to begin tabulating all such events beginning in 2015. It is because of the extraordinary effort by *The Guardian* and *The Washington Post* that accurate data are now available. Before that, the usual government sources of homicide data—the National Vital Statistics System and the Supplementary Homicide Reports compiled by the Federal Bureau of Investigation (FBI)—were missing or misclassifying approximately half of the officer-involved killings, leading to a massive undercount of "legal intervention" deaths.[6] This deficit of federal data will be repaired in the near future: The Centers for Disease Control and Prevention's National Violent Death Reporting System compiles detailed, individual-level data on homicides that provide an accurate count of citizens killed by the police.[7] But that system will not issue reports on all 50 states until 2023—and even then will do so with a 2-year delay. *The Washington Post* database provides an accurate source available within days rather than years,[8] based on a comprehensive "scrape" of media accounts. In what follows, we make extensive use of these data for the period 2015–2020.

Figure 8.1 tells a simple story: that there have been approximately 1,000 homicides per year in which a law enforcement officer shot a civilian. This count is surprisingly stable from year to year, despite all the changes that we might point to during that period. Two of those underlying changes are the growth in the U.S. population and in the overall gun homicide rate. As a rate per million U.S. residents, it evened out to 3.1 in both 2015 and 2020. But viewed as a percentage of all gun homicides, officer-involved shootings have decreased from 7.4% in 2015 to 5.3% in 2020—the COVID era's surge in civilian gun homicides diluted the relative importance of officer-involved shootings (Figure 8.2).

Depending on the point of comparison, then, lethal violence by the police is quite rare. Most police officers work their entire career without shooting a

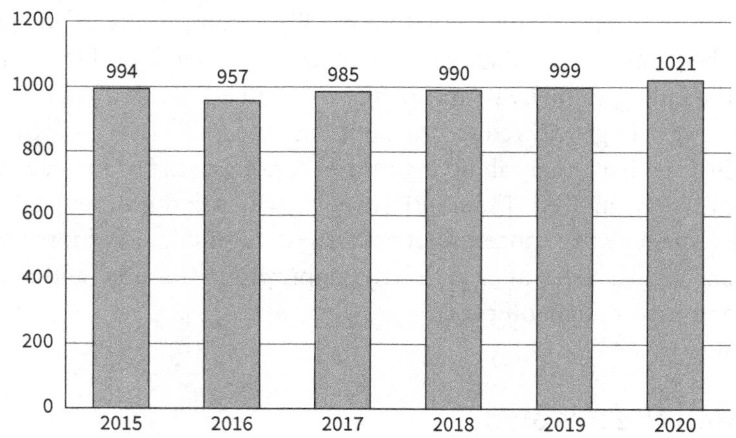


**Figure 8.1** Total officer-involved shooting deaths per year, 2015–2020.
*Source*: *The Washington Post* Fatal Police Shooting database, https://www.washingtonpost.com/graphics/investigations/police-shootings-database/.

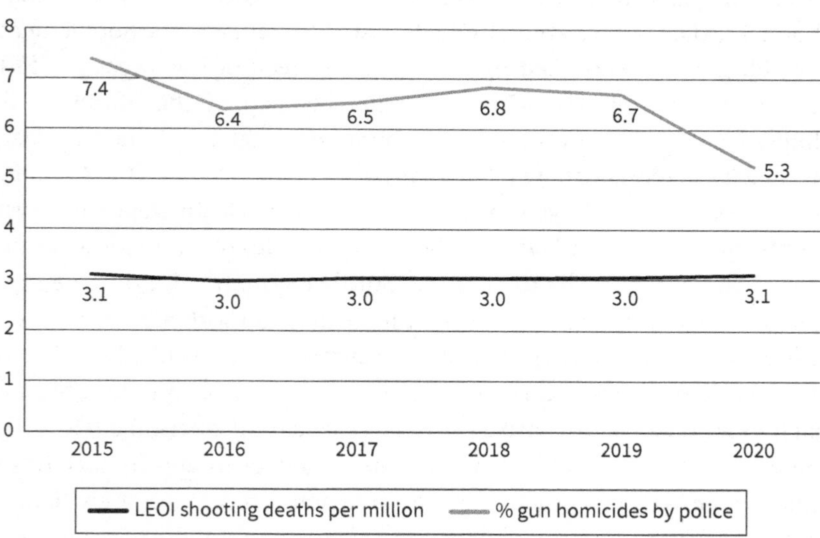


**Figure 8.2** Total officer-involved shooting deaths per million and as a percentage of all interpersonal shooting deaths, 2015–2020.
Note: LEOI = Law Enforcement Officer Involved.
*Sources*: *The Washington Post* Police Shooting database, https://www.washingtonpost.com/graphics/investigations/police-shootings-database. Data on total shooting deaths for 2015–2019 obtained from Centers for Disease Control and Prevention, "WISQARS: Web-based Injury Statistics Query and Reporting System," https://www.cdc.gov/injury/wisqars/fatal.htmls. Shooting data for 2020 obtained from *Gun Violence Archive*, https://www.gunviolencearchive.org/past-tolls.

civilian. The population-adjusted rate of officer-involved lethal shootings (3.1 per million) is far lower than in Brazil, Venezuela, Nicaragua, and some other nations of Central America and the Caribbean. But the population-adjusted rate of deadly shootings by the police in the United States is off-the-charts high in comparison with Canada and the nations of Western Europe, which typically have only a handful of police killings each year. Of course, those nations enjoy a fraction of the U.S. rate of civilian gun violence also.

## Circumstances

Policing is a dangerous profession, with routine challenges that most of us avoid. Police–citizen interactions can be uniquely *urgent* as officers are expected to respond to and resolve problems immediately, *involuntary* as officers do not have the luxury of picking and choosing clientele and situations to handle, and *public* as third parties and crowds can influence the dynamics of the encounters in unpredictable ways.[9] That most police shootings are legally justified receives support from the detailed data from *The Washington Post* database. Some summary statistics are presented in Table 8.1. Most victims were armed at the time of the shooting, usually with a gun. The victim was threatening or physically attacking the responding officers or another citizen in nearly two-thirds of the incidents. Nearly one-fourth of fatal shooting victims were reported to be exhibiting signs of mental illness. In almost 30% of the fatalities, the victim was attempting to flee the scene when shot and killed by the police. Of course, it is wise to consider the fact that this information is provided to the press by the police, and it may have a self-serving spin in some cases.

## Racial Disparities

The victims of police shootings are far from representative of the population at large. The overwhelming percentage (95%) are males. Most are youthful, with almost half (45%) in the age range 18–34 years. But the disparity that has received the greatest attention and concern is with respect to race. Approximately 27% of victims are Black, compared with just 13% of the overall population: The victimization rate from 2015 to 2020 was 33 per million for Blacks, 25 per million for Hispanics, and 13 per million for non-Hispanic Whites (Figure 8.3).

**Table 8.1** Circumstances of Officer-Involved Fatal Shootings, 2015–2020 Combined ($N = 5{,}946$)

| Victim Characteristics | | | |
|---|---|---|---|
| *Gender* | % | *Age (Years)* | % |
| Male | 95.6 | 17 or younger | 1.8 |
| Female | 4.4 | 18–24 | 14.1 |
| | | 25–29 | 15.3 |
| *Race* | | 30–35 | 18.7 |
| White | 46.6 | 36–45 | 22.0 |
| Black | 24.3 | 46 or older | 24.1 |
| Hispanic | 17.2 | Unknown | 4.0 |
| Other | 3.9 | | |
| **Circumstances** | | | |
| *Signs of Mental Illness Reported* | % | *Threat Level Reported* | % |
| Yes | 76.4 | Attacked officer/citizen | 65.0 |
| No | 23.6 | Other circumstances | 32.3 |
| | | Undetermined | 2.7 |
| *Armed* | | *Fleeing Scene* | |
| Firearm | 58.2 | Not fleeing | 61.9 |
| Knife/cutting instrument | 18.3 | Fleeing in car/on foot | 29.4 |
| Air pistol/toy weapon | 3.8 | Other | 3.3 |
| Vehicle | 3.7 | Unknown | 5.4 |
| Blunt instrument | 2.4 | | |
| Other/undetermined weapon | 3.3 | | |
| Unarmed | 6.8 | | |
| Unknown | 3.5 | | |

*Source*: *The Washington Post* Police Shooting database, https://www.washingtonpost.com/graphics/investigations/police-shootings-database/.

It is not surprising that in these respects, the pattern of police shootings has some similarity with patterns in gun homicide generally. Among both victims and shooters, there is a considerable overrepresentation of males (~80%), youths aged 18–34 years (~60%), and minority groups—especially Blacks. Overall, 60% of victims of gun homicide are Black. The implication is that police shootings are actually a smaller portion of Black gun homicide than White gun homicide. Figure 8.4 makes that point. Whereas officer-involved shootings constitute just 2.9% of gun homicides with Black victims, they constitute 7.3% of White and fully 8.7% of Hispanic cases.

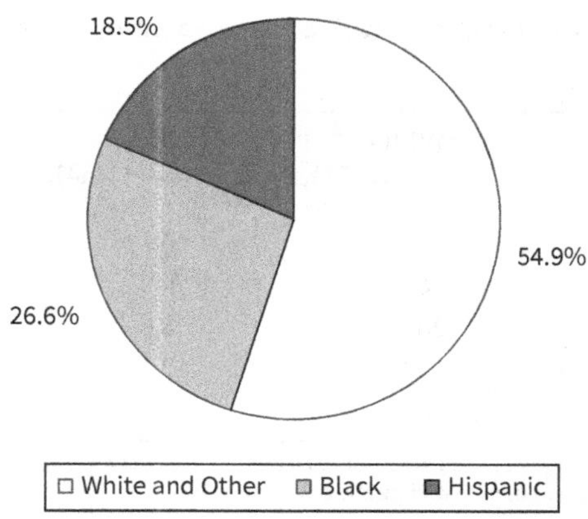


**Figure 8.3** Victim race in officer-involved shooting deaths, 2015–2020 combined.
*Source*: *The Washington Post* Police Shooting database, https://www.washingtonpost.com/graphics/investigations/police-shootings-database.

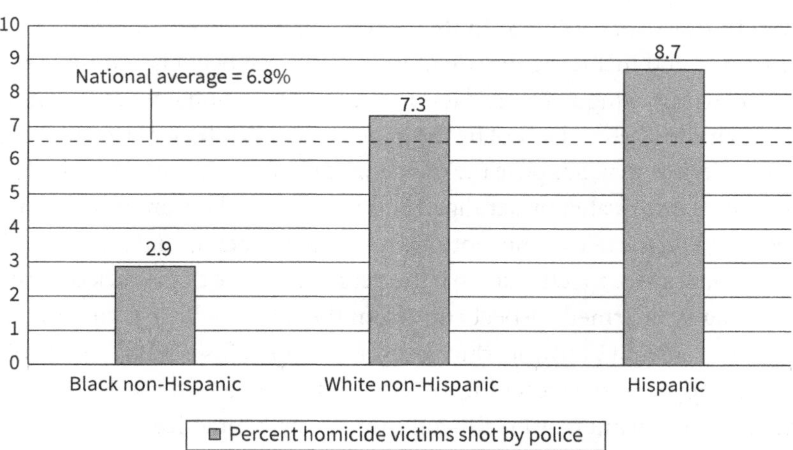


**Figure 8.4** Percentage of homicide victims shot by police, 2015–2019.
*Sources*: *The Washington Post* Police Shooting database, https://www.washingtonpost.com/graphics/investigations/police-shootings-database. Data on total shooting deaths for 2015–2019 obtained from Centers for Disease Control and Prevention, "WISQARS: Web-based Injury Statistics Query and Reporting System," https://www.cdc.gov/injury/wisqars/fatal.html.

Despite these disparities, the circumstances in which members of the three groups are shot by police are quite similar, as shown in Table 8.2. The norm is still an armed individual who is reasonably viewed as an imminent threat. Although much is made of those victims who are unarmed, they in fact constitute a small portion of the total, albeit somewhat more likely for Black and Hispanic victims than White.

**Table 8.2** Circumstances of Officer-Involved Fatal Shootings by Race, 2015–2020 Combined[a]

| Circumstance | White ($n$ = 2,771), % | Black ($n$ = 1,444), % | Hispanic ($n$ = 1,022), % |
|---|---|---|---|
| Armed with firearm | 59.7 | 60.1 | 51.8 |
| Unarmed | 6.1 | 9.2 | 7.5 |
| Fleeing scene | 26.3 | 35.6 | 30.6 |
| Attacking officer | 66.7 | 67.2 | 58.7 |
| Signs of mental illness | 30.0 | 15.7 | 18.0 |

[a] Percentages are not cumulative because multiple circumstances may apply. The sample for each racial or ethnic category excludes cases in which victim race is missing.

*Source*: *The Washington Post* Police Shooting database, https://www.washingtonpost.com/graphics/investigations/police-shootings-database/.

The race-based disparity in shooting rates contributes to a narrative that the police as a group tend to treat Black or Hispanic suspects with greater suspicion or even hostility than Whites. In the extreme, that may lead to use of excessive force—up to and including the use of their gun. That belief is widespread, but it is difficult to test using available data. The specific question is whether a minority suspect is more likely to be shot by the police than a White suspect who poses the same objective threat. Suppose the police are called to deal with an armed person who appears intoxicated or deranged and refuses to follow an order to drop the weapon. Would the officers be more likely to call for backup and try to give the individual some space to settle down if the person is White than Black or Hispanic? What about if an armed suspect runs from the officer who is trying to take the suspect into custody? Or who, during a traffic stop, refuses to follow the officer's orders and appears to be reaching for a gun? The details of these encounters may matter a great deal but may be difficult to ascertain in practice.

Here is one example of such an analysis. The economist Roland G. Fryer, Jr., utilized detailed data from Houston to create a sample of tense encounters between the police and suspects.[10] He focused on all cases in which the Houston Police Department used TASER or made an arrest for resisting or interfering with an arrest. In some of these cases, the suspect was shot by the officers. In that sample, there was no difference by suspect's race in the likelihood that the encounter escalated to the point of an officer shooting. But is that the right sample for testing for bias? It could be that the Houston police would have been more adept in the first place at avoiding a tense confrontation with a White suspect than a minority suspect.

Whether racial disparities in fatal police shooting rates can largely be explained by factors other than officer bias, few would argue that the police do not shoot too many people overall. The challenge is to reduce police shootings without undercutting their productive engagement with the task of combatting civilian violence.

## Patterns

Lawrence Sherman, an American who serves as Director of the Cambridge (England) Centre for Evidence-Based Policing, has been a pathbreaking scholar for the past half century. He has usefully classified the approaches to understanding police behavior into five "buckets": individual, situational, organizational, community, and legal.[11] All of these are relevant to understanding police use of deadly force, as summarized here.

## Community and Organization

There are large and persistent differences among cities in the rate of police shootings. Among the nation's largest cities, the rates per million residents in 2015–2020 ranged from 0.6 in New York City to 9.2 in Phoenix, fully 14 times as high (Figure 8.5). And these differences are persistent, as shown in Figure 8.6: Cities that had high rates of police shootings in the period 2015–2017 also tended to have high rates for the subsequent 3 years. This remarkable disparity among cities provides a basis for inspiration. Can other cities aspire to achieve New York's relatively low rate?

To some extent, police violence is influenced by community violence, particularly gun violence. When we look for New York's secret, a place to start is to realize that the overall homicide rate in New York is relatively low, as is the rate of gun ownership[12]—both of which are related to police violence.[13] But that is by no means the whole story. For example, compare Dallas with Phoenix. They are similar-sized cities of the Southwest, with a large Hispanic population and Whites in the minority—and a high rate of gun ownership. These similarities do not extend to police behavior, and indeed, the officer-involved gun homicides by the Phoenix Police Department are nearly five times as high (adjusted for population) as for the Dallas Police Department. That is not because Phoenix is a more violent city overall—indeed, the reverse is true. To understand the huge difference in the shooting rate, we are inclined to look for differences in the two departments rather than in the context in which they operate. A place to start is with the departmental culture and norms and, concretely, departmental protocols on dealing with tense

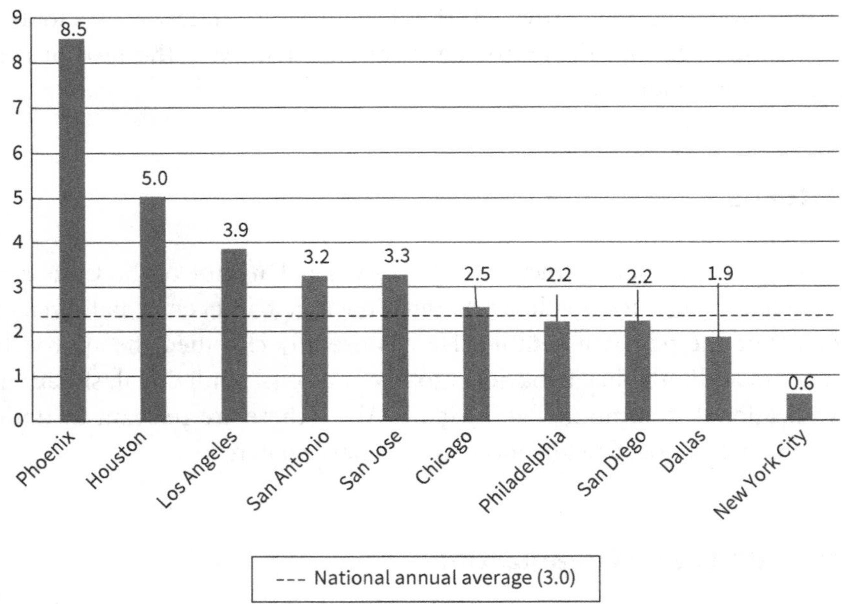


**Figure 8.5** Annual rates of officer-involved shootings deaths per million, 2015–2020 (10 most populous U.S. cities ordered by shooting rate).

*Sources*: *The Washington Post* Police Shooting database, https://www.washingtonpost.com/graphics/investigations/police-shootings-database. City population data for 2018 obtained from U.S. Census Bureau, https://data.census.gov/cedsci.

confrontations—what officer behaviors are tolerated or encouraged with respect to the use of force, and in particular the use of their guns.

An extreme case serves to illustrate the negative possibilities. The Vallejo, California, Police Department (VPD) was profiled in 2020 by *The New Yorker* as an organization with a culture that seemed to embrace violence by its officers.[14] Since 2010, VPD officers have killed 19 people in a city of approximately 122,000 residents: With the exception of St. Louis, Missouri, the VPD killing rate was higher than that of any of the 100 largest police departments in the United States. The VPD had a long history of not holding officers accountable for problematic behaviors. The police union has perpetuated pro-violence norms, protecting officers who were behaving unlawfully, bullying local politicians, and resisting reform efforts. When a reform-minded Black chief was appointed to lead the VPD, the head of the union stated that the chief "can't speak English" and that he would not follow the chief's orders if he does not like them. A long-time public defender who worked in Vallejo commented, "Chiefs come and go. . . . It's the sergeants and the shift lieutenants

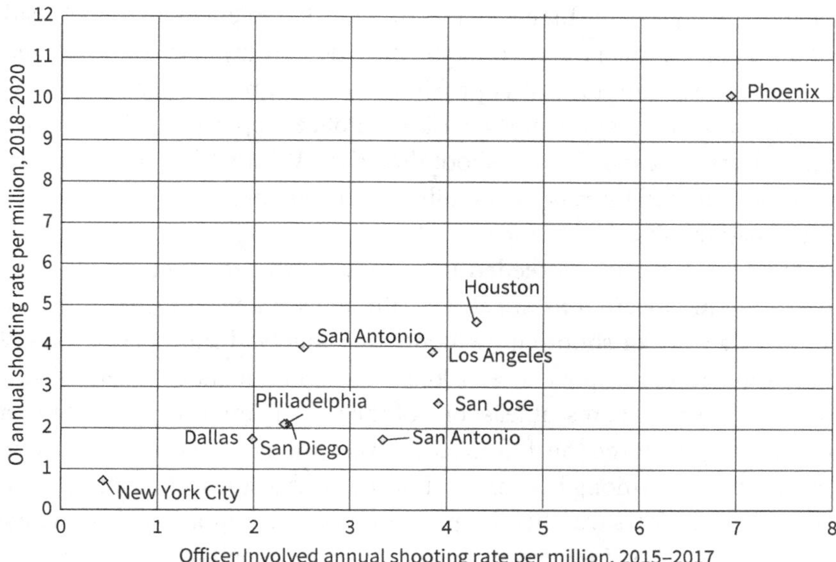


**Figure 8.6** Officer-involved shooting deaths per million, 2015–2017 versus 2018–2020. OI, officer-involved.

*Sources*: Data on total shooting deaths for 2015–2019 obtained from Centers for Disease Control and Prevention, "WISQARS: Web-based Injury Statistics Query and Reporting System," https://www.cdc.gov/injury/wisqars/fatal.html. 2020 data from *Gun Violence Archive*, https://www.gunviolencearchive.org/past-tolls. City population data for 2018 obtained from U.S. Census Bureau, https://data.census.gov/cedsci.

and the captains that really control the tenor of the department and that resist change."

## Individual and Situational

Although a focus on the police organization, with its culture and protocols, is entirely warranted, public outrage generated by prominent police shootings tends to focus on the villainy of the individual officer or on the character of police officers in general. It is true that not all officers are equally likely to end up shooting a civilian, and understanding why some do is of great interest. Some of the observed differences are associated with the officer's character, but the officer's assignment—their beat—may also make a considerable difference.

For instance, in the New York Police Department (NYPD) during the 1970s, minority officers were more likely to be involved in deadly shooting incidents than their White counterparts.[15] A careful analysis found that Black officers were more likely to have high-risk assignments in violent areas, which, rather than a difference in character or style, provided an explanation for different involvement in shootings. At approximately the same time, the same lesson was offered by an analysis of the Chicago Police Department (CPD), where Black officers were *less* likely to shoot than their White colleagues, apparently because in the CPD it was White officers who tended to get the more dangerous assignments.[16]

Some analyses have succeeded in estimating the effect of officer characteristics in similar circumstances. Criminologist Greg Ridgeway developed a unique data set of shooting incidents that involved multiple officers: 291 NYPD officers in all, present at 106 shooting incidents between 2004 and 2006.[17] In these incidents, at least one of the officers involved fired at the suspect. Ridgway explored the difference between the shooters and non-shooters in each incident. Among his various findings was a suggestion that character was an issue: Officers who had frequent misconduct reports were more likely to shoot during these incidents than those who did not have such problematic work histories.

An alternative approach is to track a cohort of new recruits to the police department, who presumably end up having a similar variety of assignments. One such study, involving nearly 2,000 Philadelphia Police Department officers, was able to use information on their personality collected when they first joined the force to predict subsequent behavior.[18] Of particular interest was their self-control. Officers working violent beats frequently find themselves being challenged verbally or even physically and are expected to show self-restraint in these cases, something that may not come naturally. Five percent of these officers ended up shooting at someone during the early part of their careers. The study found that officers with lower self-control were much more likely to shoot than those with greater self-control. For every additional point on a self-control scale that ranged from 1 to 7, the odds that officers shot their guns increased by 21%.

Officers who do turn out to be bad actors may influence their colleagues. In each large department, a relative few officers generate a disproportionate number of complaints for mistreatment of civilians. Officers who generate high levels of complaints are more likely to be transferred to different assignments within their departments. But such "shuffling" of problematic officers may make shooting problems within police departments worse. One creative analysis drew on a database of 38,442 complaints against CPD officers between 2000 and 2003.[19] Officers with many complaints proved to be more likely than their colleagues to shoot a civilian. But more than that, these officers appeared to have a negative influence on others in their social network, increasing the chance that associates would shoot. That analysis begins to illuminate how "bad apples" may "spoil the barrel."

## What Can Be Done?

In some cases, officer-involved shootings and other attacks on civilians are not legally justified and are deservedly subject to criminal prosecution. We believe that the bulk of all police shootings, although legally justified, could be prevented through better training, accountability, and rules of engagement—together with strong leadership. To use our previous example, the Phoenix Police Department could lower its rate of officer-involved shootings to the level of shootings by the Dallas Police Department (if not that of the NYPD) and do so without degrading its crime-prevention mission. There is no proven recipe for success, but there is enough experience to formulate best-practice guidelines.

## Law and Police Department Policy

The Fourth Amendment to the U.S. Constitution protects citizens against unlawful searches and seizures. When police officers are not justified in their use of deadly force in the line of duty, this extreme "apprehension" of the suspect is regarded as an illegal seizure. Two noteworthy U.S. Supreme Court cases establish the federal legal framework that governs police use of deadly force. In *Tennessee v. Garner*, 471 U.S. 1 (1985), the Supreme Court ruled that police may only use deadly force to apprehend or to ensure the arrest of someone fleeing from the commission of a felony if the officer reasonably believes that the fleeing person at the time of flight poses a threat of death or serious bodily injury to others. In *Graham v. Connor*, 490 U.S. 386 (1989), the Supreme Court further clarified remaining questions regarding excessive use of force by setting the "objective reasonableness" standard. This requires that all police use of force incidents be judged from the perspective of a reasonable officer dealing with a tense and rapidly evolving situation. Law enforcement officers should use only the force that is objectively reasonable to effectively bring an incident under control, while protecting the safety of the officer, suspect, and others.

Although rather vague, the *Garner* decision appears to have generated a positive effect on police use of deadly force after its passage,[20] especially in states that had police use-of-deadly force laws that were unconstitutional under the new standard. Federal and state laws serve as important guideposts to govern police use of force behaviors, and federal oversight in the form of "pattern and practice" investigations can be helpful in reining in the use of excessive force.[21] However, as Franklin Zimring rightly observes in his book *When Police Kill*,[22] the main arena for the changes required to save civilian lives lies with the local police department, and in particular the police executives who shape and enforce policies and set the tone.[23] Of course, police leadership is subject to politics and public opinion (sometimes expressed in street demonstrations) as well as legal constraints and mandates.

Many police departments have policy guides that are used to train officers in the appropriate escalation of their actions during an encounter with a civilian. The better developed policies provide a clear guide as to when force can be used and when it cannot.[24] Force is a last resort, after other feasible tactics have been tried to deescalate the situation. The use of deadly force is restricted to cases in which there is an imminent threat of physical harm to the officer or to bystanders or the escape of a dangerous felony suspect. More generally, force must be proportional to the situation and follow the "use-of-force continuum." The continuum is intended to guide officers in how to control suspects who resist their commands, and it covers the spectrum from verbal commands to minor exertions of force and lethal force.[25] These use-of-force protocols clarify what may be considered "objectively reasonable" force in specific situations, including de-escalation once suspect resistance has declined or ended.[26]

The International Association of Chiefs of Police (IACP) and 10 other law enforcement organizations developed a model use-of-force continuum and encouraged police executives to improve compliance through officer pre-employment and in-service training, ongoing officer assessment and tracking of performance, early warning systems to identify problem officers and address their deficits, and community outreach and relationship-building efforts.[27] Furthermore, these professional police organizations argued for the importance of incident review and accountability. To facilitate organizational learning, key findings should be communicated internally via "after action" or "lessons learned" reports. More than 96% of the 18,000 U.S. police departments report having policies governing firearms discharges, use of deadly force, and use of less-than-lethal force,[28] but the extent to which these policies follow the systematic approach outlined by IACP and others has not been documented.

Best-practice guidelines could also seek to establish a "stop shooting" protocol for those instances in which an officer is compelled to shoot. In a number of well-documented cases, officers have continued to fire after the suspect has been incapacitated and is no longer a threat, or the suspect is trying to flee the scene and is not an immediate threat.[29]

The use-of-force continuum is intended to establish norms for how to respond to a defiant suspect who poses a serious threat. One emphasis in department policy and training efforts is to manage potentially dangerous encounters to buy time.[30] The relevant concept here has become known as tactical decision-making, serving as a guiding principle for police department policies, training, and supervision. A basic tactic involves "slowing down" an encounter in order to buy time to better assess the situation, consider different options, and possibly call in backup officers if appropriate.[31] The Police Executive Research Forum (PERF), one of the important professional associations, has developed this notion in a series of reports. At one PERF conference, a commander for the Los Angeles Police Department is reported to have summarized this line of thinking to a short formula: "distance = time = options = resources."[32]

## Accountability

Clear department policies governing use of force, coupled with appropriate training and consistent leadership, can shape police use of force and ultimately reduce the number of civilians shot.[33] Accountability for officers who violate departmental directives is an important part of the mix. In the most egregious cases, accountability entails a criminal proceeding against the offending officer. But usually an internal sanction is more appropriate and feasible. The high-wire act in this area is for the department to make it clear that excessive force by officers will not be tolerated while at the same time assuring officers that they can and should do what is reasonably necessary to handle threatening situations. We do not want officers to simply stay in their vehicles and avoid getting in trouble.

Since first authorized by a federal law in 1994, the U.S. Department of Justice has conducted scores of "pattern or practice" investigations of law enforcement agencies that had poor track records with respect to use of excessive force and related problems. In 40 such cases, the investigation led to a judicially enforced consent decree, or a memo of understanding.[34] From these settlements have emerged a list of best practices for police accountability. Officers are required to promptly file reports if they used force against a suspect, and these reports are to be reviewed by supervisors and ultimately by command staff, with appropriate interventions with officers in violation of departmental policies. Best practice also provides citizens with the option of filing complaints against officers, and it specifies training so that the rules are clear. A number of state laws adopted in recent years have required an independent investigation in some cases.

But departmental proceedings against an officer can be encumbered by union rules and state laws known as Law Enforcement Officers' Bill of Rights, now in 15 states. These laws provide extensive due-process protections for officers in internal investigations that could lead to demotion or dismissal, including a right to an attorney, advanced notification, access to any relevant evidence, and confidentiality if the investigation does not result in sanction. In the Maryland law, for example, officers under investigation have up to 5 days to make a statement (while they are finding an attorney), and they can only be interrogated by sworn officers. Needless to say, most workers do not have protections of this sort!

Even in states that do not have Law Enforcement Officers' Bill of Rights, collective bargaining provisions with the police union frequently provide similar due process. Unions are committed to represent or defend members accused of misconduct and criminal behavior.[35] And, as the Vallejo police union story suggests, they can be purveyors of highly problematic behaviors when a pro-violence culture is present in the rank and file. In general, unionized police departments receive complaints about their members' use of force at a rate that is more than one-third higher than that of non-unionized departments.[36] A more recent study found that violent misconduct by sheriff's deputies in Florida increased by 40% when the deputies unionized.[37]

Police accountability has been rare even in cases in which the police clearly violated the law or standard operating procedures. Video evidence of illegal police shootings, such as the infamous 2014 killing of 17-year-old Lacquan McDonald by Chicago Police Officer Jason Van Dyke, has taught the world that police sometimes engage in cover-ups—they lie to protect themselves and each other—which has further generated distrust. Strong unions can make it difficult to hold officers accountable for their misconduct because sanctions can be appealed through multiple reviews and appeals are often heard by an arbiter who is usually selected in part by the union. Even officers with a long history of violence can be difficult to fire. When they are fired, their records are invisible, and they get hired by other departments. In the aftermath of the shooting of 12-year-old Tamir Rice who was playing with a toy gun, Cleveland Police Officer Timothy Loehmann was not fired for poor decision-making. Rather, Loehmann was fired for concealing the fact during his hiring process that he was previously asked to resign from another police department for being too emotionally unstable for police work.

A 2017 investigative report by *The Washington Post* found that, largely following union-mandated appeals, nearly one-fourth (451 of 1,881) of police officers fired for misconduct from departments throughout the country were reinstated after arbiters overruled police chief decisions.[38] The arbiters who reviewed the firing process often accepted the underlying misconduct by fired officers but usually concluded that there was not enough evidence to support termination or the departments were too harsh in their firing decisions. Former Philadelphia Commissioner Ramsey commented, "It's demoralizing to the rank and file who really don't want to have those kinds of people in their ranks. . . .It causes a tremendous amount of anxiety in the public. Our credibility is shot whenever these things happen."

There is some support for the idea that reforms to police unions may be effective mechanisms to control officer behavior if unions can be incentivized to "self-regulate" the actions of their membership by transferring the burden of liability insurance from municipalities to unions.[39] Police leaders can also engage unions directly by holding regular meetings to discuss officer work conditions, tactics and strategies, and other matters. Departmental policies and positions on use of deadly force and officer safety can be discussed and reinforced to union memberships.[40] This can facilitate candid discussions on officer concerns about their personal safety and liability exposure when performing their work duties. Engaging line-level officers on policy matters and developing new efforts to address legitimate safety and liability concerns could energize the rank and file to modify their behaviors.[41]

## Body-Worn Cameras

The ultimate device for holding line officers accountable for their actions is the body-worn camera (BWC). The presence of BWCs during police–citizen encounters has become a prominent feature of urban policing throughout the world. By 2016, roughly 80% of large local police departments (agencies with 500 or more full-time sworn officers) had acquired BWCs, and 70% had started outfitting active duty officers with the technology.[42] The growth in the adoption of BWCs in the United States was fueled in response to persistent problems with police–community relations and concerns with police shootings of unarmed Black citizens.[43]

The first program evaluations considering the effects of BWC on police officer use of force during interactions with citizens produce mixed findings.[44] But two recent studies provide more robust evidence in support of a positive result.[45] Braga led an evaluation of the introduction of BWCs in 40 precincts in New York City that experienced a high level of civilian complaints against the police.[46] These 40 precincts were sorted into 20 pairs of precincts in the same borough, with a coin toss determining which member of each pair got the experimental "treatment" of equipping officers with BWCs. The treatment precincts had fewer civilian complaints (a 21% reduction), although there was no effect on the recorded use of force. A second study analyzed the effect of BWC adoption in a large sample of cities, finding that they did reduce officer-involved homicides.[47]

We would expect some variation in effectiveness, depending on usage—whether the officers in a department that has adopted BWCs actually wear them in practice and keep them switched on.[48] But they do have considerable potential to provide an objective record of the sequence of events in a tense encounter.[49] Knowing that may encourage officers to follow departmental guidelines in managing confrontations. BWCs may also constrain civilians from filing false complaints against officers, a fact that has made them popular with the rank and file.

## Making Police Encounters with People in Behavioral Crisis Less Dangerous

People in behavioral crisis (PBCs), such as those who suffer from serious mental health challenges or persistent substance abusers, are far more likely than other individuals to encounter the police. PBCs have an elevated risk of violent behavior, are more likely to be crime victims, and are more prevalent among homeless populations.[50] In these situations, PBCs may be aggressive, agitated, and difficult to understand. As such, police encounters with PBCs are more likely to escalate and are at greater risk of negative outcomes. Indeed, in approximately one in four officer-involved fatal shootings, the victim is mentally ill.[51] Training officers to provide time, distance, and cover during encounters with PBCs can be helpful in avoiding unnecessary police shootings. There is promising evidence that mental health experts can provide a wider range of options for de-escalating PBC encounters through their involvement in Crisis Intervention Teams (CITs). Even if a department is not large enough to staff a CIT, training individual officers in the same principles could be helpful in improving police responses to these complicated situations.

CITs seem to be producing notable reductions in police shootings in Miami–Dade County, Florida.[52] The 40-hour CIT training teaches officers how to identify people in a mental health crisis, how to de-escalate tense encounters with individuals, and where to take them for treatment rather than simply arresting them. The training also teaches them to be more empathetic toward PBCs who have serious mental illnesses and have a past history of trauma.

From 2010 to 2019, the City of Miami and Miami–Dade County police departments handled 105,268 mental health calls and made only 198 arrests. They diverted 18,608 individuals from jail and assisted 66,556 in accessing treatment.[53] The county experienced roughly 90 police shootings during the 5 years preceding the establishment of the CIT. Miami–Dade County experienced only approximately 30 shootings in the 5 years after the CIT was launched. But more systematic evaluations of the impact of CITs on police shootings lack strong and consistent findings.[54]

There are a number of other practices worth considering to reduce police shootings.[55] These include risk-based gun removal strategies such as "red flag" laws that use gun violence restraining orders to temporarily restrict an individual's access to guns when they are in crisis. And there is considerable interest in using available data to identify calls for service involving a behavioral crisis; instead of a standard response, such cases may call for the dispatch of a CIT, a social service unit. Clues about the appropriate response may be as obvious as the identity of the caller, who may be well known to the police, or the location, such as a camp for the homeless.

It is also important to note that effective responses to encounters with PBCs require officers themselves to be in control of their emotions. Being a police officer is a highly stressful job, and it is well known that officers suffer from high rates of substance use disorders, depression, and suicide.[56] Providing improved mental health services to police officers could be helpful in preparing them to handle these difficult encounters and to exercise good judgment when following departmental policies.

## Reducing Fatality Rates When Police Shoot

The number of citizens killed in police shootings is of course closely related to the number who are shot, but a majority of civilians who are shot actually survive. The likelihood of survival may depend on the quality of medical care for the wounded.[57] Some observers suggest that lives could be saved if police officers were allowed to transport injured people to hospitals when emergency medical services are not available or delayed.[58] This practice, informally called "scoop and run," is of course not limited to the victims of police shootings. Outfitted with battlefield-grade hemostatic bandages,[59] officers can provide victims with immediate medical attention to halt the bleeding and then transport them to trauma centers. Police departments would need to equip officers with these bandages and work with local medical systems to train officers in how to properly administer such aid and safely transport victims.

In fact, most police departments in the United States do not allow officers to use their vehicles for this purpose, nor do officers necessarily want to provide that service. The Philadelphia Police Department is one of the few U.S. police departments to have a written policy allowing officers to transport victims to trauma centers and to use the practice regularly to save lives.[60] Approximately 30% of assault victims are transported by the police to Philadelphia trauma centers on an annual basis, and in 2016, more than 50% of victims with penetrating injuries were transported by the police.[61] The available research evidence indicates that survival rates are at least equivalent when police transport and emergency medical services transport are compared,[62] with some studies suggesting that victims are more likely to survive penetrating injuries when transported by the police.[63] Although not researched yet, "scoop and run" programs could plausibly help improve police–community relations in minority communities suffering from high levels of gun homicides.[64]

## TASERs

It seems like common sense that if officers have a less lethal way to stop an attack without using their gun, lives will be saved. Most local police departments have authorized their officers to be equipped with TASERs, and other conducted-energy devices (CEDs) have been adopted as well.[65] One analysis of 12 police agencies and more than 24,000 use-of-force cases showed that the odds of suspect injury decreased when a CED was used.[66]

The evidence is less positive about CED effects on police shootings. In 2010, the CPD modified its policies to allow TASERs to be used by patrol officers. This policy change unsurprisingly led to a sharp increase in the use of TASERs, but unfortunately no decline in the use of firearms.[67] Officers continued to deploy firearms (rather than CEDs) when they believed that their lives or the lives of others were seriously threatened. Officers used CEDs to deal with less threatening situations. It appears that some officers use CEDs in situations that could be de-escalated with words or softer tactics; one study referred to this pattern as "lazy cop syndrome."[68] But as with the use of firearms, excess use of TASERs can be moderated by a clear departmental directive.[69]

CEDs could plausibly reduce fatal police shootings if police departments developed policies that encouraged officers to use these less lethal weapons rather than firearms in appropriate situations, such as a knife attack.[70] New technologies need to be supported by changes to internal police organizational influences such as strong policies governing use of force and robust accountability mechanisms.

## Lethal Violence Against the Police

Roughly 10% of all police officers are assaulted per year.[71] After taxi drivers, police officers suffer the second highest occupational homicide rate.[72] When fatal and nonfatal assaults are combined, police experience the highest rate of violent victimization in the workplace.[73] Police perceptions of on-the-job risks of violent victimization have become more acute in recent years in the wake of high-profile lethal attacks on officers, most notoriously in Brooklyn (two officers killed, December 2014); Dallas (five officers killed, July 2016); and Baton Rouge, Louisiana (three officers killed, July 2016).[74]

The threat of lethal attack is a palpable part of the job of serving as a U.S. police officer. Relative to police officers in other wealthy nations, U.S. police officers face much higher risks of being killed in the line of duty: approximately 25 times the risk of police death from assault in England and Wales and more than 40 times that of Germany.[75]

The good news is that the yearly rate of U.S. law enforcement officers killed in the line of duty as a result of felonious incidents has decreased over time. Drawing on nearly 50 years of data on all police officer line-of-duty deaths (1970–2016) from the Officer Down Memorial Page, we see that the policing profession is much safer today than it was in the 1970s.[76] Felonious officer deaths dropped by more than 80% over the course of this period (from 52 per 100,000 in 1970 to an average of 10 per 100,000 between 2012 and 2016). There is no evidence of a post-Ferguson "war on cops," as suggested by some observers commenting on recent high-profile killings of police officers.[77] Rather, there has been remarkable stability in geographic-, temporal-, and incident-level characteristics of felonious killings of police officers over time. A total of 51 officers were shot dead in 2019; that number dropped to 48 during the tumultuous year of 2020. Unfortunately, the number of officers killed by gunfire increased to 62 in 2021.[78]

The most recent data available from the FBI's Law Enforcement Officers Killed and Assaulted reports 31% were conducting investigative and enforcement activities (e.g., conducting traffic stops, interacting with wanted individuals, and performing drug investigations), nearly 19% were involved in tactical situations (e.g., serving warrants and dealing with hostage situations), approximately 10% were the victims of unprovoked attacks, and some 8% were responding to crimes in progress.[79] Most of the officers (92%) were killed with firearms.

A comprehensive study of more than 20,000 assaults on police officers between 2002 and 2010 identified several incident-level characteristics that were associated with increased assault risks, including outdoor crime scene locations, increased numbers of offenders present, male offenders, intoxicated offenders, and response to a violent crime (specifically, robberies and assaults).[80] Research has consistently documented that the level of violence in the communities in which police work is a risk factor for officer victimization.[81] Studies have also linked increased rates of assaults on officers with aggressive patrol styles.[82] Body armor provides a clear protective effect.[83]

There is considerable overlap in the characteristics and contexts of police–citizen encounters that lead to negative outcomes for both sets of participants in these interactions. Indeed, the same kinds of system changes that can lead to reductions in police-involved shootings may also reduce shootings of police officers.[84] Critics of police violence should collaborate with advocates for increased officer safety to demand and implement meaningful reforms.

## Conclusion

Too many people die in avoidable officer-involved shootings. To the extent that police departments make a reduction in the number of killings by their officers a priority, creating new rules of engagement reinforced through extensive training, then there would be fewer deaths and, presumably, less damage to police–community relationships. This result could be achieved without diminishing officer safety. In a departmental regime that stresses that "lives matter," nonlethal means of responding to tense situations would be given even more attention in training and departmental policy. Better training for dealing with crises due to mental health problems and strategies to prevent people from dying after being shot should be on the agenda as well.

Some police departments need to improve their internal accountability mechanisms if they are going to launch a powerful response to officer-involved shooting programs. It is a false dichotomy to ask whether the problem is a few bad apples or a bad system. It is a bad system that protects the bad apples—and fails to provide sufficient training, guidance, and options to the great majority of officers who want to do the right thing in challenging circumstances.

# 9

# Policing Firearms Trafficking, Theft, and Illegal Diversion

The transactions usually took place in a car parked near West 166th Street and St. Nicholas Avenue in Manhattan. Abdul Davis would arrive from New Jersey, carrying guns in a bag, the authorities said. He sold them in batches of three or four: revolvers, semiautomatic pistols, shotguns, assault rifles.

All told, prosecutors said, he unloaded 82 weapons over 13 months in exchange for about $94,000, with the money wired to his bank account in advance. What Mr. Davis did not know was that his customer was an undercover police officer, and that the Manhattan district attorney's office had obtained a wiretap on his phone.

On Monday, Mr. Davis, 52, and his girlfriend, Shelita Funderberk, 50, who is accused of helping him with the sales, were arrested in Linden, N.J., where they live, and await extradition. They are charged with criminal sale of firearms, conspiracy and other crimes, Cyrus R. Vance Jr., the Manhattan district attorney, said.

Three men in Virginia and one in Georgia were also arrested near their homes on conspiracy and gun-selling charges. Mr. Vance said they served as straw purchasers for Mr. Davis, buying guns at shops and shows in those states. Mr. Davis negotiated sales with them over the phone, wired them money and traveled to their homes to pick up the weapons, according to a 119-count indictment.

"It was clear, through the evidence, they knew they were selling weapons to come to New York State," he said. Robert K. Boyce, the chief of detectives, said there was evidence that Mr. Davis, who had a previous conviction for drug trafficking, had been peddling guns in the city for at least 10 years. The police discovered his business after an informant tipped them off and had the undercover officer pose as a street dealer, he said. Among the weapons the officer bought were five assault rifles, including a Bushmaster Firearms model that had been outfitted with a 100-round drum magazine, court papers said.[1]

*Policing Gun Violence.* Anthony A. Braga and Philip J. Cook, Oxford University Press. © Oxford University Press 2023.
DOI: 10.1093/oso/9780199929283.003.0009

Many major cities have units and specific police personnel investigating and seeking to curtail criminal access to guns. And the Bureau of Alcohol, Tobacco, Firearms and Explosives (ATF) works with state and local law enforcement agencies to interdict trafficking, straw purchases, and illicit manufacture, where the goal is to enforce regulations on gun commerce. For instance, the New York Police Department (NYPD) has a Gun Violence Suppression Division that identifies individuals and organizations responsible for the trafficking and sale of illegal firearms in New York City and attempts to dismantle criminal enterprises such as the one described above. The division uses several avenues, including undercover police officers and confidential informants, to reduce the number of guns on the streets. ATF details special agents to support the work of these local gun enforcement teams. Other city police departments address illegal firearms diversions by assigning personnel to serve as ATF task force officers.

These kinds of gun enforcement efforts are usually modest and not well documented or evaluated. But the rationale for these efforts is well founded: Reducing the illegal supply of guns to criminals can reduce gun violence. Underground gun markets are "thin"—relatively few buyers and sellers—and if they cannot find each other or trust each other, the transaction will be blocked. Supply-side interventions seek to further limit illegal transactions and thereby enhance the incentive for those who cannot shop at a gun store to economize on gun possession and use. Both regulatory and focused enforcement efforts can impact the supply lines through which criminals get guns. But few police departments are much invested in disrupting supply.

## The Illegal Supply of Guns to Criminals

Recall that approximately 15 million new firearms are sold each year for private use nationwide, and there are several million more transactions involving used firearms. As described in Chapter 3, most new guns and some of the secondhand guns are sold by licensed dealers from stores. Privately manufactured firearms, often called "ghost guns" due to their lack of traceable serial numbers, have become more common as assembly has grown simpler and cheaper through commercial availability of parts kits, unfinished firearms frames or receivers, and compact computer numerical control milling devices. Most of these transactions and private manufacture are legal. The sales and transfers that are illegal include thefts, transfers to people who are disqualified due to their youth or criminal record, and transactions that are in technical violation of firearms regulations (e.g., a state regulation requiring that the buyer have a permit, or a federal ban on selling ghost guns). A large percentage of the transactions that arm dangerous offenders are illegal under current law.[2] Also relevant is whether the transaction is in the primary market—a documented sale by a licensed dealer—or in the informal secondary market. Figure 9.1 is an attempt to represent these distinctions with a Venn diagram and locate the transactions that arm dangerous offenders.

In Figure 9.1, the transactions that arm dangerous offenders (those likely to use the gun to injure another person) are divided into four segments, as shown schematically in the relevant circle. The shaded segment represents illegal transactions in the secondary market, which probably constitutes most of the transactions of interest.[3] But as represented in the diagram, some—perhaps most—of the transactions that are illegal do not arm people who are likely to use the guns in violent crime, and some of the transactions that do arm dangerous people are legal. In the latter category may be sales to individuals who have numerous arrests for violence or drug and alcohol problems but no felony convictions, which is what is required to disqualify someone by federal law and in the law of most states.[4]

Most guns used in crime are not obtained by purchase from a licensed dealer but, rather, in informal transactions that are likely illegal for any of a variety of reasons. As described in Chapter 3, this underground market is

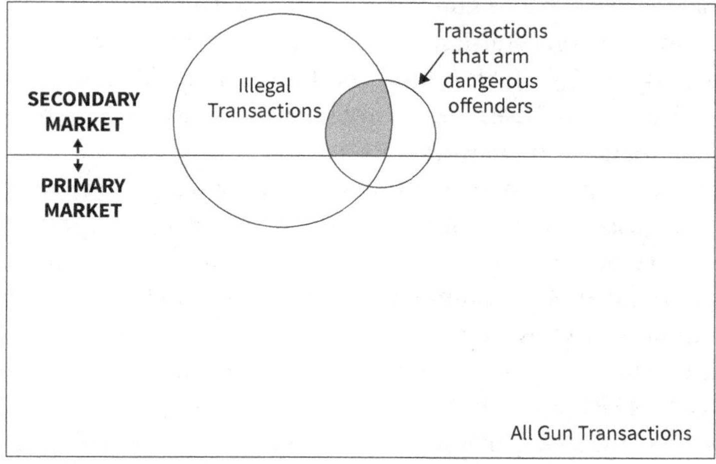


**Figure 9.1** Venn diagram of gun transactions by legal status.

*Source*: Philip J. Cook and Harold A. Pollack, "Reducing Access to Guns by Violent Offenders," *Russell Sage Foundation Journal of the Social Sciences* 3, no. 5 (2017): 2–36.

supplied by used guns diverted from licit commerce. One prominent means of diversion is theft, although it is not clear how important that is in practice.[5] Another channel by which guns are diverted from the licit market to offenders is systematic trafficking. The general picture is of guns flowing from less regulated to more regulated states, typically in small shipments. There is no indication of large crime organizations playing an important role, perhaps because anyone with suitable connections in an unregulated state is in a position to obtain guns and transport them to their home city where, again with the right connections, they will be worth more.

Chapter 3 introduced ATF and described its general capacities to enforce federal firearms laws. Local gun diversions, such as theft and in-state transfers in violation of state laws, can be investigated by state and local police departments. However, ATF is responsible for investigating interstate gun trafficking and regulating firearms commerce more generally. Disrupting the illegal supply lines of guns to criminals requires productive partnerships between ATF, U.S. Attorneys, and state and local authorities. ATF plays key investigative roles in interagency task forces and, through its crime gun tracing and ballistics imaging efforts, provides an information foundation to focus gun law enforcement efforts. ATF launched its Crime Gun Intelligence Centers (CGICs) in July 2016 as an interagency collaboration designed to collect, analyze, and distribute intelligence data about crime guns, mass shootings, and major incidents across multiple jurisdictions. These data resources are used to uncover patterns of firearms trafficking, identify illegal and "straw" firearms purchasers, and develop leads to recover firearms used in violent crimes.

An analysis of 2,608 ATF gun trafficking investigations made between 1999 and 2002 provides a general, if somewhat dated, account of the nature of illegal gun market dynamics.[6] Table 9.1 presents the gun trafficking pathways identified by ATF agents in these investigations. An updated account would include a more differentiated framework for firearms diverted over the internet with illicit surface, deep, and dark web transactions featured.[7] There has also been a concerning rise in the number of privately manufactured firearms recovered by police in violent gun crimes, including hate violence and domestic terrorism. In 2019, ATF estimated that more than 10,000 of these off-the-books, untraceable ghost guns had been seized by law enforcement agencies.[8] In 2021, 19,344 ghost guns were recovered by law enforcement agencies and submitted to ATF for tracing.[9]

Many gun trafficking investigations involve close-to-retail diversions of guns from legal firearms commerce. Firearms trafficking investigations are initiated through varied means, ranging from traditional methods—such as through confidential informants or a referral of illegal activity by other law

**Table 9.1** Gun Trafficking Pathways Identified in ATF Trafficking Investigations ($N = 2{,}068$)

| Source | No. | %[a] |
|---|---|---|
| Firearms diverted by straw purchaser or straw purchasing ring | 1,078 | 41.3 |
| Firearms diverted by unregulated private sellers[b] | 708 | 27.1 |
| Prohibited persons lying and buying firearms | 364 | 14.0 |
| Diverting firearms stolen from residence or vehicle | 338 | 13.0 |
| Diverting firearms stolen from FFL | 239 | 9.2 |
| Diverting firearms at gun shows | 185 | 7.1 |
| Firearms diverted by licensed dealer, including pawnbroker | 163 | 6.3 |
| Diverting firearms at flea markets, auctions, or want ads and gun magazines | 112 | 4.3 |
| Diverting firearms stolen from common carrier | 28 | 1.1 |
| Diverting firearms over the internet | 22 | 0.8 |
| Other | 5 | 0.2 |

[a] Sum exceeds 100% because investigations may be included in more than one category. Gun trafficking investigations can be complex and involve a variety of illegal gun sources.

[b] As distinct from straw purchasers and other traffickers.

FFL, Federal Firearms Licensees.

*Source*: Anthony A. Braga, Garen J. Wintemute, Glenn L. Pierce, Philip J. Cook, and Greg Ridgeway, "Interpreting the Empirical Evidence on Illegal Gun Market Dynamics," *Journal of Urban Health* 89, no. 5 (2012): 779–793e.

enforcement agencies or licensed dealers—to innovative analyses of firearms trace, multiple sales, and other commerce data suggesting suspicious purchase and sales patterns. A plurality (41.3%) of investigations involved straw purchasing from federally licensed dealers (Federal Firearms Licensees [FFLs]), with firearms trafficked by straw purchasers either themselves or indirectly. The investigations also involved trafficking by unlicensed sellers (27.1%), trafficking by FFLs (6.3%), illegal diversions at gun shows (7.1%), and illegal diversions from flea markets and other secondary market sources (4.3%). When aggregated into one category, firearms stolen from FFLs, residences, and common carriers were involved in 22.5% of the trafficking investigations.

Although 117,138 firearms were involved altogether, most investigations involved relatively small numbers of guns. The mean and median were 45 and 8 guns per case, respectively; a majority involved 10 firearms or less. Large-scale trafficking was uncommon; roughly 5% of investigations involved more than 100 firearms. One investigation involved 30,000 firearms. Different trafficking pathways were associated with large differences in the numbers of guns linked to the investigations. FFLs, including pawnbrokers, have access to a large volume of firearms, so a corrupt licensed dealer can illegally divert large numbers of firearms. FFL traffickers were involved in only 6% of investigations but had by far the largest mean number of guns per case and accounted for 47% of all guns linked to the investigations.

Drawing on the parlance of environmental regulation, illegal gun markets consist of "point sources"—ongoing diversions through scofflaw dealers and trafficking rings—and "diffuse sources"—acquisitions through small-scale straw purchasing, informal transfers, and theft.[10] Both point and diffuse sources of guns are important. When controlling pollution, authorities need to regulate point source factories that belch filth into the skies and dump waste into water supplies. Pollution levels are also powerfully influenced by the cumulative effects of vehicle exhaust, and these diffuse emission sources need to be controlled. A well-rounded gun market disruption strategy needs to identify and shut down point sources that flood city streets with illegal guns and develop complementary strategies to curtail diffuse sources that cumulatively arm many violent criminals.

As suggested by the Biden administration's recently announced gun violence reduction plans,[11] apprehending scofflaw FFLs is clearly an important task given their potential for generating great harm. Experimental studies suggest that some licensed dealers will knowingly participate in illegal gun sales.[12] Fortunately, there are not many corrupt licensed dealers in the United States. A recent firearm licensee survey asked respondents what percentage of licensees might be bad apples who participate knowingly in illegal gun sales. The median response was 3%.[13] While the ATF has limited capacity to regulate retailers, it appears to be quite effective in gaining compliance.[14] The challenge to police departments seeking to curtail the underground gun market is the variety of sources.

## Can Underground Gun Markets Be Disrupted?

It seems reasonable to believe that guns are readily available in the United States, and for that reason it would be difficult to prevent a motivated person, whether legally qualified or not, from obtaining one.[15] That view is reinforced by the recent Supreme Court finding of a personal right to gun ownership, which places a Constitutional limit on the types of regulations that government may impose on gun ownership and transactions. Yet there is reason to believe that existing regulations are better than nothing, as suggested by the evidence presented in Chapter 3.

## The Efficacy of Regulations

Current regulations are effective in keeping offenders from buying their guns from retail dealers and in influencing interstate trafficking patterns and other aspects of the underground gun market. Interstate gun flows change in response to a change in regulations. A notable example is the dramatic change in sources of crime guns to Chicago following the adoption of the Brady Act in 1994; the percentage coming from the deep South states, where gun stores for the first time were required to run background checks, dropped abruptly by 15 points, replaced by in-state sales.[16] Other examples of how interstate movements respond to changes in state regulations have also been well documented.[17] For instance, the likelihood that a Boston handgun would be traced to a Virginia FFL nearly doubled after Virginia repealed its law limiting consumers to one handgun per month.[18] Such evidence helps document the importance of systematic trafficking into jurisdictions with tight controls.

This same evidence is suggestive of the importance of retail dealers as the source of guns to traffickers. In Virginia, for example, private sales are largely unregulated, so a reduction in trafficking from Virginia attributed to the old one-gun-a-month regulation implies both that the dealers were compliant with that provision and that collectively they were an important source of guns to traffickers. Indeed, it appears that FFLs are largely compliant with federal and state regulations, or at least sufficiently compliant as to profoundly influence the channels by which guns are obtained by disqualified offenders. That is rather remarkable, given the historically light touch of ATF's regulatory efforts.

The bottom-line question is whether regulatory effects on transaction patterns translate into reduced gun violence. A noteworthy example is the Brady Act, which imposed a nationwide requirement that FFLs conduct background checks of would-be buyers. Since fully implemented in 1998, 3 million transactions have been blocked as a result of these background checks, for the most part because the customer had a felony conviction. Nonetheless, according to one evaluation, the direct effect of the Brady Act on homicide rates was statistically negligible.[19] Closing the secondary market or "private sale" loophole may be a necessary precondition for effective screening.[20] But several federal and state regulations have proven their worth in reducing gun violence. Strong evidence suggests that expansions in the categories of people disqualified from owning guns could save lives. Violent recidivism by those convicted of misdemeanor violence fell after they were disqualified from owning guns in California.[21] Similarly, domestic murders involving guns fell after the Gun Control Act was amended by Congress in 1996 to expand the federal ban on felons to include those convicted of misdemeanor-level domestic violence.[22]

In summary, there are various examples in which gun regulations have been carefully evaluated and shown effective at reducing criminal misuse of firearms. Chapter 3 presents this evidence. The lesson is not that all such regulations are effective but, rather, that regulations can be effective and should not automatically be written off as futile given the alleged efficiency of the underground market. But there is no such thing as a free lunch when it comes to regulatory effectiveness, and in particular jurisdictions that adopt regulations but do not enforce them will be disappointed.[23] Importantly, this body of research supports the idea that police can be effective in reducing gun violence by limiting criminal access to firearms.

## Prices of Guns to Criminals

The prices of heroin, cocaine, and other illicit drugs are carefully monitored as an indicator of regulatory and enforcement effectiveness. Defining prices in underground gun market settings is much more complicated than for drugs. Guns are durable goods with prices that are highly differentiated by type, manufacture, condition, source, and other factors. Gun purchases are low-frequency events compared to drug purchases. As such, it is not surprising ATF has largely ignored street prices of guns in measuring the effectiveness of their enforcement and regulatory efforts. In contrast to the routine purchasing of drugs from street sources by the Drug Enforcement Administration, ATF does not make controlled buys of guns to develop comparative data on firearms prices across jurisdictions over time. Still, we do know that regulatory efforts are successful in the sense that guns cost much more in some underground markets than buying them from an FFL.

Efforts to reduce the supply of available guns should increase the price of guns sold to prohibited persons and increase the "effective price" of acquiring guns—the time and hassle required to make a "connection" to buy guns.[24] The benefit of this approach would be an increased incentive for criminals and youths to economize on gun possession and use. As guns become scarcer and more valuable, they will be slower to buy and quicker to sell, thus reducing the percentage of their criminal careers in which they are in possession of a gun.[25] For police departments, raising street prices of guns would entail launching effective illegal gun market disruption strategies. But what is the evidence that retail prices are linked to the prices or other availability measures in the market for guns that supply offenders?

There is, unfortunately, scant research to consider here. The little that is known about gun prices suggests noteworthy markups for guns purchased in underground markets, with higher street prices in cities located in jurisdictions with stronger gun commerce laws and regulations. For instance, non-gang-affiliated Chicago youth reported paying between $250 and $400 for low-quality pistols that were available on legal market websites for as little as $50 to $100.[26] In an older study, anecdotal evidence provided by law enforcement agencies suggested a low-quality Davis .380 semiautomatic pistol cost $90 at a retail outlet; $250 on the streets of Charlotte or Raleigh, North Carolina; and $400 on the streets of New York or Washington, DC.[27] In our New York City study, reported gun prices ranged from $200 for a used, small-caliber handgun (i.e., .22 Davis pistol) to more than $1,000 for a new, high-quality large-caliber handgun (i.e., .45 Desert Eagle pistol). Bronx and Brooklyn respondents typically paid between $300 and $400 for their most recent handgun.[28]

The most detailed work on gun prices is an analysis of guns purchased by gangs in Boston led by our colleague David Hureau.[29] Through his personal connections with gang members, Hureau was able to get detailed information on make, model, and condition of a number of these guns and compare the price paid by the gang with the "Blue Book" price that reflects prices in the licit market. The two sets of prices are positively correlated for cheaper guns, valued at less than $350 in the licit market, with a large markup and considerable "noise." The markup, which averages out to be a factor of three, may be higher than in most cities because Boston has one of the lowest gun ownership rates of any city in the nation. Unfortunately, comparable data are not available for other cities.

The variability of money prices extends the finding that transactions costs differ widely within the same jurisdiction. In a well-functioning market, the "law of one price" prevails. But in a thin market in which trust is important and gun transactions are often based on personal connections, the equilibrating force is weak.

## What Can the Police Do to Reduce the Supply of Guns to Criminals?

Local police departments can quite possibly be effective at disrupting local gun markets, but only if they concern themselves with gathering the necessary intelligence and acting on it. Most police departments have been focused on getting guns off the street instead of focusing on the sources of these guns.[30] Beginning in the mid-1990s, however, police practices have changed in many major cities due in part to efforts by ATF and the U.S. Department of Justice to form partnerships to reduce the availability of guns to youth and criminals. CGICs are currently staffed by ATF special agents, industry operations investigators, state and local law enforcement agencies, forensics experts, intelligence specialists, and prosecutors focused on stopping violent gun crimes and illegal gun trafficking. Heightened enforcement of federal laws against illegal gun trafficking is also a core component of the U.S. Department of Justice–sponsored Project Safe Neighborhoods initiative to reduce gun violence in each of the 94 U.S. Attorney judicial districts in the United States. A key practice in these partnerships is the comprehensive tracing of all firearms recovered in a jurisdiction to their first retail sale, and the strategic analysis of trace information to identify suspicious purchase and sales patterns indicative of illegal gun trafficking.[31]

Local problem-oriented policing projects hold great promise for creating a strong response to illicit firearms markets. The problem-oriented approach provides an appropriate framework to uncover the complex mechanisms at play in illicit firearms markets and to develop tailor-made interventions to disrupt the gun trade. The complexity and diversity of illegal gun markets suggest that there is no single best policy or approach to disrupting the illegal supply of guns. Jurisdictions interested in reducing the availability of guns should develop a portfolio of interventions based on problem-solving partnerships between federal, state, and local authorities. By analyzing the nature of specific gun trafficking problems, law enforcement can develop a systematic plan to shut down supply lines rather than simply pursuing ad hoc enforcement actions.

## Analyzing Underground Gun Markets

City-level studies of underground gun markets shed further insight into how illegal diversions arm high-risk people in particular urban environments. Intelligence gathering is the foundation of designing effective interventions. Here is an example.

Braga, Cook, and colleagues partnered with the NYPD to analyze New York City's underground gun market by examining the flow of guns into the two boroughs where gun violence and crime gun recoveries were most prevalent: the Bronx and Brooklyn.[32] The study analyzed 2010–2015 ATF firearms trace data and in-depth interviews with individuals considered to be at high risk for involvement in gun violence. Guns recovered by the NYPD in the

Bronx and Brooklyn were not notably different from firearms elsewhere in the city. Firearms recovered by the NYPD throughout the city were primarily handguns and most likely to be semiautomatic pistols, usually medium-caliber firearms (e.g., .38, .380, and 9 mm), and mostly made by reputable manufacturers (e.g., Smith & Wesson, Glock, and Ruger). ATF was able to successfully trace almost two-thirds of the recovered firearms to their first known retail sale.

Table 9.2 presents gun trafficking indicators for the traced New York City study guns. Large shares of traced guns originated from first retail sales at I-95 southern states with comparatively permissive gun laws (specifically, Florida, Georgia, North Carolina, South Carolina, and Virginia; Figure 9.2). FFLs located in New York state generated 13% of the traced recovered guns, whereas FFLs located in Pennsylvania, a proximate state with weaker gun

**Table 9.2** Selected Gun Trafficking Indicators for Traced Firearms Recovered in New York City, 2010–2015

| Characteristic | Citywide ($n$ = 15,092), % | Bronx and Brooklyn ($n$ = 9,477), % | Rest of New York City ($n$ = 5,615), % |
|---|---|---|---|
| **Source state** | | | |
| I-95 southern states | 48.6 | 51.1 | 44.5 |
| New York | 13.3 | 10.6 | 17.9 |
| Pennsylvania | 10.4 | 11.4 | 8.7 |
| Other states | 27.7 | 27.0 | 28.9 |
| **Retail purchaser sex** | | | |
| Male | 84.3 | 83.8 | 85.1 |
| Female | 15.7 | 16.2 | 14.9 |
| **Purchaser and possessor identification** | | | |
| Purchaser and possessor are different people | 94.9 | 97.6 | 90.4 |
| Purchaser and possessor is the same person | 5.1 | 2.4 | 9.6 |
| **Time to crime** | | | |
| Recovered over 3 years after first retail sale | 83.0 | 83.8 | 81.5 |
| Recovered within 3 years of first retail sale | 17.0 | 16.2 | 18.5 |
| Median time to crime | 12.6 years | 12.7 years | 12.6 years |

*Source*: Anthony A. Braga, Rod K. Brunson, Philip J. Cook, Brandon S. Turchan, and Brian Wade, "Underground Gun Markets and the Flow of Illegal Guns into the Bronx and Brooklyn: A Mixed Methods Analysis," *Journal of Urban Health* 98 (2021): 596–608, https://link.springer.com/article/10.1007/s11524-020-00477-z. Accessed August 28, 2021.

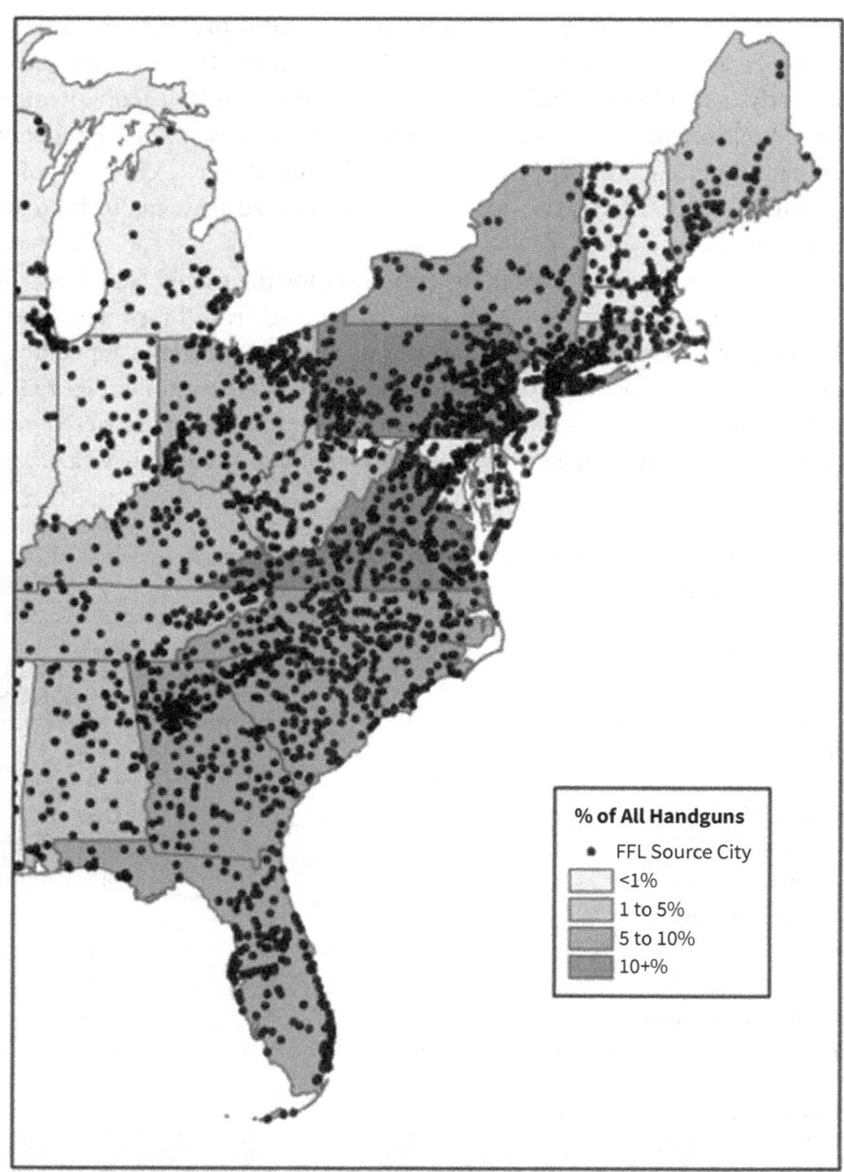


**Figure 9.2** Source states for traced firearms recovered in New York City, 2010–2015. The percentages reflect the source state for handguns successfully traced to their first purchase. FFL, Federal Firearms Licensees.

controls, were the first retail sale sources for 10% of the traced guns. Most traced guns were first purchased by males (84%) rather than females; the vast majority were recovered in the hands of someone other than the first retail purchaser (95%), suggesting that at some point in their life span, these guns were likely transferred from a legal owner to a criminal possessor. Traced guns tended to be quite old (median time to crime = 12.6 years), and only 17% of traced guns were recovered by the NYPD within 3 years of the first retail sale. Further statistical analysis of these data revealed that guns recovered in the Bronx and Brooklyn were significantly more likely to originate in states with less restrictive gun laws and more likely to have changed ownership in unregulated transactions relative to guns recovered elsewhere in New York City.[33]

Consistent with the NYPD trace data analyses, study participants (85% of 103 subjects) reported that most crime guns in their neighborhoods originated from I-95 southern states with lax gun laws. In fact, the interviewees routinely and casually referred to "the south" or "down south" when speaking about the flow of illegal guns into their neighborhoods.[34] Nearly one-fifth of the sample also mentioned Pennsylvania, Ohio, and upstate New York as sources. Interviews revealed three primary avenues for illegal guns reaching Bronx and Brooklyn neighborhoods: high-volume gun brokers, middlemen, and individuals who make small episodic acquisitions from straw purchasers in other states. However, subjects suggested that most illegal firearm acquisitions occurred through low-level individual transactions on the street; the majority asserted that illicit gun sales were not centralized to a handful of individuals but instead spread out among many market participants. For example, one gang member explained, "It's not like one person. It's widespread. It's various people that have [them] (guns) and various people that know people who have [them]."[35] No one identified theft as a meaningful source of crime guns in their Bronx and Brooklyn neighborhoods.

Many participants (57%) reported difficulty in obtaining guns, although gang members typically were better connected to the underground market than others. For example, a gang member explained, "basically, people in gangs . . . they got guns ready. . . . They know more people . . . got more connects (potential dealers)." Furthermore, an individual gang member's access to guns was not restricted to merely their own personal networks; rather, gang members shared "connects." As another gang member illustrated, "[Someone in] a gang knows more people. I might know a couple, you might know a couple, he might know a couple. That might add up."[36]

The New York City results complement studies completed by Braga and collaborators in Boston, a city with similarly tight gun controls in place. Boston gang members also tended to acquire older handguns diverted by illicit gun runners who exploit unregulated secondary market transactions in states with weak gun controls.[37] Further analyses found that Boston crime guns with trafficking indicators were more likely to be recovered from gang members, drug sellers, and other high-risk offenders who faced the greatest risk of both committing shootings and suffering gunshot wounds.[38]

## Comprehensive Crime Gun Intelligence

The New York and Boston findings show that systematic intelligence is helpful in understanding the workings of a local underground gun market. Targeted interventions can then be aimed at curtailing illegal transfers of firearms to gang members and other high-risk individuals and, ultimately, to decrease gun violence. Gun trafficking and shooting investigations are facilitated by comprehensive processing of recovered crime guns and related evidence to understand the principal sources of guns to shooters.[39] Importantly, prosecutors are much more likely to adopt gun trafficking cases when investigators can demonstrate the tangible harm generated by linking trafficked guns to subsequent violence.

What data are useful in this effort? Evidence that can usefully be obtained from recovered guns known or suspected to have been used in crime includes the following:

- Ballistics (which also applies to recovered casings and projectiles)
- DNA, latent fingerprints, and trace evidence
- ATF trace information on the last known purchaser
- Theft reports, both local and filed with the National Crime Information Center.[40]

Also important is cooperation in information sharing among the various law enforcement agencies operating within the region.

The National Integrated Ballistics Information Network (NIBIN), maintained by ATF, is an underutilized source of clues for individual investigations as well as a research tool for understanding criminal networks. Shell casings and bullets are automatically scanned for marks imprinted during firing; there are microscopic differences among firearms that can be used to associate a casing or bullet fragment with a particular gun. NIBIN maintains a database of this ballistic information that can be utilized by the police to link shootings to guns and to other shootings. Cold hits that link recovered crime guns, bullets, and cartridge casings across gun crime events sometimes generate investigative leads.[41]

Detectives and ATF agents advance shooting and gun trafficking investigations forward when "information chains" are constructed around the events linked by ballistics evidence. The amount and types of information associated with linked gun crime events can differ tremendously across matches (Figure 9.3). All matches provide investigators with the caliber, crime types, dates, times, and locations of shots fired from a particular gun or from a recovered gun that is subsequently test fired by firearms examiners. If a gun is recovered, ATF can initiate a trace of the firearm to determine the identity of the last known purchaser. However, other key information that may be critical to solving a particular

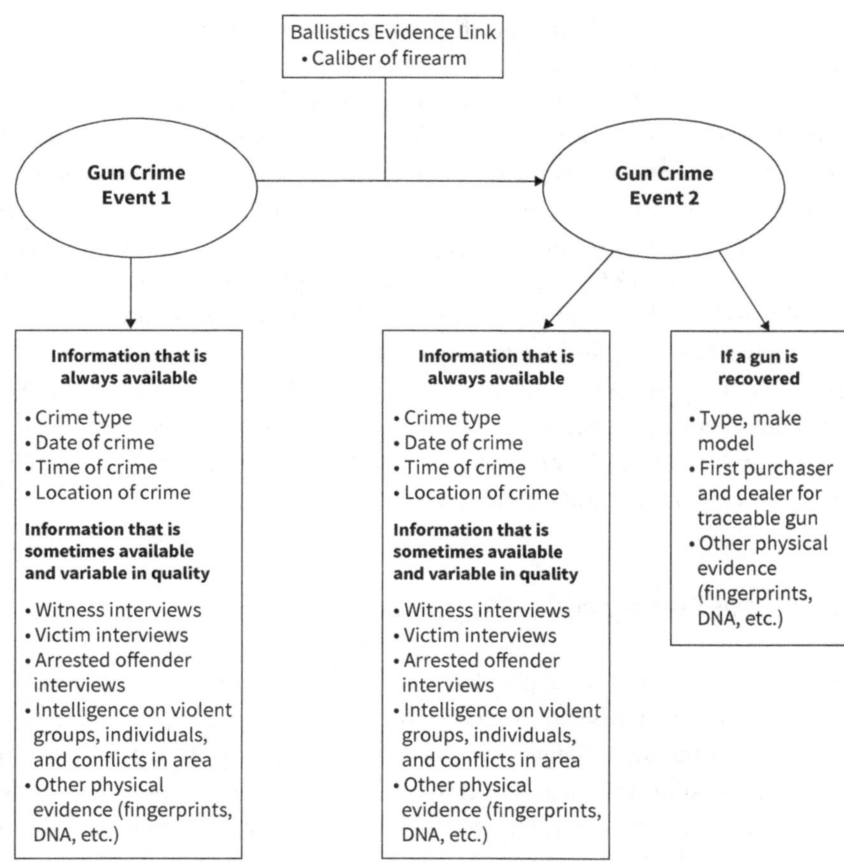


**Figure 9.3** Types of investigative information linked by ballistic matches.

*Source*: Anthony A. Braga, "Gun Enforcement and Ballistics Imaging Technology in Boston," in *Ballistics Imaging*, eds. Daniel L. Cork, John E. Rolph, Eugene S. Meieran, and Carol V. Petrie, National Research Council and National Academy of Engineering (Washington, DC: National Academies Press, 2008), 296.

violent crime may or may not be available to investigators, depending on the nature of the incidents linked by ballistics evidence.

NIBIN-suggested matches also provide important opportunities for law enforcement agencies to better understand and respond to street violence. The links help guide violence prevention efforts by establishing patterns of violence in particular areas and among specific individuals. When ballistic hit reports are organized as a network analysis, detectives can identify and target the key nodes in a criminal network.[42] Arrested offenders can then be debriefed on the sources of their guns, and this information can guide gun-market disruption efforts.

Braga's interviews with Boston Police Department detectives confirmed the considerable investigative value of NIBIN cold-hit matches and the resulting information chains built around the linked events.[43] For instance, a Taurus .40 Model PT 140 Pro semiautomatic pistol recovered from a suspect in a nonfatal gun assault was linked to a triple homicide incident that occurred 4 months earlier. A subsequent interview with this individual (following his arrest) revealed that the lead suspect in the triple homicide incident had provided the Taurus .40 semiautomatic pistol to him. The lead investigator on the triple homicide case commented, "The bullet match was a significant lead in the . . . investigation of a triple homicide. Through further investigation, we were able to link the recovered firearm to the homicide offender and obtain an arrest warrant."[44] A gun trafficking investigation then developed from this case as a subsequent ATF trace of the recovered firearm revealed that a third party had recently purchased the Taurus .40 semiautomatic pistol at a licensed dealer in an Interstate 95 southern state with lax gun control laws compared to Massachusetts' tighter gun control laws.

## Successful Supply-Side Programs

A prominent example of a problem-oriented approach is the Boston Gun Project/Operation Ceasefire intervention described in Chapter 6. Based on an analysis of the local illegal gun market, the resulting strategy was appropriately focused on the illegal diversion of new handguns from retail outlets in Massachusetts, southern states along Interstate 95, and elsewhere.[45] For investigative and tactical purposes, guns with quick "time to crime" (the time between the last known purchase and its ultimate recovery by the police) offer law enforcement an opportunity to identify illegal gun traffickers. New guns have passed through fewer hands, which makes it much easier for law enforcement to investigate their diversion and their diverters and to mount prosecutions. Records are likely to be more complete and more available; individuals listed on paperwork are easier to find; guns are less likely to have been resold, given away, or stolen; and the chain of transfers to illicit consumers is likely to be shorter. The key elements of the Ceasefire gun market disruption strategy were as follows:[46]

- Expand the focus of local, state, and federal authorities to include *intrastate* firearms trafficking in Massachusetts in addition to interstate trafficking.
- Focus enforcement attention on traffickers of the makes and calibers of handguns most used by gang members.
- Focus enforcement attention on traffickers of newer handguns, in which the first retail buyer was likely to have been complicit. The ATF Boston Field Division implemented an in-house tracking system that flagged handguns whose traces revealed a short time-to-crime interval.
- Focus enforcement attention on traffickers of handguns used by the city's most violent gangs.
- Attempt to restore obliterated serial numbers of confiscated handguns and subsequently investigate trafficking based on these restorations.
- Support these enforcement priorities through strategic analyses of data generated by the Boston Police Department and ATF's comprehensive tracing of crime guns and by developing leads from the systematic debriefing of gang-affiliated arrestees and those involved in violent crime.
- Advertise successful investigations and prosecutions of gun traffickers to deter others from diverting firearms from retail sources to criminals and youth in Boston.

A quasi-experimental evaluation found that Operation Ceasefire's focus on close-to-retail diversions of handguns was associated with significant decreases in the percentage of handguns recovered by the Boston Police that were new.[47] Although data on street prices of new handguns paid by criminals were not available, the evaluation findings suggest that the supply-side enforcement strategy increased the effective price of new handguns by making it riskier to acquire these firearms for illegal possession and criminal use. This conclusion was supported by an increased percentage of older recovered handguns, suggesting that traffickers and underground gun market sellers sought to avoid detection by diverting secondhand firearms.

There is also an interesting example from the West Coast. In the early 2000s, the Los Angeles Police Department (LAPD), ATF, and the RAND Corporation initiated a research and program development effort to understand the nature of illegal gun markets operating in Los Angeles.[48] Braga was a key member of the working group that managed this effort. The primary goal of this project was to determine whether a data-driven, problem-solving approach could yield new interventions aimed at disrupting the workings of local illegal gun markets serving criminals, gang members, and juveniles in the LAPD's 77th Street Policing District area (South Los Angeles). The analyses of illegal gun markets serving criminals in the target area revealed that many crime guns were first purchased at local licensed dealers. That is, rather than the conventional wisdom that crime guns were being trafficked across state borders from places with less stringent regulations such as Arizona and Nevada, most crime guns were purchased in Los Angeles County.

Based on their investigative experience, LAPD detectives and ATF case agents suggested that the local nature of the market was driven by prohibited possessors who were having local friends or family members conduct straw purchases for them.[49] These investigators suggested that because the people conducting the straw purchases do not have a criminal history forbidding them from making legal purchases, this population could potentially be deterred from initiating this illegal activity. These friends and family members were not organized gun runners. Most transactions by an individual purchaser only involved one gun. Yet, this diffuse source represented a common way for gang members in South Los Angeles to acquire guns.

In partnership with the California Department of Justice, the LAPD and RAND researchers organized a "letter campaign" intervention that attempted to dissuade legal firearm purchasers from selling or transferring their firearms to others without filing the necessary paperwork with the state (Figure 9.4). New gun buyers received a notification letter during their 10-day waiting period, before they picked up their newly purchased firearm, that informed them of their responsibilities as a gun owner and that the firearm can be traced back to them if used in a crime. The key idea of this new gun market disruption strategy was to deter small-scale straw purchasers from picking up their firearms and from making other illegal purchases in the future.

It turned out that the rate at which guns were reported stolen for those who received the letter was more than twice the rate for those who did not receive the letter.[50] Of those receiving the letter, nearly 2% reported their gun stolen during the study period compared to only 1% for those who did not receive the letter. The letter campaign apparently increased straw-purchaser perceptions of apprehension risk as they sought to distance themselves from the illegal transfer by reporting the gun stolen. This research suggested that simple, targeted gun law awareness campaigns can modify new gun buyers'

*Office of the Attorney General for the State of*
*California Office of the Los Angeles* City Attorney
*Los Angeles Police Department*

Name
Address

Dear Mr./Ms. Name,

As you know, gun violence is a serious problem in Los Angeles. We understand that you have recently purchased a gun. It is important that we all do our part to store guns safely and keep guns out of the hands of kids and criminals. We are working in collaboration with the federal program called Project Safe Neighborhood (PSN).

As partners in keeping the streets safe in your neighborhood we want to remind you of your obligations as a gun owner.

**If you ever decide to sell or give your gun to someone, you must complete a "Dealer Record of Sale" (DROS) form. These forms can be obtained and completed at any gun store. Remember, it is a crime to transfer a gun to anyone without first filling out this form.**

If the police recover a gun that was involved in a crime, the Los Angeles City Attorney will prosecute the gun's previous owner if that owner did not complete the "Dealer Record of Sale" form. Please make sure you go to a firearms dealer and fill out that form if you want to sell or give away your firearm.

You can help us make Los Angeles a safer community by preventing your gun from ending up in the wrong hands.

Thank you,

Rockard J. Delgadillo
Los Angeles City Attorney

Bill Lockyer, Attorney General
State of California

William J. Bratton, Chief
Los Angeles Police Department

**Figure 9.4** Scanned image of CA state letter to gun purchasers.

*Source*: Greg Ridgeway, Anthony A. Braga, George E. Tita, and Glenn L. Pierce, "Intervening in Gun Markets: An Experiment to Assess the Impact of Targeted Gun Law Messaging," *Journal of Experimental Criminology* 7, no. 1 (2011): 108.

behaviors. It also suggests that diffuse sources of illegal guns can be addressed through strategic action.

There are other examples of law enforcement efforts to shut down the illegal diversion of guns from retail commerce.[51] Unfortunately, very few have been evaluated. Those that have been evaluated have shown notable changes to local gun market dynamics. For instance, in Detroit and Chicago, the flow of new guns to crime through straw purchasing was sharply reduced after undercover police stings and lawsuits targeted scofflaw retail dealers.[52] Milwaukee achieved the same result when a notorious gun dealer (who had led the nation in selling guns that were later put to criminal use) was persuaded to voluntarily reform its sales practices.[53] New York City Mayor Michael Bloomberg broke new ground in 2006 by suing 27 out-of-state gun dealers whose guns were frequently showing up on the streets of New York; the result was a sharp reduction in their role in supplying criminal use.[54]

Gun buybacks, amnesties, and exchange programs have wide appeal for communities affected by gun violence, for understandable reasons. Advocates suggest these programs reduce the number of firearms available to criminals, those with mental illnesses, and other high-risk individuals who may harm themselves or others with a gun. Moreover, these programs arguably empower participants and supporters to take an active role in the fight against gun violence. Unfortunately, there is no scientific evidence that these programs reduce gun violence.[55]

Given the popularity of gun buybacks, police departments will continue to participate in these efforts. The design of gun buybacks, however, could affect the nature of the firearms that are recovered and improve their potential effectiveness as violence prevention measures. In Boston, program features such as higher prices for handguns, proof of Boston residency to prevent suburban FFLs from dumping unwanted inventory, and community drop-off locations yielded much higher numbers of semiautomatic pistols and other handguns.[56] Most gun buybacks are relatively brief, one-time events. In contrast, the NYPD has a permanent "Cash for Guns" buyback program that offers $200 per gun surrendered. New Yorkers can turn in guns anonymously. The fact that this buyback has been in place for years could be generating a desirable effect on the availability of guns on city streets by creating a $200 price floor. (Guns worth less than $200 on the street should be turned in to the NYPD for the more profitable price.) That economic logic should be tested in New York and other jurisdictions, since it has a clear implication for the design of buyback programs. Brief buybacks accomplish little or nothing, but sustained buybacks are likely to transform the underground market.

## What About Gun Theft?

As suggested in Chapter 3, theft is one plausible source of guns to offenders, but it is an open question whether controlling theft would have a noticeable effect on gun violence. There are easily enough guns stolen every year, mostly from homes and vehicles, to supply all the offenders who commit robbery and assault. But it is unknown how thieves dispose of stolen guns, and particularly whether it is any more likely that they are sold to gang members and robbers than would be true for a stolen computer or necklace. Convicted offenders, when asked where they obtained their guns, rarely mention theft as a source.[57] But theft may be playing a hidden role in trafficking and diversion to the underground market.

Problem-oriented policing approaches have been shown to be effective in controlling a wide range of theft problems, including burglary, thefts from vehicles, and shoplifting.[58] The approach has also been used to analyze and shrink markets for stolen goods.[59] The practical lessons learned from these experiences could be applied in specific jurisdictions to address guns stolen emanating from residential burglaries, vehicle break-ins, "smash-and-grab" theft operations that target licensed dealers, and street fences who transfer stolen guns to criminals.

## Conclusion

Reducing gun availability to criminal use requires systematic intelligence and planning. Local police departments may take a problem-oriented approach to understand how criminals access guns in their jurisdictions and collaborate with federal and state law enforcement partners to implement interventions to shut down specific gun trafficking pathways. This strategy is particularly promising in areas where gun ownership is less common (e.g., Northeastern cities) and state regulations are stringent. Certainly, the flows of guns to offenders look much different in Nashville or Phoenix, for example, than in New York City and Boston. And in this area, good intelligence on both local diversion patterns and interregional movements is key to crafting an effective strategy.

It is also important to recognize that the underground market is not static—far from it. The emergence of ghost guns as a problem in California and elsewhere stands as a vivid example. Individuals with criminal records and others who would not pass background checks to obtain guns can assemble them at home—often with the help of online videos and instructions—after legally buying kits and individual parts. In Los Angeles County, the Sheriff estimated that the recovery of untraceable ghost guns increased by roughly 50% between 2018 and 2019.[60] In Oakland, the percentage of ghost guns among recovered crime guns increased dramatically from 1.4% in 2017 to 24% in 2021; ghost guns were more likely to be recovered in violent crime relative to guns produced by licensed manufacturers.[61] The bottom line is that the underground market in guns can be disrupted and curtailed, but only through a well-informed strategy and with the knowledge that it is a moving target.

# 10
# There's Much to Be Done

The surge in criminal firearms violence that began in the "year from hell," 2020, continued full force through 2021, with no end in sight. Both the social and the economic burden of this surge have been enormous. Public safety is a precondition of individual well-being and community prosperity, and in many cities public safety has been a casualty of all that went wrong in that year.

Gun violence is a multifaceted problem requiring a multifaceted response. An essential component of any comprehensive effort is more effective policing. That is a controversial assertion, seemingly the antithesis of the progressive "defund the police" movement. But we believe that an investment in better policing would save thousands of lives every year and markedly improve the quality of life, notably but not only in low-income minority communities. The "great crime drop" from 1993 to 2014 did just that, with homicide and other violence rates cut in half and a resulting renaissance in many depressed neighborhoods. Now is the time to restart that process.

The way forward, we submit, is not to defund the police but, rather, to devote more of the police (and other law enforcement) resources to what matters most while respecting the interests and rights of citizens. Additional resources and evidence-informed management can make policing more effective in preventing gun violence. A great deal has been learned about intervening in hot spots, improving shooting investigations, communicating a retail-deterrence message to gang members, and interdicting illegal gun transactions.

Gun control is sometimes offered as a substitute for effective law enforcement. But regulations on gun commerce and use require enforcement if they are to be effective. Furthermore, the future of gun regulation is in doubt, given that the new majority on the U.S. Supreme Court has favored a very expansive interpretation of the Second Amendment. And even if some regulations survive Constitutional review, they are more a complement than a substitute for law enforcement. For example, enforcement actions to reduce illegal gun carrying in public require that gun carrying be illegal, at least under some

*Policing Gun Violence.* Anthony A. Braga and Philip J. Cook, Oxford University Press. © Oxford University Press 2023.
DOI: 10.1093/oso/9780199929283.003.0010

circumstances. And for police homicide investigations to link the guns to the shooters, gun commerce must be regulated to ensure appropriate recordkeeping.

Of course, the police are far from perfect instruments. They need to be motivated and guided to do the right thing. The "wrong" thing includes excessive use of force, disparate treatment by race, and heavy-handed interactions with the public that lack procedural justice. But the challenge is not just curtailing police abuse of citizens—it is also the real possibility of neglect. We need officers to get out of their patrol cars, engage with an often-hostile public, and investigate serious crimes of violence even when the victims and other witnesses are uncooperative. Arrest and conviction rates in many violence-plagued cities currently fall below 10% for nonfatal shootings and are not much higher for fatal shootings. The result is near impunity for shooters. "Failure to serve" is a common citizen complaint. Black communities feel both oppressed and underserved by the police.

The stakes are high. Gun violence in all its forms reduces our standard of living—whether community violence, domestic violence, shootings by law enforcement, mass shootings, or intimidation by militia groups. The burden falls particularly heavily on Blacks, who constitute a majority of victims for community and domestic violence and suffer population-adjusted victimization rates an order of magnitude higher than for Whites. In that sense, more effective enforcement becomes a matter of social justice. The goal is public safety for all.

## The Police Have Evolved, But Challenges Persist

During the post-Vietnam War era, the police have become less corrupt, better educated, more professional, better paid, and far more diverse with respect to race and sex. They have by and large become more respectful of citizen rights, due in part to exclusionary rules, court settlements, citizen review boards, and other accountability efforts. Excessive use of force remains a real problem, but it is not a new problem. The reality of improved police behavior clashes with public perception, which has been shaped in recent years by bystanders' ability to video record confrontations and post the results on social media. Vivid instances of police brutality, when publicized, may trump more systematic evidence of reform. Minority communities in particular do not trust the police nor believe that the police are concerned with public safety in their neighborhoods, which in turn induces hostility and lack of cooperation. Public hostility serves to undercut police morale, leading to disengagement and recruitment problems. This dynamic can be reversed—not only through police reform but also by improving service to these neighborhoods. The most important service is providing greater public safety.

The police have a unique role in crime prevention, and the prevention of gun violence in particular. The traditional tasks of investigating gun crime, arresting suspects, and building cases that will hold up in court are sometimes dismissed as "reactive," although in fact the main purpose (and effect) is to prevent future crime. The relevant mechanisms include deterrence and incapacitation, as well as interrupting retaliatory cycles. The police also engage in proactive efforts to gather intelligence on gangs and dangerous criminals, communicate the threat of legal consequences as effectively as possible, and disrupt what might be thought of as "precursor" activities—for example, stopping a stolen vehicle with armed gang members on the way to a drive-by shooting or breaking up a street corner drug-dealing operation. Even proactive work that is not focused specifically on gun crime may help because gun crime is closely linked to other types of criminal violence.

There is every reason to think that the police are more effective in crime control than they were even a generation ago due to improved technology, focused prevention strategies, and greater resources. But there remain some generic challenges. Most centrally, the police need to be viewed as legitimate authorities in the eyes of the public. Crime control is a co-production process, and civilian cooperation in reporting crimes and providing evidence is vital. Distrust of police by the communities most affected by gun violence, together with the "no snitching" culture and fear of retaliation, impairs investigations. Police work would benefit from improved community relations. There is no simple formula. "Community policing" and "procedural justice" provide some guidance in that respect. Ultimately, most victims of serious crime want their case to be taken seriously, and they will be more inclined to cooperate with the police if they believe that it will lead to a good result. Just as violence breeds violence, so will success breed success in police investigations.

Nonetheless, the pursuit of public safety may conflict with other community values. Perhaps the most notable such conflict in recent years has involved proactive efforts to get guns off the street known as "stop, question, and frisk." The approach involved high-volume stops of suspect individuals in violence-plagued neighborhoods for the purpose of questioning them and perhaps frisking them for illegal weapons. Although this tactic may well have had some effect in deterring gun carrying and thus saving lives in cities such as New York, Chicago, and Los Angeles, it came at unacceptable cost. Many residents of poor minority communities felt harassed and oppressed rather than served. Public safety is a vital concern, but it is not the only relevant value.

We do not envy police chiefs, who find that their officers are vilified and demoralized, their budgets are under attack, and their lead responsibility of controlling serious violence seems out of reach. But there is much that can be done to rectify this situation.

## A Portfolio of Effective Gun Violence Reduction Programs

In this book, we have not claimed that any single policing program represents a silver bullet to control gun violence. Given the multiple dimensions of gun violence problems, the quest is for a portfolio of somewhat effective programs, developed through systematic analysis of local conditions. Success also requires that police departments be properly staffed and supported and also held publicly accountable for results. Given that context, we attempt to offer guidance in five key areas.

### Address Gun Violence Hot Spots

In May 2021, faced with a surge in gun violence, the mayor and police chief of Washington, DC, announced that extra officers and resources would be deployed into six historically crime-ridden neighborhoods. A total of 45 blocks were selected on the basis of high concentrations of homicides, sounds of gunshots, robberies, and overall violent crime. Washington leaders were following the "hot spots" playbook.[1]

The police are responsible for the safety of the entire community. But given finite resources, effective crime prevention requires focus on the places where crime is concentrated. That concentration is baked into reactive policing. A 911 call about a shooting will ordinarily direct several patrol cars to that area, and the areas with the most shootings will cumulatively get the most attention. But for routine "preventive" patrol in between calls, the capacity to reduce crime is very limited. To increase the productivity of patrol in that respect, departments typically inform officers about problematic places, groups, and individuals. That guidance has gotten more systematic with the advent of hot spots policing and other tactics guided by data analysis. There have also been well-known innovations that provide guidance to officers on how to engage—and how *not* to engage—with the public for maximum impact. Among these innovations are a well-thought-out approach to selecting suspects for proactive street stops and, more generally, problem-oriented policing. These approaches have been refined and evaluated by analysts and in some cases by the courts.

The bulk of gun violence occurs away from home and requires that the shooter has transported the gun. Guns in public pose a public threat that has long been recognized. A traditional police goal has been to keep guns off the street, and in some cities, notably Chicago, there is a long tradition of searching for and confiscating guns that are being carried illegally by suspects. Based on the experience with programs of this sort in several mid-sized cities, the New York Police Department (NYPD) took it to the next level, implementing an aggressive stop, question, and frisk program by patrol officers, with the intent of deterring illegal gun carrying. In practice, only a small percentage of stops yielded guns or other contraband, but there is some evidence that it was effective in reducing the number of guns on the street. The program was challenged in the courts for its disparate impact on Blacks and sometimes questionable justifications for frisks. This high-volume approach has now been abandoned. The NYPD has replaced it with "precision" policing, which focuses enforcement on specific individuals known to the police. That experience illustrates the costs of aggressive police tactics and the potential trade-offs involved. A more selective approach reduces the costs of this program while arguably preserving much of the benefit. Unfortunately, the deregulation of gun carrying in most states has the effect of curtailing the scope for any effort to preempt gun use in crime.

The goal is nonetheless valid: reducing illegal gun carrying by dangerous offenders in public spaces. A tight focus on high-risk people in hot spots should be limited enough to help safeguard against harms such as undue racial disparities and perception of police harassment. Even in states that have deregulated gun carrying, felons, juveniles, and others prohibited from gun possession are of course also barred from carrying in public places. Police can still stop and question people on a selective basis and frisk them or search their cars given probable cause. A reduction in routine gun carrying by gang members and other dangerous people can reduce the rate of opportunistic shootings. When implementing this approach, police departments need to ensure that their officers are properly supervised and well trained to uphold civil rights and conduct procedurally-just encounters.

More ambitiously, patrol officers are in a prime position to notice crime patterns in particular hot spots and how they relate to underlying criminal opportunities. Violent crime may be linked to vacant lots, abandoned buildings, taverns that spawn fights, traffic patterns that facilitate street-corner drug dealing, or the routes that teens take to get to and from school.

Given encouragement, officers can diagnose problems and propose new tactics for the department or even interventions by other city agencies and organizations.

## Deal with Gangs, Street Crews, and Other Dangerous Offenders

The notion that violent gangs, drug crews, and other high-rate offenders could be deterred from gun misuse by the threat of arrest meets with widespread skepticism. But in fact there is very strong evidence in support of this claim.

The best evidence derives from the well-known Boston Gun Project/Operation Ceasefire strategy and similar programs in "retail" or "focused" deterrence. Working with David Kennedy, Anne Piehl, and local practitioners, Braga helped develop the Boston approach, and Chapter 6 tells that story from his direct experience. The Boston Police Department (BPD) and analytic team identified the most dangerous gangs in the city. Gang violence was given high priority in police investigations, with a comprehensive response when there was a shooting. In a unique innovation, the response was not limited to seeking arrest of the particular individuals involved in the shootings: The BPD and its community, social service, and criminal justice partners called for meetings with the violent gangs that were involved. The message to the gang members was that BPD and its criminal justice partners would pull every enforcement lever available against all the gang members if the gang continued to be involved in gun violence. On the other hand, gang members would be connected with resources and support for stepping away from the violence. Church ministers and other community groups provided public support for this intervention.

A number of other cities have adopted some version of this intervention, and much has been learned from disparate experiences. The Oakland version of focused deterrence is noteworthy not only for its success in reducing gang-related gun violence but also for its development of a citywide management structure to ensure effective implementation by the police, social service, and community-based organizations. The Oakland Mayor's Office established a directive designating that the initiative would be managed through weekly shooting reviews, biweekly coordination meetings, and bimonthly performance appraisals.

The most important ingredient for success appears to be a credible threat of arrest for specific behaviors. Credibility requires both a real increase in the likelihood of arrest and an effective communication program to make credible the claim that the police were monitoring gang behavior and were in a position to act effectively. However, as focused deterrence has continued to develop, other aspects of the intervention have received heightened prominence. Participating agencies increasingly promote changing the pro-violence norms held by gang members and paying attention to legitimacy and procedural justice. Community members, and those targeted by the intervention, seem to appreciate these aspects of the strategy. In their eyes, there is an inherent fairness in offering targeted offenders a choice and providing resources to support their transition away from violent behavior rather than simply arresting and prosecuting them.

## Strengthen Shooting Investigations

In a large majority of cases, violent gun offenders are not held accountable for their crimes and justice is denied to victims and their loved ones. Because most shootings involve Black or Brown victims, the failure to solve shooting cases is of particular concern to minority communities. The absence of justice in these cases signals to minority citizens that the police do not care about serious violence in their communities. It follows that increasing arrest and conviction rates for shootings could simultaneously reduce gun violence and improve police–community relations.

Investments and innovations in police investigations of shootings can improve their capacity to hold violent gun criminals accountable. Some of the strongest evidence in support of this perspective comes from our recent experiences working with the BPD as it sought to improve its homicide clearance rates and enhance its investigations of nonfatal shootings. An important outcome of this research and development exercise was to document the fact that whether the victim lives or dies in a shooting is essentially random—nonfatal and fatal cases are nearly identical with respect to circumstances and intent. One implication is that an increased arrest rate for nonfatal cases would have the same deterrent and incapacitation effects as an increase in arrests for the fatal cases (homicides). But in practice, fatal cases have higher clearance rates because those investigations have higher priority, and the additional resources translate into gaining greater witness cooperation and making more extensive use of forensic evidence. If nonfatal shootings had similar priority, there would be more arrests and thus less gun violence.

In addition to investigator time and access to other resources, there are common-sense reforms that will improve clearance rates. The Boston experience demonstrates that enhanced investigative resources and improved management structures and oversight processes can increase homicide clearance rates in even the most challenging types of cases, such as gang- and drug-related gun homicides. Approximately 10% of shooting cases, both fatal and nonfatal, "solve themselves," but the rest require sustained and well-managed investigative effort. Ultimately, the effective investigation of shootings can help prevent further cascades of gun violence in cities by deterring retaliation and incapacitating violent individuals who could persist in their shooting behaviors or end up being victims of retaliatory shootings.

## Reduce Shootings by the Police

Law enforcement officers shoot and kill roughly 1,000 people in the line of duty each year. Only recently have data become available to illuminate the scope and nature of this problem. Police shootings often result from encounters with people who are brandishing weapons and refusing to cooperate with the officer's requests. Mental illness and intoxication play an important role. A majority of victims are White, although the population-adjusted rates are much higher for Hispanics and especially Blacks. Most of the shootings are legally justifiable but nonetheless problematic and preventable.

Year after year, some departments have much higher rates of police shootings than others that are facing similar populations and crime situations. Why does Phoenix have five times the rate of police shootings as Dallas? That sort of comparison suggests that police shootings are influenced by factors specific to the department, and indeed, it appears that a strong commitment on the part of leadership to reduce officer-involved shootings can make a considerable difference. Engagement protocols, organizational culture, and training are all salient. Within police departments, a small number of officers generate disproportionate numbers of citizen complaints and are more likely to be involved in shootings relative to their peers.

A variety of ideas have been put forward on how to reduce police shootings of civilians. The following are some of the most promising approaches:

- Provide clear guidance on engaging with people who are making threats and resisting commands. Common sense can inform these protocols, instructing officers to maintain distance when possible and summon backup. Departmental guidelines on drawing a gun, and actually using it to shoot someone (e.g., a fleeing suspect), are vital and need to be reinforced through training.

- Hold officers accountable when they have violated department gun policy or shot someone in circumstances that appear criminal. Fire officers with problematic records of abuse and excess violence, and take steps to keep them from joining another department. That effort may in practice be facilitated by changes in state law and police union contracts.
- Body-worn cameras are no panacea, but on balance they appear to reduce excessive use of violence by the police (as well as reducing false complaints against the police). Body armor may make officers more relaxed about engaging without using their gun, and in any event it has saved many officer lives.

An attractive idea that has not worked in practice is to equip officers with TASERs, a nonlethal option for controlling a suspect. The TASER option does not appear to have reduced police shootings.

## Disrupt Underground Gun Markets

Most guns used in crime are not obtained by purchase from a licensed dealer but, rather, in informal transactions that may be illegal for any of a variety of reasons. The underground market is supplied by used guns diverted from licit commerce. Indeed, the use of guns in crime is closely linked to the prevalence of legal gun ownership. One prominent means of diversion is theft, although it is not clear how important that is in supplying the guns used in crime. In any event, many major cities have units and specific police personnel (task force officers assigned to the Bureau of Alcohol, Tobacco, Firearms and Explosives [ATF]) investigating and curtailing gun theft. ATF and other law enforcement agencies also devote some attention to interdicting gun trafficking and illicit manufacture, where the goal is to enforce regulations on gun commerce. Overall, this sort of enforcement effort is thin and has not been well documented or evaluated, but there is a strong justification to allocating more resources. Regulations do not enforce themselves.

Multiple sources of guns supply underground gun markets for criminals: negligent or corrupt licensed dealers, straw purchasers who buy on behalf of prohibited individuals, unregulated private sellers who make undocumented gun transfers, and traffickers who obtain guns in one jurisdiction (usually one with weak regulation) to sell in another. In recent years, privately manufactured firearms (or "ghost guns"), which are entirely untraceable, have become common among criminals, terrorists, and extremist groups. The ease and increasing popularity of internet-based gun transactions have also been exploited by violent criminals.

Despite all these possibilities, it is still difficult for some individuals to obtain a gun, especially in jurisdictions in which there are relatively few in private hands (e.g., New York, Boston, and other Northeastern cities). For people who lack connections with the underground market, such as through a gang, the search time may be long and prices high. The difficulty in obtaining a gun, and concern about the legal consequences of carrying one, may account for why only 40% of robberies are committed with a gun rather than a less intimidating weapon. Supply-side enforcement programs seek to raise the monetary and nonmonetary costs associated with acquiring a gun and to decrease the length of time that high-risk people possess guns during their criminal careers.

## Closing Thoughts

For many cities, reducing gun violence is of the highest priority. In heavily impacted neighborhoods, it depreciates the quality of life, discourages economic investment, and interferes with the successful and healthy development of children into productive adults. Because those neighborhoods are usually poor and predominantly minority, gun violence reduction is a matter of social justice. But the negative impact of gun violence is by no means limited to the residents of those neighborhoods.

Our theme has been that the police are an essential component to controlling gun violence—and that the police have the potential to do more in that respect. Best practice requires police agencies to give the highest priority to investigations of nonfatal shootings as well as fatal, engage directly with violent gangs to deter them from misusing their guns, and work with other city agencies in reducing the settings and opportunities for violent crimes. Even under an expansive definition of gun rights under the Second Amendment, the police could do more to interdict the flow of guns into the underground market and discourage gun carrying by those who are legally barred from possession.

Needless to say, our thesis appears as a challenge to progressive rhetoric about the police and gun violence. That rhetoric focuses on the police use of excessive force and denies their essential role in preventing serious violence. Prevention, in this view, can be accomplished through gun control and programs to improve opportunities for youth, and the police are largely irrelevant. That rhetoric is naive at best. The police are obviously not the only answer, and of course they are far from perfect, but they are essential. We submit that it is entirely feasible to improve police effectiveness in gun violence prevention while curbing the use of excessive force in agencies in which that has been common. A clear demonstration that gun violence prevention is a priority will also improve their relationships with low-income minority communities that bear the lion's share of the burden of gun violence and recognize that their public safety concerns have been neglected.

Devastatingly high rates of violence are not inevitable. The Great Crime Drop took the nation from the highest homicide rate in recorded history (in 1993) down to the much more civilized level over the course of 20 years. Part of the credit goes to smarter, better resourced policing. The renewed surge of violence starting in 2020 threatens all that was gained from those years of relative peace on the streets. Reclaiming public safety is an urgent priority, and gun violence reduction should be the top priority for the police in violence-plagued cities. There is much that can be done.

# Notes

## Chapter 1

1. For example, see David H. Bayley, *Police for the Future* (New York, NY: Oxford University Press, 1994); Michael R. Gottfredson and Travis Hirschi, *A General Theory of Crime* (Stanford, CA: Stanford University Press, 1990).
2. William J. Bratton and Peter Knobler, *The Turnaround: How America's Top Cop Reversed the Crime Epidemic* (New York, NY: Random House, 1998).
3. Philip J. Cook and Jens Ludwig, "Understanding Gun Violence: Public Health vs. Public Policy," *Journal of Policy Analysis and Management* 38, no. 3 (2019): 788–795; David Hemenway and Matt Miller, "Counterpoint: Reducing Gun Violence—Why a Public Health Approach Is Helpful," *Journal of Policy Analysis and Management* 38, no. 3 (2019): 795–801.
4. "Sir Robert Peel's Nine Principles of Policing," *The New York Times*, April 15, 2014, https://www.nytimes.com/2014/04/16/nyregion/sir-robert-peels-nine-principles-of-policing.html. Accessed August 8, 2021.
5. Alfred Blumstein and Joel Wallman, eds., *The Crime Drop in America*, 2nd ed. (New York, NY: Cambridge University Press, 2006); Steven D. Levitt, "Understanding Why Crime Fell in the 1990s: Four Factors That Explain the Decline and Six That Do Not," *Journal of Economic Perspectives* 18, no. 1 (2004): 163–190.
6. Tanaya Devi and Roland G. Fryer, Jr., "Policing the Police: The Impact of 'Pattern-or-Practice' Investigations on Crime," NBER working paper 27324 (2020), https://www.nber.org/papers/w27324.

## Chapter 2

1. Philip J. Cook and Jens Ludwig, "The Costs of Gun Violence Against Children," *The Future of Children* 12, no. 2 (2002): 86–99.
2. Interview with "Mary Jones" about her experience in the Boston projects, quoted in Jeffrey R. Kling, Jeffrey B. Liebman, and Lawrence F. Katz, "Bullets Don't Got No Name: Consequences of Fear in the Ghetto," in *Discovering Successful Pathways in Children's Development: Mixed Methods in the Study of Childhood and Family Life*, ed. Thomas S. Weisner (Chicago, IL: University of Chicago Press, 2005), 251–252.
3. Luca Berardi, "Neighborhood Wisdom: An Ethnographic Study of Localized Street Knowledge," *Qualitative Sociology* 44, no. 1 (2021): 103–124.
4. Everytown for Gun Safety Support Fund, Mayors Against Illegal Guns, and the National Urban League, *Strategies for Reducing Gun Violence in American Cities*, June 2016, https://centerforimprovinginvestigations.org/wp-content/uploads/2017/07/StrategiesReducingGunViolenceAmericanCities_2016.pdf.
5. "Facts & Statistics: Highway Safety," Insurance Information Institute, https://www.iii.org/fact-statistic/facts-statistics-highway-safety. Accessed August 8, 2021.

6. Bindu Kalesan, Mrithyunjay A. Vyliparambil, Yi Zuo, Jeffrey Siracuse, Jeffrey A. Fagan, Charles C. Branas, and Sandro Galea, "Cross-Sectional Study of Loss of Life Expectancy at Different Ages Related to Firearm Deaths Among Black and White Americans," *BMJ Evidence-Based Medicine* 24, no. 2 (2019): 55–58.
7. "Crime Data Explorer," Federal Bureau of Investigation, https://crime-data-explorer.fr.cloud.gov/explorer/national/united-states/shr. Accessed August 8, 2021.
8. Anthony A. Braga and David M. Kennedy, *A Framework for Addressing Violence and Serious Crime* (New York, NY: Cambridge University Press, 2020).
9. Laura Dugan, Daniel Nagin, and Richard Rosenfeld, "Explaining the Decline in Intimate Partner Homicide: The Effects of Changing Domesticity, Women's Status, and Domestic Violence Resources," *Homicide Studies* 3, no. 3 (1999): 187–214; Richard Rosenfeld, "Firearms Research and the Crime Drop," *Criminology and Public Policy* 4, no. 4 (2005): 799–806.
10. Angela Browne, Kirk R. Williams, and Donald G. Dutton, "Homicide Between Intimate Partners: A 20-Year Review," in *Homicide: A Sourcebook of Social Research*, eds. M. D. Smith and Margaret A. Zahn (London, UK: Sage, 1999), 149–164.
11. Jacquelyn C. Campbell, Daniel Webster, Jane Koziol-McLain, Carolyn Block, Doris Campbell, Mary Ann Curry, et al., "Risk Factors for Femicide in Abusive Relationships: Results from a Multisite Case Control Study," *American Journal of Public Health* 93, no. 7 (2003): 1089–1097.
12. Janet L. Lauritsen, Maribeth L. Rezey, and Karen Heimer, "When Choice of Data Matters: Analyses of US Crime Trends 1973–2012," *Journal of Quantitative Criminology* 32 (2016): 335–355.
13. Alfred Blumstein and Joel Wallman, eds., *The Crime Drop in America*, 2nd ed. (New York, NY: Cambridge University Press, 2006); Anthony A. Braga, "Serious Youth Gun Offenders and the Epidemic of Youth Violence in Boston," *Journal of Quantitative Criminology* 19, no. 1 (2003): 33–54; Philip J. Cook and John H. Laub, "After the Epidemic: Recent Trends in Youth Violence in the United States," *Crime and Justice* 29 (2002): 21–37; Steven D. Levitt, "Understanding Why Crime Fell in the 1990s: Four Factors That Explain the Decline and Six That Do Not," *Journal of Economic Perspectives* 18, no. 1 (2004): 163–190.
14. Blumstein and Wallman, *The Crime Drop*.
15. Philip J. Cook and Jens Ludwig, "The Economist's Guide to Crime Busting," *Wilson Quarterly* 35, no. 1 (2011): 62–66.
16. Rucker Johnson and Steven Raphael, "How Much Crime Reduction Does the Marginal Prisoner Buy?" *Journal of Law and Economics* 55, no. 2 (2012): 275–310; Steven D. Levitt, "Understanding Why Crime Fell."
17. Philip J. Cook, "Gun Markets," *Annual Review of Criminology* 1, no. 1 (2018): 359–377.
18. Franklin E. Zimring, "Is Gun Control Likely to Reduce Violent Killings?" *University of Chicago Law Review* 35, no. 4 (1968): 721–37; Franklin E. Zimring, "The Medium Is the Message: Firearm Caliber as a Determinant of Death from Assault," *Journal of Legal Studies* 1, no.1 (1972): 97–123.
19. David S. Abrams, "Estimating the Deterrent Effect of Incarceration Using Sentencing Enhancements," *American Economics Journal: Applied Economics* 4, no. 4 (2012): 32–56; Philip J. Cook and Daniel Nagin, *Does the Weapon Matter? An Evaluation of a Weapons-Emphasis Policy in the Prosecution of Violent Offenders* (Washington, DC: Institute for Law and Social Research, 1979). The instrumentality effect also appears to be important in suicide; the evidence for that claim begins with the observation that the likelihood that

a suicide attempt will result in death is far higher if a gun is used than for most other means. There is strong evidence that the ready availability of guns increases both the gun suicide rate and the overall suicide rate. See Matthew Miller, Deborah Azrael, and Catherine Barber, "Suicide Mortality in the United States: The Importance of Attending to Method in Understanding Population-Level Disparities in the Burden of Suicide," *Annual Review of Public Health* 33 (2012): 393–408.

20. Andrew R. Morral, Terry L. Schell, and Margaret Tankard, *The Magnitude and Sources of Disagreement Among Gun Policy Experts* (Santa Monica, CA: RAND Corporation, 2018), https://doi.org/10.7249/RR2088.1.
21. Anthony A. Braga and Philip J. Cook, "The Association of Firearm Caliber with Likelihood of Death from Gunshot Injury in Criminal Assaults," *JAMA Network Open* 1, no.3 (2018), https://doi.org/10.1001/jamanetworkopen.2018.0833; see also Zimring, "The Medium Is the Message."
22. Philip J. Cook, "Robbery," in *The Oxford Handbook of Crime and Public Policy*, ed. Michael Tonry (New York, NY: Oxford University Press, 2009), 102–114; Philip J. Cook, "Robbery Violence," *Journal of Criminal Law and Criminology* 78, no. 2 (1987): 357–376.
23. J. G. D'Alessio, "Gunshot Wounds: Bullet Caliber Is Increasing," *Journal of Trauma* 47, no. 5 (1999): 992–993; Arthur L. Kellermann, Roberta K. Lee, James A. Mercy, and Joyce Banton, "The Epidemiologic Basis for the Prevention of Firearm Injuries," *Annual Review of Public Health* 12, no. 1 (1999): 17–40; Michael D. McGonigal, John Cole, C. William Schwab, Donald R. Kauder, Michael F. Rotondo, and Peter B. Angood, "Urban Firearm Deaths: A Five-Year Perspective," *Journal of Trauma* 35, no. 4 (1993): 532–536; Daniel W. Webster, Howard R. Champion, Patricia S. Gainer, and Leon Sykes, "Epidemiologic Changes in Gunshot Wounds in Washington, DC, 1983–1990," *Archives of Surgery* 127, no. 6 (1992): 694–698; Garen J. Wintemute, "The Relationship Between Firearm Design and Firearm Violence: Handguns in the 1990s," *JAMA* 275, no. 22 (1996): 1749–1753.
24. Anthony A. Braga, "Long-Term Trends in the Sources of Boston Crime Guns," *Russell Sage Foundation Journal of the Social Sciences* 3, no. 5 (2017): 76–95.
25. Garen J. Wintemute, "Guns and Gun Violence," in *The Crime Drop in America* (2nd ed.), eds. Alfred Blumstein and Joel Wallman (New York, NY: Cambridge University Press, 2006), 45–96.
26. Philip J. Cook and John J. Donohue, "Regulating assault weapons and large capacity magazines for ammunition," *Journal of the American Medical Association* 328, no. 12 (September 22, 2022): 1191–1192.
27. Franklin E. Zimring and Gordon Hawkins, *Crime Is Not the Problem: Lethal Violence in America* (Oxford, UK: Oxford University Press, 1997); Erin Grinshteyn and David Hemenway, "Violent Death Rates in the US Compared to Those of the Other High-Income Countries, 2015," *Preventive Medicine*, 123 (June 2019): 20–26, https://repository.usfca.edu/nursing_fac/130.
28. All four U.S. presidents who were assassinated (Lincoln, Garfield, McKinley, and Kennedy), and both presidents who were wounded in an assassination attempt (T. Roosevelt and Reagan), were shot. See "List of United States Presidential Assassination Attempts and Plots," Wikipedia, https://en.wikipedia.org/wiki/List_of_United_States_presidential_assassination_attempts_and_plots. Accessed August 8, 2021.
29. Patrick Sharkey, *Uneasy Peace: The Great Crime Decline, the Renewal of City Life, and the Next War on Violence* (New York, NY: Norton, 2018).

30. Philip J. Cook and Jens Ludwig, *Gun Violence: The Real Costs* (New York, NY: Oxford University Press, 2000).
31. Franklin E. Zimring, *The City That Became Safe* (New York, NY: Oxford University Press, 2011); Sharkey, *Uneasy Peace*.
32. See Petula Dvorak, "Millions of Kids Fear Being Killed at School. It's Time for Adults to Say: Enough," *The Washington Post*, December 27, 2018, https://www.washingtonpost.com/local/millions-of-kids-fear-being-killed-at-school-its-time-for-adults-to-say-enough/2018/12/27/faa0cf62-0a06-11e9-88e3-989a3e456820_story.html? utm_term=.2527fa10965a.
33. Thomas Schelling, "The Life You Save May Be Your Own," in *Problems in Public Expenditure Analysis*, ed. Samuel B. Chase (Washington, DC: The Brookings Institution, 1968), 127–162.
34. Jens Ludwig and Philip J. Cook, "The Benefits of Reducing Gun Violence: Evidence from Contingent-Valuation Survey Data," *Journal of Risk and Uncertainty* 22, no. 3 (2001): 207–226.
35. Arrow et al. (1993) report the views of a distinguished group of economists on how best to conduct a contingent valuation study. We followed their guidance. See Kenneth Arrow, Robert Solow, Paul R. Portney, Edward E. Leamer, and Howard Radner, "Report of the NOAA Panel on Contingent Valuation," *Federal Register* 58, no. 10 (1993): 4601–4614.
36. Philip J. Cook and Jens Ludwig, "Understanding Gun Violence: Public Health vs. Public Policy," *Journal of Policy Analysis and Management* 38, no. 3 (1990): 788–795; Cook and Ludwig, *Gun Violence*; Mark Follman, Julia Lurie, Jaeah Lee, and James West, "The True Cost of Gun Violence in America," *Mother Jones*, April 15, 2015, https://www.motherjones.com/politics/2015/04/true-cost-of-gun-violence-in-america.

## Chapter 3

1. "2 Arrested for 'Ghost Gun' Trafficking in San Jose," *CBS San Francisco Bay Area*, March 2, 2021, https://sanfrancisco.cbslocal.com/2021/03/02/san-jose-police-arrested-two-for-trafficking-illegal-ghost-guns.
2. Philip J. Cook and Jens Ludwig, "Understanding Gun Violence: Public Health vs. Public Policy," *Journal of Policy Analysis and Management* 38, no.3 (2019): 788–795.
3. Philip J. Cook, "The Great American Gun War: Notes from Four Decades in the Trenches," *Crime and Justice* 42, (2013): 19–73.
4. Gary Kleck, *Point Blank* (New York, NY: Aldine de Gruyter, 1991).
5. Bryan Burrough, *Public Enemies: America's Greatest Crime Wave and the Birth of the FBI, 1933–34*, 2nd ed. (New York, NY: Penguin, 2009).
6. Franklin E. Zimring, "Firearms and Federal Law: The Gun Control Act of 1968," *Journal of Legal Studies* 4, no.1 (1975): 133–197.
7. Jens Ludwig and Philip J. Cook, "Homicide and Suicide Rates Associated with Implementation of the Brady Handgun Violence Prevention Act," *JAMA* 284, no. 5 (2000): 585–591.
8. Charles DiMaggio, Jacob Avraham, Cherisse Berry, Marko Bukur, Justin Feldman, Michael Klein, Noor Shah, Manish Tandon, and Spiros Frangos, "Changes in US Mass Shooting Deaths Associated with the 1994–2004 Federal Assault Weapons Ban: Analysis of Open-Source Data," *Journal of Trauma and Acute Care Surgery* 86, no. 1 (2019): 11–19.

9. Elizabeth Richardson Vigdor and James A. Mercy, "Do Laws Restricting Access to Firearms by Domestic Violence Offenders Prevent Intimate Partner Homicide?" *Evaluation Review* 30, no. 3 (2006): 313–346; Kerri M. Raissian, "Hold Your Fire: Did the 1996 Federal Gun Control Act Expansion Reduce Domestic Homicides?" *Journal of Policy Analysis and Management* 35, no.1 (2016): 67–93.
10. The cause of action against the cigarette manufacturers focused on the costs to the states of paying for treatment of smoking-related illnesses through the Medicaid program. The Master Settlement Agreement was signed by the four largest manufacturers and 46 attorneys general. Among other things, it obligated the manufacturers to make annual payments to the states in exchange for some exemption from subsequent liability.
11. Joseph Blocher and Darrell A. H. Miller, *The Positive Second Amendment: Rights, Regulation, and the Future of Heller* (New York, NY: Cambridge University Press, 2018).
12. Robert J. Spitzer, *Politics of Gun Control*, 8th ed. (New York, NY: Routledge, 2020).
13. Winnie Stachelberg, Arkadi Gerney, and Chelsea Parsons, "Blindfolded, and with One Hand Tied Behind the Back." Center for American Progress, March 19, 2013. https://www.americanprogress.org/issues/courts/reports/2013/03/19/56928/blindfolded-and-with-one-hand-tied-behind-the-back.
14. Philip J. Cook and Kristin Goss, *The Gun Debate* (New York, NY: Oxford University Press, 2020).
15. U.S. Government Accountability Office, *Few Individuals Denied Firearms Purchases Are Prosecuted and ATF Should Assess Use of Warning Notices in Lieu of Prosecutions* (Washington, DC: U.S. Government Accountability Office, 2020).
16. U.S. Bureau of Alcohol, Tobacco, Firearms, and Explosives, *Firearms Commerce in the United States, Annual Statistical Update 2020* (Washington, DC: U.S. Department of Justice, 2020).
17. U.S. Bureau of Alcohol, Tobacco, Firearms, and Explosives, "Firearms Compliance Inspections," n.d., https://www.atf.gov/firearms/compliance-inspections.
18. Philip J. Cook, Jens Ludwig, and Anthony A. Braga, "Criminal Records of Homicide Offenders," *JAMA* 294, no. 5 (August 3 2005): 598–601; Katherine A. Vittes, Jon S. Vernick, and Daniel W. Webster, "Legal Status and Source of Offenders' Firearms in States with the Least Stringent Criteria for Gun Ownership," *Injury Prevention* 19 (2013): 26–31.
19. Tom W. Smith and Jaesok Son, *General Social Survey Final Report: Trends in Gun Ownership in the United States, 1972–2014* (Chicago, IL: NORC at the University of Chicago, March 2015), https://www.norc.org/PDFs/GSS%20Reports/GSS_Trends%20in%20Gun%20Ownership_US_1972-2014.pdf.
20. James D. Wright, Jana L. Jasinski, and Drew N. Lanier, "Crime, Punishment, and Social Disorder: Crime Rates and Trends in Public Opinion over More Than Three Decades," in *Social Trends in American Life: Findings from the General Social Survey Since 1972*, ed. Peter V. Marsden (Princeton, NJ: Princeton University Press, 2012), 146–174.
21. Smith and Son, *General Social Survey Final Report*.
22. Philip J. Cook, "Notes on the Availability and Prevalence of Firearms," *American Journal of Preventive Medicine* 9, no. 1 (1993): 33–38.
23. Matthew Miller, Lisa Hepburn, and Deborah Azrael, "Firearm Acquisition Without Background Checks: Results of a National Survey," *Annals of Internal Medicine* 166, no. 4 (2017): 233–239.

24. Deborah Azrael, Lisa Hepburn, David Hemenway, and Matthew Miller, "The Stock and Flow of US Firearms: Results from the 2015 National Firearms Survey," *Russell Sage Foundation Journal of Social Sciences* 3, no. 5 (2017): 38–57.
25. Miller et al., "Firearm Acquisition."
26. Philip J. Cook and Jens Ludwig, *Guns in America: Results of a Comprehensive National Survey on Private Ownership and Use of Firearms* (Washington, DC: Police Foundation, May 1997), http://www.ncjrs.gov/pdffiles/165476.pdf.
27. Philip J. Cook and Harold A. Pollack, "Reducing Access to Guns by Violent Offenders," *Russell Sage Foundation Journal of the Social Sciences* 3, no. 5 (2017): 2–36.
28. Pew Research Center, *Why Own a Gun? Protection Is Now Top Reason* (Washington, DC: Pew Research Center, 2013), https://www.pewresearch.org/politics/2013/03/12/why-own-a-gun-protection-is-now-top-reason.
29. Miller et al., "Firearm Acquisition."
30. Garen J. Wintemute, "Firearms Licensee Characteristics Associated with Sales of Crime-Involved Firearms and Denied Sales: Findings from the Firearms License Survey," *Russell Sage Foundation Journal of the Social Sciences* 3, no. 5 (2017): 58–74.
31. Miller et al., "Firearm Acquisition."
32. Deborah Azrael, Philip J. Cook, and Matthew Miller, "State and Local Prevalence of Firearms Ownership: Measurement, Structure, and Trends," *Journal of Quantitative Criminology* 20, no. 1 (2004): 43–62.
33. Jacquelyn C. Campbell, Daniel Webster, Jane Koziol-McLain, Carolyn Block, Doris Campbell, Mary Ann Curry, et al., "Risk Factors for Femicide in Abusive Relationships: Results from a Multisite Case Control Study," *American Journal of Public Health* 93, no. 7 (2003): 1089–1097.
34. Philip J. Cook and Jens Ludwig, "The Effects of Gun Prevalence on Burglary: Deterrence Versus Inducement," in *Evaluating Gun Policy*, eds. Jens Ludwig and Philip J. Cook (Washington, DC: Brookings Institution Press, 2003), 77–148.
35. Philip J. Cook and Karen Hawley, "North Carolina's Pistol Permit Law: An Evaluation," *Popular Government* 46, no. 4 (Spring 1981): 1–6.
36. "Licensing 2021," Giffords Law Center, accessed August 9, 2021, https://giffords.org/lawcenter/gun-laws/policy-areas/owner-responsibilities/licensing.
37. Lisa Hepburn, Matthew Miller, Deborah Azrael, and David Hemenway, "The U.S. Gun Stock: Results from the 2004 National Firearms Survey," *Injury Prevention* 13, no.1 (2007): 15–19.
38. Alfred Blumstein, Jacqueline Cohen, and Paul Hsieh, *The Duration of Adult Criminal Careers, Final Report* (Washington, DC: U.S. Department of Justice, National Institute of Justice, 1982), https://www.ojp.gov/pdffiles1/Digitization/89569NCJRS.pdf.
39. James B. Jacobs, *Can Gun Control Work?* (New York, NY: Oxford University Press, 2002).
40. Philip J. Cook, "Gun Markets," *Annual Review of Criminology* 1, no. 1 (2018): 359–377.
41. Philip J. Cook, "Crime Control in the City: A Research-Based Briefing on Public and Private Measures," *Cityscape* 11, no. 1 (2009): 53–79.
42. Terry L. Schell, Samuel Peterson, Brian G. Vegetabile, Adam Scherling, Rosanna Smart, and Andrew R. Morral, *State-Level Estimates of Household Firearm Ownership* (Santa Monica, CA: RAND Corporation, 2020), https://www.rand.org/pubs/tools/TL354.html.
43. Alexandra M. Ciomek, Anthony A. Braga, and Andrew V. Papachristos, "The Influence of Firearms Trafficking on Gunshot Injuries in a High-Risk Social Network," *Social Science & Medicine* 259, no. 2 (2020), https://doi.org/10.1016/j.socscimed.2020.113114; Elizabeth

Roberto, Anthony A. Braga, and Andrew V. Papachristos, "Closer to Guns: The Role of Street Gangs in Facilitating Access to Illegal Firearms," *Journal of Urban Health* 95, no. 3 (2018): 372–382.

44. Philip J. Cook, Jens Ludwig, Sudhir Venkatesh, and Anthony A. Braga, "Underground Gun Markets," *Economic Journal* 117, no. 524 (2007): 588–618.
45. Philip J. Cook, Harold A. Pollack, and Kailey White, "The Last Link: From Gun Acquisition to Criminal Use," *Journal of Urban Health* 96, no. 5 (2019): 784–791.
46. Anthony A. Braga, Rod K. Brunson, Philip J. Cook, Brandon Turchan, and Brian Wade, "Underground Gun Markets and the Flow of Illegal Guns into the Bronx and Brooklyn: A Mixed Methods Analysis," *Journal of Urban Health* 98 (2021): 596–608, https://doi.org/10.1007/s11524-020-00477-z.
47. Philip J. Cook and Anthony A. Braga, "Comprehensive Firearms Tracing: Strategic and Investigative Uses of New Data on Firearms Markets," *Arizona Law Review* 43, no. 2 (2001):277–309.
48. Philip J. Cook, Richard J. Harris, Jens Ludwig, and Harold A. Pollack, "Some Sources of Crime Guns in Chicago: Dirty Dealers, Straw Purchasers, and Traffickers," *Journal of Criminal Law and Criminology* 104, no. 4 (2015): 717–759.
49. Brian Knight, "State Gun Policy and Cross-State Externalities: Evidence from Crime Gun Tracing," *American Economic Journal: Economic Policy* 5, no. 4 (2013): 200–229; Glenn L. Pierce, Anthony A. Braga, Raymond R. Hyatt, and Christopher S. Koper, "The Characteristics and Dynamics of Illegal Firearms Markets: Implications for a Supply-Side Enforcement Strategy," *Justice Quarterly* 21, no. 2 (2004): 391–422; David M. Kennedy, Anne M. Piehl, and Anthony A. Braga, "Youth Violence in Boston: Gun Markets, Serious Youth Offenders, and a Use-Reduction Strategy," *Law and Contemporary Problems* 59, no. 1 (1996): 147–196.
50. Mark H. Moore, "The Police and Weapons Offenses," *Annals of the American Academy of Political and Social Science* 452, no. 1 (1980): 22–32; David M. Hureau and Anthony A. Braga, "The Trade in Tools: The Market for Illicit Guns in High-Risk Networks," *Criminology* 56, no. 3 (2018): 510–545.
51. Cook et al., "Crime Guns in Chicago."
52. Brian Freskos, "Gun Theft from Legal Owners Is on the Rise, Quietly Fueling Violent Crime Across America," NBC Philadelphia, November 17, 2017, https://www.nbcphiladelphia.com/news/national-international/gun-theft-from-legal-owners-is-on-the-rise/2054480.
53. See, e.g., Brian Freskos, "Why Thieves Target Gun Stores," *New Yorker*, https://www.newyorker.com/news/news-desk/why-thieves-target-gun-stores. Accessed July 25, 2021.
54. Freskos, "Gun Theft from Legal Owners Is on the Rise."
55. Philip J. Cook, "Gun Theft and Crime," *Journal of Urban Health* 95, no. 3 (2018): 305–312.
56. Jake Charles, *Strict Gun Laws Likely Saved Lives During the Capitol Insurrection* (Durham, NC: Duke Center for Firearms Law, 2021), https://firearmslaw.duke.edu/2021/01/strict-gun-laws-likely-saved-lives-during-the-capitol-insurrection.
57. Adam Winkler, *Gunfight: The Battle over the Right to Bear Arms in America* (New York, NY: Norton, 2011).
58. Jeff Dege, "History of Handgun Carry Permit Laws, 1986–Present," *Wikimedia Commons*, https://commons.wikimedia.org/wiki/File:Right_to_Carry,_timeline.gif. Accessed August 9, 2021.
59. "Coronavirus: Armed Protesters Enter Michigan Statehouse," BBC News, May 1, 2020, https://www.bbc.com/news/world-us-canada-52496514.

60. John R. Lott, *More Guns, Less Crime*, 2nd ed. (Chicago, IL: University of Chicago Press, 2000); Charles F. Wellford, John V. Pepper, and Carol V. Petrie, eds., *Firearms and Violence: A Critical Review* (Washington, DC: National Academies Press, 2004); John J. Donohue, Abhay Aneja, and Kyle D. Weber, "Right-to-Carry Laws and Violent Crime: A Comprehensive Assessment Using Panel Data and a State-Level Synthetic Control Analysis," *Journal of Empirical Legal Studies* 16, no. 2 (2019): 198–247.
61. Garen J. Wintemute, Veronica A. Pear, Julia P. Schleimer, Rocco Pallin, Sydney Sohl, Nicole Kravitz-Wirtz, and Elizabeth A. Tomsich, "Extreme Risk Protection Orders Intended to Prevent Mass Shootings: A Case Series," *Annals of Internal Medicine* 171, no. 9 (2019): 655–658; Rocco Pallin, Julia P. Schleimer, Veronica A. Pear, and Garen J. Wintemute, "Assessment of Extreme Risk Protection Order Use in California from 2016 to 2019," *JAMA Network Open* 3, no. 6 (2020), https://jamanetwork.com/journals/jamanetworkopen/fullarticle/2767259; Jeffrey W. Swanson, "Understanding the Research on Extreme Risk Protection Orders: Varying Results, Same Message," *Psychiatric Services* 70, no.10 (2019): 953–954; Shannon Frattaroli, Elise Omaki, Amy Molocznik, Adelyn Allchin, Renee Hopkins, Sandra Shanahan, and Anne Levinson, "Extreme Risk Protection Orders in King County, Washington: The Epidemiology of Dangerous Behaviors and an Intervention Response," *Injury Epidemiology* 7, no. 1 (2020): 1–9.
62. Veronica A. Pear, Christopher D. McCort, Nicole Kravitz-Wirtz, Aaron B. Shev, Ali Rowhani-Rahbar, and Garen J. Wintemute, "Risk Factors for Assaultive Reinjury and Death Following a Nonfatal Firearm Assault Injury: A Population-Based Retrospective Cohort Study," *Preventive Medicine* 139 (October 2020), https://pubmed.ncbi.nlm.nih.gov/32652134.

## Chapter 4

1. Summary excerpts from Anthony Braga's notes during a ride-along with a Baltimore Police Department officer in the Western District of Baltimore on April 21, 2021.
2. Philip J. Cook and John H. Laub, "After the Epidemic: Recent Trends in Youth Violence in the United States," *Crime and Justice* 29, no. 1 (2002): 1–37; William Bennett, John J. DiIulio, Jr., and John P. Walters, *Body Count: Moral Poverty . . . and How to Win America's War Against Crime and Drugs* (New York, NY: Simon & Schuster, 1996).
3. Franklin E. Zimring, *The City That Became Safe* (New York, NY: Oxford University Press, 2011); Alfred Blumstein and Joel Wallman, eds., *The Crime Drop in America*, 2nd ed. (New York, NY: Cambridge University Press, 2006).
4. Aaron Chalfin and Justin McCrary, "Are U.S. Cities Underpoliced? Theory and Evidence," *Review of Economics and Statistics* 100, no. 1 (March 2018): 167–186; Aaron Chalfin, Benjamin Hansen, Emily Weisburst, and Morgan Williams, Jr., "Police Force Size and Civilian Race," *American Economic Review* 4, no. 2 (2022): 139–158, https://www.aeaweb.org/articles?id=10.1257/aeri.20200792&&from=f; William N. Evans and Emily G. Owens, "COPS and Crime," *Journal of Public Economics* 91, no. 1–2 (2007): 181–201; Steven Mello, "More COPS, Less Crime," *Journal of Public Economics* 172 (April 2019): 174–200.
5. Chalfin et al., "Police Force Size and Civilian Race"; Evans and Owens, "COPS and Crime."
6. Andrew Gelman, Jeffrey Fagan, and Alex Kiss, "An Analysis of the New York City Police Department's "Stop-and-Frisk" Policy in the Context of Claims of Racial Bias," *Journal of the American Statistical Association* 102, no. 479 (September 2007): 813–823; John

M. MacDonald and Anthony A. Braga, "Did Post-*Floyd et al.* Reforms Reduce Racial Disparities in NYPD Stop, Question, and Frisk Practices? An Exploratory Analysis Using External and Internal Benchmarks," *Justice Quarterly* 36, no. 5 (2019): 954–983.

7. Chalfin et al., "Police Force Size and Civilian Race."
8. Richard Auxier, "What Police Spending Data Can (and Cannot) Explain amid Calls to Defund the Police," Urban Institute, June 9, 2020, https://www.urban.org/urban-wire/what-police-spending-data-can-and-cannot-explain-amid-calls-defund-police. Accessed August 9, 2021.
9. Bureau of Justice Statistics, *Local Police Departments, 2016: Personnel*, U.S. Department of Justice, Office of Justice Programs, https://bjs.ojp.gov/content/pub/pdf/lpd16p.pdf. Accessed July 29, 2021.
10. Bureau of Justice Statistics, *LEMAS 2016*. Accessed July 29, 2021.
11. "Policing by the Numbers," Council on Criminal Justice Task Force on Policing, https://counciloncj.foleon.com/policing/assessing-the-evidence/policing-by-the-numbers. Accessed May 10, 2021.
12. Jeff Asher and Ben Horwitz, "How Do the Police Actually Spend Their Time?" *The New York Times*, June 19, 2020, https://www.nytimes.com/2020/06/19/upshot/unrest-police-time-violent-crime.html. Accessed October 7, 2022.
13. Los Angeles Police Department, "Sworn Personnel by Rank Gender, and Ethnicity Report," February 14, 2021, https://www.lapdonline.org/sworn-and-civilian-report/. Accessed May 8, 2021.
14. These statistics were produced in May 2021 by using the U.S. Census to identify the 50 largest U.S. cities and then visiting city police department webpages to determine the race and sex of the chief at that time.
15. Jayson Rydberg and William Terrill, "The Effect of Higher Education on Police Behavior," *Police Quarterly* 13, no. 1 (2010): 92–120; David L. Carter and Allen Sapp, "The Evolution of Higher Education in Law Enforcement: Preliminary Findings from a National Study," *Journal of Criminal Justice Education* 1, no. 1 (1990): 59–85.
16. Christie Gardiner, *Policing Around the Nation: Education, Philosophy, and Practice*, Center for Public Policy at California State University (Washington, DC: Police Foundation, 2017), https://www.policefoundation.org/publication/policing-around-the-nation-education-philosophy-and-practice. Accessed October 7, 2022.
17. See, e.g., Christopher Chapman, "Use of Force in Minority Communities Is Related to Police Education, Age, Experience, and Ethnicity," *Police Practice and Research* 13, no. 5 (2012): 1–16; Bernard Cohen and Jan Chaiken, *Police Background Characteristics and Performance* (Lexington, MA: Lexington Books, 1973); Roy Roberg and Scott Bonn, "Higher Education and Policing: Where Are We Now?" *Policing*, 27, no. 4 (2004): 469–486; Rydberg and Terrill, "The Effect of Higher Education on Police Behavior."
18. Lawrence W. Sherman and Dennis P. Rogan, "Effects of Gun Seizures on Gun Violence: 'Hot Spots' Patrol in Kansas City," *Justice Quarterly* 12, no. 4 (1995): 673–694; Anthony A. Braga, Brandon Turchan, David M. Hureau, and Andrew V. Papachristos, "Hot Spots Policing and Crime Reduction: An Update of an Ongoing Systematic Review and Meta-Analysis," *Journal of Experimental Criminology* 15, no.3 (2019): 289–311; Anthony A. Braga, David L. Weisburd, and Brandon Turchan. "Focused Deterrence Strategies and Crime Control: An Updated Systematic Review and Meta-Analysis of the Empirical Evidence," *Criminology & Public Policy* 17, no. 1 (2018): 205–250; Aaron Chalfin, Michael LaForest, and Jacob Kaplan, "Can Precision Policing Reduce Gun Violence? Evidence from Gang Takedowns

in New York City," *Journal of Policy Analysis and Management* 40, no. 4 (2021): 1047–1082, https://onlinelibrary.wiley.com/doi/10.1002/pam.22323.

19. Aaron Chalfin, Benjamin Hansen, Jason Lerner, and Lucie Parker, "Reducing Crime Through Environmental Design: Evidence from a Randomized Experiment of Street Lighting in New York City," *Journal of Quantitative Criminology* 38 (2022): 127–157, https://doi.org/10.1007/s10940-020-09490-6; Santiago Gómez, Daniel Mejía, and Santiago Tobón, "The Deterrent Effect of Surveillance Cameras on Crime," *Journal of Policy Analysis and Management* 40, no. 2 (2021): 553–571; Jennifer L. Doleac, "The Effects of DNA Databases on Crime," *American Economic Journal: Applied Economics* 9, no. 1 (2017): 165–201.
20. Samuel Walker, *The Police in America*, 2nd ed. (New York, NY: McGraw-Hill, 1992).
21. Alfred Blumstein, "Youth Violence, Guns, and the Illicit Drug Industry," *Journal of Criminal Law and Criminology* 86, no. 1 (1995): 10–36; Anthony A. Braga, "Serious Youth Gun Offenders and the Epidemic of Youth Violence in Boston," *Journal of Quantitative Criminology* 19, no. 1 (2003): 33–54; Cook and Laub, "After the Epidemic."
22. Michael R. Gottfredson and Travis Hirschi, *A General Theory of Crime* (Stanford, CA: Stanford University Press, 1990), 270.
23. David H. Bayley, *Police for the Future* (New York, NY: Oxford University Press, 1994), 3.
24. William J. Bratton and Peter Knobler, *The Turnaround: How America's Top Cop Reversed the Crime Epidemic* (New York, NY: Random House, 1998), 202.
25. Bratton and Knobler, *The Turnaround*, xi.
26. David L. Weisburd and Anthony A. Braga, eds., *Police Innovation: Contrasting Perspectives*, 2nd ed. (New York, NY: Cambridge University Press, 2019).
27. William J. Bratton, "How to Win the War Against Crime," *The New York Times*, April 5, 1996, https://www.nytimes.com/1996/04/05/opinion/how-to-win-the-war-against-crime.html. Accessed August 8, 2021.
28. Eli B. Silverman, *NYPD Battles Crime: Innovative Strategies in Policing* (Boston, MA: Northeastern University Press, 1999).
29. David L. Weisburd, Stephen D. Mastrofski, Ann Marie McNally, Rosann Greenspan, and James J. Willis, "Reforming to Preserve: CompStat and Strategic Problem Solving in American Policing," *Criminology and Public Policy* 2, no. 2 (2003): 421–457.
30. Uniform Crime Report (UCR) data were gathered from the annual *Crime in the United States* report and from the FBI's UCR website at http://www.fbi.gov/about-us/cjis/ucr/ucr (accessed August 12, 2021).
31. Steven D. Levitt, "Understanding Why Crime Fell in the 1990s: Four Factors That Explain the Decline and Six That Do Not," *Journal of Economic Perspectives* 18, no. 1 (2004): 163–190; Blumstein and Wallman, *The Crime Drop in America*.
32. National Research Council, *Fairness and Effectiveness in Policing*, Committee to Review Research on Police Policy and Practices (Washington, DC: National Academies Press, 2004): https://nap.nationalacademies.org/catalog/10419/fairness-and-effectiveness-in-policing-the-evidence; Blumstein and Wallman, *The Crime Drop in America*.
33. See, e.g., Carl B. Klockars, "The Rhetoric of Community Policing," in *Community Policing: Rhetoric or Reality*, eds. Jack R. Greene and Stephen D. Mastrofski (New York, NY: Praeger, 1998), 239–258; Jerome H. Skolnick and David H. Bayley, *The New Blue Line: Police Innovation in Six American Cities* (New York, NY: Free Press, 1998).
34. John E. Eck and William Spelman, *Problem Solving: Problem-Oriented Policing in Newport News* (Washington, DC: Police Executive Research Forum, 1987); Anthony A. Braga, *Problem-Oriented Policing and Crime Prevention*, 2nd ed. (Boulder, CO: Rienner, 2008).

35. National Research Council, *Proactive Policing: Effects on Crime and Communities*, Committee on Proactive Policing: Effects on Crime, Communities, and Civil Liberties (Washington, DC: The National Academies Press, 2018): https://doi.org/10.17226/24928; Braga, *Problem-Oriented Policing and Crime Prevention*; Joshua Hinkle, David L. Weisburd, Cody W. Telep, and Kevin Petersen, "Problem-Oriented Policing for Reducing Crime and Disorder: An Updated Systematic Review and Meta-Analysis," *Campbell Systematic Reviews* 16, no. 2 (2020): e1089.
36. Herman Goldstein, *Problem-Oriented Policing* (Philadelphia, PA: Temple University Press, 1990); Braga, *Problem-Oriented Policing and Crime Prevention*.
37. William H. Sousa and George L. Kelling., "Of Broken Windows, Criminology, and Criminal Justice," in *Police Innovation: Contrasting Perspectives* (2nd ed.), eds. David L. Weisburd and Anthony A. Braga (New York, NY: Cambridge University Press, 2019), 121–141: George L. Kelling and Catherine M. Coles, *Fixing Broken Windows* (New York, NY: Free Press, 1996).
38. Anthony A. Braga and Brenda J. Bond, "Policing Crime and Disorder Hot Spots: A Randomized Controlled Trial," *Criminology* 46, no.3 (2008): 577–608; Anthony A. Braga., David L. Weisburd, Elin J. Waring, Lorraine G. Mazerolle, William Spelman, and Francis Gajewski, "Problem-Oriented Policing in Violent Crime Places: A Randomized Controlled Experiment," *Criminology* 37, no. 3 (1999): 541–580.
39. Anthony A. Braga, Brandon C. Welsh, and Cory Schnell, "Can Policing Disorder Reduce Crime? A Systematic Review and Meta-Analysis," *Journal of Research in Crime and Delinquency* 52, no. 4 (2015): 567–588.
40. Charles C. Branas, Eugenia South, Michelle C. Kondo, Bernadette C. Hohl, Philippe Bourgois, Douglas J. Wiebe, and John M. MacDonald, "Citywide Cluster Randomized Trial to Restore Blighted Vacant Land and Its Effects on Violence, Crime, and Fear," *Proceedings of the National Academy of Sciences of the USA* 115, no. 12 (2018): 2946–2951; Ruth Moyer, John M. MacDonald, Greg Ridgeway, and Charles C. Branas, "Effect of Remediating Blighted Vacant Land on Shootings: A Citywide Cluster Randomized Trial," *American Journal of Public Health* 109, no. 1 (2019): 140–144.
41. Glenn L. Pierce, Susan Spaar, and LeBaron R. Briggs, *The Character of Police Work: Strategic and Tactical Implications* (Boston, MA: Center for Applied Social Research, 1998); Lawrence W. Sherman, L., Patrick R. Gartin, and Michael E. Buerger, "Hot Spots of Predatory Crime: Routine Activities and the Criminology of Place," *Criminology* 27, no. 1 (1989): 27–56; David L. Weisburd, Elizabeth R. Groff, and Sue-Ming Yang, *The Criminology of Place* (New York, NY: Oxford University Press, 2012).
42. Police Executive Research Forum, *Violent Crime in America: What We Know About Hot Spots Enforcement* (Washington, DC: Police Executive Research Forum, 2008); Weisburd et al., "Reforming to Preserve."
43. Anthony A. Braga, "The Effects of Hot Spots Policing on Crime," *Annals of the American Academy of Political and Social Science* 578 (November 2001): 104–125; Anthony A. Braga, Andrew V. Papachristos, and David M. Hureau, "The Effects of Hot Spots Policing on Crime: An Updated Systematic Review and Meta-Analysis," *Justice Quarterly* 31, no. 4 (2014): 633–663.
44. Anthony A. Braga, Brandon S. Turchan, David M. Hureau, and Andrew V. Papachristos, "Hot Spots Policing and Crime Reduction: An Update of an Ongoing Systematic Review and Meta-Analysis," *Journal of Experimental Criminology* 15, no. 3 (2019): 289–311.
45. David M. Kennedy, *Don't Shoot: One Man, a Street Fellowship, and the End of Violence in Inner-City America* (New York, NY: Bloomsbury, 2008); Anthony A. Braga and David M.

Kennedy, *A Framework for Addressing Violence and Serious Crime: Focused Deterrence, Legitimacy, and Prevention* (New York, NY: Cambridge University Press, 2020).

46. Anthony A. Braga., David M. Kennedy, Elin J. Waring, and Anne M. Piehl, "Problem-Oriented Policing, Deterrence, and Youth Violence: An Evaluation of Boston's Operation Ceasefire," *Journal of Research in Crime and Delinquency* 38, no. 3 (2001): 195–225.
47. Braga and Kennedy, *A Framework for Addressing Violence and Serious Crime*.
48. Anthony A. Braga, David L. Weisburd, and Brandon Turchan, "Focused Deterrence Strategies and Crime Control: An Updated Systematic Review and Meta-Analysis of the Empirical Evidence," *Criminology & Public Policy* 17, no. 1 (2018): 205–250.
49. Cynthia Lum, Christopher S. Koper, and James Willis, "Understanding the Limits of Technology's Impact on Police Effectiveness," *Police Quarterly* 20, no. 2 (2017): 135–163.
50. Jerry H. Ratcliffe, "Predictive Policing," in *Police Innovation: Contrasting Perspectives* (2nd ed.), eds. David L. Weisburd and Anthony A. Braga (New York, NY: Cambridge University Press, 2019), 347–365.
51. National Research Council, *Proactive Policing: Effects on Crime and Communities*.
52. Bureau of Justice Statistics, *Local Police Departments, 2016: Personnel* (Washington, DC: U.S. Department of Justice, October 2019), https://bjs.ojp.gov/content/pub/pdf/lpd16p.pdf.
53. Police Executive Research Forum, *Future Trends in Policing* (Washington, DC: U.S. Department of Justice, 2014), https://www.policeforum.org/assets/docs/Free_Online_Documents/Leadership/future%20trends%20in%20policing%202014.pdf.
54. See, e.g., Ronald V. Clarke, "Defining Police Strategies: Problem Solving, Problem-Oriented Policing and Community-Oriented Policing," in *Problem-Oriented Policing: Crime-Specific Problems, Critical Issues, and Making POP Work*, eds. Tara O'Connor Shelley and Anne C. Grant (Washington, DC: Police Executive Research Forum, 1998), 315–329; John E. Eck, "Problem-Oriented Policing and Its Problems: The Means over Ends Syndrome Strikes Back and the Return of the Problem-Solver," unpublished manuscript, University of Cincinnati, 2000.
55. Anthony A. Braga and David L. Weisburd, "Problem-Oriented Policing: The Disconnect Between Principles and Practice," in *Police Innovation: Contrasting Perspectives* (2nd ed.), eds. David L. Weisburd and Anthony A. Braga (New York, NY: Cambridge University Press, 2019), 182–204. National Research Council, *Fairness and Effectiveness in Policing*; Cody W. Telep and Steve Winegar, "Police Executive Receptivity to Research: A Survey of Chiefs and Sheriffs in Oregon," *Policing* 10, no. 3 (2016): 241–249.
56. Kathryne M. Young and Joan Petersilia, "Keeping Track: Surveillance, Control and the Expansion of the Carceral State," *Harvard Law Review* 129 (2016): 1318–1360.
57. John A. Eterno and Eli B. Silverman, *The Crime Numbers Game: Management by Manipulation* (New York, NY: CRC Press, 2012).
58. Dorothy Guyot, "Bending Granite: Attempts to Change the Rank Structure of American Police Departments," *Journal of Police Science and Administration* 7, no. 3 (September 1979): 253–284.
59. Weisburd et al., "Reforming to Preserve."
60. See, e.g., Catherine Fisk and L. Song Richardson, "Police Unions," *George Washington Law Review* 85, no. 3 (2017): 712–800.
61. Tom R. Tyler, *Why People Obey the Law: Procedural Justice, Legitimacy, and Compliance*, rev. ed. (Princeton, NJ: Princeton University Press, 2006).

62. Tom R. Tyler., Philip A. Goff, and Robert J, MacCoun, "The Impact of Psychological Science on Policing in the United States: Procedural Justice, Legitimacy, and Effective Law Enforcement," *Psychological Science in the Public Interest* 16, no. 3 (December 2015): 75–109.
63. Daniel S. Nagin and Cody W. Telep, "Procedural Justice and Legal Compliance," *Annual Review of Law and Social Science* 13, no. 1 (2017): 5–28; National Research Council, "Proactive Policing."
64. David L. Weisburd, Cody W. Telep, Heather Vovak, Taryn Zastrow, Anthony A. Braga, and Brandon Turchan, "Reforming the Police Through Procedural Justice Training: A Multicity Randomized Trial at Crime Hot Spots," *Proceedings of the National Academy of Sciences of the USA* 119, no. 14 (2022): e2118780119, https://www.pnas.org/doi/10.1073/pnas.2118780119.
65. Tyler, *Why People Obey the Law.*
66. President's Task Force on 21st Century Policing, *Final Report of the President's Task Force on 21st Century Policing* (Washington, DC: Office of Community Oriented Policing Services, 2015), https://cops.usdoj.gov/pdf/taskforce/taskforce_finalreport.pdf.

## Chapter 5

1. Kerry Burke, Graham Rayman, and Bill Sanderson, "'They End Up Shooting Whoever'—Rising Gun Mayhem Across NYC Hits Brooklyn Housing Project Hardest, with Four Deaths," *New York Daily News*, October 24, 2020, https://www.nydailynews.com/new-york/nyc-crime/ny-brooklyn-project-shootings-20201025-76rqjsfmvbhgtldem3i2be6voi-story.html. Accessed December 28, 2020.
2. Mark H. Moore, "The Police and Weapons Offenses," *Annals of the American Academy of Political and Social Science* 452, no. 1 (1980): 22–32.
3. Jacqueline Cohen and George Tita, "Diffusion in Homicide: Exploring a General Method for Detecting Spatial Diffusion Processes," *Journal of Quantitative Criminology* 15, no. 4 (1999): 451–493; Richard Rosenfeld, Timothy M. Bray, and Arlen Egley, "Facilitating Violence: A Comparison of Gang-Motivated, Gang-Affiliated, and Nongang Youth Homicides," *Journal of Quantitative Criminology* 15, no. 4 (1999): 495–516.
4. Anthony A. Braga, "Serious Youth Gun Offenders and the Epidemic of Youth Violence in Boston," *Journal of Quantitative Criminology* 19, no. 1 (2003): 33–54; David M. Kennedy, Anthony A. Braga, and Anne M. Piehl, "The (Un)Known Universe: Mapping Gangs and Gang Violence in Boston," in *Crime Mapping and Crime Prevention*, eds. David L. Weisburd and J. Thomas McEwen, *Crime Prevention Studies*, 8 (Monsey, NY: Criminal Justice Press, 1997), 219–262.
5. Anthony A. Braga, David M. Hureau, and Christopher Winship, "Losing Faith? Police, Black Churches, and the Resurgence of Youth Violence in Boston," *Ohio State Journal of Criminal Law* 6, no. 1 (2008): 141–172.
6. Joel M. Caplan, Leslie W. Kennedy, and Joel Miller, "Risk Terrain Modeling: Brokering Criminological Theory and GIS Methods for Crime Forecasting," *Justice Quarterly* 28, no. 2 (2011): 360–381.
7. Jie Xu and Elizabeth Griffiths, "Shooting on the Street: Measuring the Spatial Influence of Physical Features on Gun Violence in a Bounded Street Network," *Journal of Quantitative Criminology* 33, no. 2 (2017): 237–253.

8. Jerry H. Ratcliffe and George F. Rengert, "Near-Repeat Patterns in Philadelphia Shooting," *Security Journal* 21, no. 1–2 (2008): 58–76.
9. William Wells, Ling Wu, and Xinyue Ye, "Patterns of Near-Repeat Gun Assaults in Houston," *Journal of Research in Crime and Delinquency* 49, no. 2 (2012): 186–212.
10. Anthony A. Braga, Andrew V. Papachristos, and David M. Hureau, "The Concentration and Stability of Gun Violence at Micro Places in Boston, 1980–2008," *Journal of Quantitative Criminology* 26, no. 1 (2010): 33–53.
11. David L. Weisburd, John E. Eck, Anthony A. Braga, Cody W. Telep, Breanne Cave, Kate Bowers, Gerben Bruinsma, et al., *Place Matters: Criminology for the 21st Century* (New York, NY: Cambridge University Press, 2016).
12. Braga et al., "The Concentration and Stability of Gun Violence."
13. Emily Davies and Peter Herman, "Amid Rising Homicides, District Launches Effort to Target Hot Spots for Violence," *The Washington Post*, May 3, 2021, https://www.washingtonpost.com/local/public-safety/washington-gun-violence-bowser-/2021/05/03/cc74a06e-ac0c-11eb-b476-c3b287e52a01_story.html. Accessed August 10, 2021.
14. James Q. Wilson, "Just Take Away Their Guns," *The New York Times*, March 20, 1994, https://www.nytimes.com/1994/03/20/magazine/just-take-away-their-guns.html. Accessed August 19, 2021.
15. *Terry v. Ohio*, 392 U.S. 1 (1968); *Whren v. United States*, 517 U.S. 806 (1996).
16. Franklin E. Zimring and Gordon J. Hawkins, *Deterrence: The Legal Threat in Crime Control* (Chicago, IL: University of Chicago Press, 1973); Philip J. Cook, "Research in Criminal Deterrence: Laying the Groundwork for the Second Decade," in *Crime and Justice: An Annual Review of Research* (vol. 2), eds. Norval Morris and Michael Tonry (Chicago, IL: University of Chicago Press, 1980), 211–268.
17. Lawrence W. Sherman, "Gun Carrying and Homicide Prevention," *JAMA* 283, no. 9 (2000): 1193–1195.
18. Lawrence W. Sherman and Dennis P. Rogan, "Effects of Gun Seizures on Gun Violence: 'Hot Spots' Patrol in Kansas City," *Justice Quarterly* 12, no. 4 (1995): 673–694.
19. Sherman and Rogan, "Effects of Gun Seizures on Gun Violence."
20. Sherman and Rogan, "Effects of Gun Seizures on Gun Violence."
21. Sherman and Rogan, "Effects of Gun Seizures on Gun Violence."
22. James W. Shaw, "Community Policing Against Guns: Public Opinion of the Kansas City Gun Experiment," *Justice Quarterly* 12, no. 4 (1995): 695–710.
23. Edmund F. McGarrell, Steven Chermak, Alexander Weiss, and Jeremy M. Wilson, "Reducing Firearms Violence Through Directed Police Patrol," *Criminology and Public Policy* 1, no. 1 (2001): 119–148; Jacqueline Cohen and Jens Ludwig, "Policing Crime Guns," in *Evaluating Gun Policy*, eds. Philip J. Cook and Jens Ludwig (Washington, DC: Brookings Institution Press, 2002), 217–250; Richard Rosenfeld, Michael J. Deckard, and Emily Blackburn, "Effects of Directed Patrol and Self-Initiated Enforcement on Firearm Violence: A Randomized Controlled Study of Hot Spot Policing," *Criminology* 52, no. 3 (2014): 428–449.
24. William J. Bratton and Peter Knobler, *Turnaround: How America's Top Cop Reversed the Crime Epidemic* (New York, NY: Random House, 1998); George L. Kelling and Catherine M. Coles, *Fixing Broken Windows* (New York, NY: Free Press, 1996); Franklin E. Zimring, *The City That Became Safe* (New York, NY: Oxford University Press, 2011).
25. See, e.g., Alfred Blumstein and Joel Wallman, eds., *The Crime Drop in America*, 2nd ed. (New York, NY: Cambridge University Press, 2006).

26. Among other innovations launched by the NYPD in the early to mid-1990s, CompStat is a data-driven management accountability structure for allocating police resources. CompStat meetings grew from the need for a mechanism to ensure precinct commanders' accountability and improve performance in crime prevention. These routine strategy meetings require precinct commanders to discuss crime trends and crime fighting plans with the upper echelons of the NYPD hierarchy. Crime maps, as well as quantitative analyses of complaints, arrests, patterns and trends, and qualitative information about precinct–community relationships in effective crime fighting, were intensely scrutinized and discussed. See Eli B. Silverman, *NYPD Battles Crime: Innovative Strategies in Policing* (Boston, MA: Northeastern University Press, 1999).
27. Jack Maple, *The Crime Fighter: How You Can Make Your Community Crime-Free* (New York, NY: Random House, 1999), 128.
28. Jeffrey Fagan, Franklin E. Zimring, and June Kim, "Declining Homicide in New York City: A Tale of Two Trends," *Journal of Criminal Law and Criminology* 88, no. 4 (1998): 1277–1324.
29. David L. Weisburd, Cody W. Telep, and Brian A. Lawton, "Could Innovations in Policing Have Contributed to the New York City Crime Drop Even in a Period of Declining Police Strength? The Case of Stop, Question and Frisk as a Hot Spots Policing Strategy," *Justice Quarterly* 31, no. 1 (2014): 129–153; David L. Weisburd., Alese Wooditch, Sarit Weisburd, and Sue-Ming Yang, "Do Stop, Question, and Frisk Practices Deter Crime? Evidence at Micro Units of Space and Time," *Criminology & Public Policy* 15, no. 1 (2016): 31–56.
30. Office of Juvenile Justice and Delinquency Prevention, *Promising Strategies to Reduce Gun Violence*, U.S. Department of Justice, Office of Justice Programs (Washington, DC: U.S. Department of Justice, 1999), https://ojjdp.ojp.gov/sites/g/files/xyckuh176/files/pubs/gun_violence/173950.pdf.
31. Judith A. Greene, "Zero Tolerance: A Case Study of Police Practices and Policies in New York City," *Crime & Delinquency* 45, no. 2 (1999): 171–181.
32. Jeffrey Fagan and Garth Davies, "Street Stops and Broken Windows: Terry, Race, and Disorder in New York City," *Fordham Urban Law Journal* 28, no. 2 (2000): 457–504; Andrew Gelman, Jeffrey Fagan, and Alex Kiss, "An Analysis of the New York City Police Department's 'Stop-and-Frisk' Policy in the Context of Claims of Racial Bias," *Journal of the American Statistical Association* 102, no. 479 (2007): 813–823.
33. New York City Global Partners, *New York City's Operation Impact*, July 2008, http://www.nyc.gov/html/unccp/gprb/downloads/pdf/NYC_Safety%20and%20Security_Operation%20Impact.pdf. Accessed August 20, 2021.
34. Michael R. Bloomberg, "'Stop and Frisk' Keeps New York Safe," *The Washington Post*, August 18, 2013, https://www.washingtonpost.com/opinions/michael-bloomberg-stop-and-frisk-keeps-new-york-safe/2013/08/18/8d4cd8c4-06cf-11e3-9259-e2aafe5a5f84_story.html. Accessed August 20, 2021; Ray Kelly, *Vigilance: My Life Serving America and Protecting Its Empire City* (New York, NY: Hachette, 2015).
35. John A. Eterno and Eli B. Silverman, *The Crime Numbers Game: Management by Manipulation* (New York, NY: CRC Press, 2012).
36. Al Baker, "New York Minorities More Likely to Be Frisked," *The New York Times*, May 12, 2020, https://www.nytimes.com/2010/05/13/nyregion/13frisk.html. Accessed August 20, 2021.
37. Ray Rivera, Al Baker, and Janet Roberts, "A Few Blocks, 4 Years, 52,000 Police Stops," *The New York Times*, July 11, 2010, https://www.nytimes.com/2010/07/12/nyregion/12frisk.html. Accessed August 18, 2021.

38. National Research Council, *Proactive Policing: Effects on Crime and Communities*, Committee on Proactive Policing: Effects on Crime, Communities, and Civil Liberties, eds. David L. Weisburd and Malay K. Majmunder (Washington, DC: National Academies Press, 2018).
39. Weisburd et al., "Could Innovations in Policing Have Contributed to the New York City Crime Drop Even in a Period of Declining Police Strength?"; Weisburd et al., "Do Stop, Question, and Frisk Practices Deter Crime?"
40. John M. MacDonald, Jeffrey Fagan, and Amanda Geller, "The Effects of Local Police Surges on Crime and Arrests in New York City," *PLoS One*, 11, no. 6 (2016): e0157223.
41. MacDonald et al., "Effects of Local Police Surges."
42. Fagan and Davies, "Street Stops and Broken Windows"; Delores Jones-Brown, Jaspreet Gill, and Jennifer Trone, *Stop, Question, and Frisk Policing Practices in New York City: A Primer*, Center on Race, Crime and Justice (New York, NY: John Jay College of Criminal Justice, 2010).
43. Amanda Geller, Jeffrey Fagan, Tom R. Tyler, and Bruce G. Link, "Aggressive Policing and the Mental Health of Young Urban Men," *American Journal of Public Health* 104, no. 12 (2014): 2321–2327.
44. Joscha Legewie and Jeffrey Fagan, "Aggressive Policing and the Educational Performance of Minority Youth," *American Sociological Review* 84, no. 2 (2019): 220–247.
45. Emily Jacobs, Carl Campanile, and Bruce Golding, "Bloomberg in Leaked 2015 Clip: '95% of Murderers Fit One Description, Xerox It'," *New York Post*, February 11, 2020, https://nypost.com/2020/02/11/leaked-bloomberg-audio-shows-him-defending-throw-them-up-against-the-walls-stop-and-frisk. Accessed August 20, 2021.
46. Jeffrey Fagan, expert report in *David Floyd et al. v. City of New York et al.*, U.S. District Court for the Southern District of New York, 08 Civ. 01034 (SAS); Gelman et al., "An Analysis of the New York City Police Department's 'Stop-and-Frisk' Policy"; however, see Greg Ridgeway, *Analysis of Racial Disparities in the New York Police Department's Stop, Question, and Frisk Practices* (Santa Monica, CA: RAND Corporation, 2007), https://www.rand.org/pubs/technical_reports/TR534.html.
47. John M. MacDonald and Anthony A. Braga, "Did Post-*Floyd et al.* Reforms Reduce Racial Disparities in NYPD Stop, Question, and Frisk Practices? An Exploratory Analysis Using External and Internal Benchmarks," *Justice Quarterly* 36, no. 5 (2019): 954–983.
48. William J. Bratton and Jon Murad, "Precision Policing," *City Journal*, Summer 2018, https://www.city-journal.org/html/precision-policing-16033.html. Accessed August 20, 2021.
49. Elaine Loughin, "'NY Precision Policing' Key to Fighting Crime," *Irish Examiner*, December 5, 2016, https://www.irishexaminer.com/ireland/ny-precision-policing-key-to-fighting-city-crime-433665.html. Accessed August 20, 2021.
50. Aaron Chalfin, Michael LaForest, and Jacob Kaplan, "Can Precision Policing Reduce Gun Violence? Evidence from Gang Takedowns in New York City," *Journal of Policy Analysis & Management* 40, no. 4 (2021): 1047–1082, https://onlinelibrary.wiley.com/doi/10.1002/pam.22323.
51. Ali Watkins, "N.Y.P.D. Disbands Plainclothes Units Involved in Many Shootings," *The New York Times*, June 15, 2020, https://www.nytimes.com/2020/06/15/nyregion/nypd-plainclothes-cops.html. Accessed October 28, 2020.
52. Tina Moore, "NYC Shootings and Homicides Soared in 2020, Crime Data Shows," *New York Post*, January 6, 2020, https://nypost.com/2021/01/06/nyc-shootings-and-homicides-soared-in-2020-crime-data-shows. Accessed February 21, 2021.

53. Tanaya Devi and Roland G. Fryer, Jr., "Policing the Police: The Impact of 'Pattern-or-Practice' Investigations on Crime," NBER working paper 27324 (Cambridge, MA: National Bureau of Economic Research, June 2020), https://www.nber.org/papers/w27324.
54. Jerry H. Ratcliffe, Travis Taniguchi, Elizabeth R. Groff, and Jennifer D. Wood, "The Philadelphia Foot Patrol Experiment: A Randomized Controlled Trial of Police Patrol Effectiveness in Violent Crime Hot Spots," *Criminology* 49, no. 3 (2011): 795–831; Elizabeth R. Groff, Jerry H. Ratcliffe, Cory P. Haberman, Evan T. Sorg, Nola M. Joyce, and Ralph B. Taylor, "Does What Police Do at Hot Spots Matter? The Philadelphia Policing Tactics Experiment," *Criminology* 53, no. 1 (2015): 23–53.
55. Anthony A. Braga, Brandon Turchan, David M. Hureau, and Andrew V. Papachristos, "Hot Spots Policing and Crime Reduction: An Update of an Ongoing Systematic Review and Meta-Analysis," *Journal of Experimental Criminology* 15, no.3 (2019): 289–311.
56. Anthony A. Braga., David L. Weisburd, Elin J. Waring, Lorraine G. Mazerolle, William Spelman, and Francis Gajewski, "Problem-Oriented Policing in Violent Crime Places: A Randomized Controlled Experiment," *Criminology* 37, no. 3 (1999): 541–580.
57. Braga et al., "Losing Faith?"
58. Anthony A. Braga and Brenda J. Bond, "Policing Crime and Disorder Hot Spots: A Randomized Controlled Trial," *Criminology* 46, no. 3 (2008): 577–608.
59. Anthony A. Braga, David M. Hureau, and Andrew V. Papachristos, "An Ex-Post-Facto Evaluation Framework for Place-Based Police Interventions," *Evaluation Review* 35, no. 6 (2011): 592–626.
60. Braga et al., "An Ex-Post-Facto Evaluation Framework."
61. Charles C. Branas, Eugenia South, Michelle C. Kondo, Bernadette C. Hohl, Philippe Bourgois, Douglas J. Wiebe, and John M. MacDonald, "Citywide Cluster Randomized Trial to Restore Blighted Vacant Land and Its Effects on Violence, Crime, and Fear," *Proceedings of the National Academy of Sciences of the USA* 115, no. 12 (2018): 2946–2951; Ruth Moyer, John M. MacDonald, Greg Ridgeway, and Charles C. Branas, "Effect of Remediating Blighted Vacant Land on Shootings: A Citywide Cluster Randomized Trial," *American Journal of Public Health* 109, no. 1 (2019): 140–144.
62. Eugenia Garvin, Charles C. Branas, Shimrit Keddem, Jeffrey Sellman, and Carolyn Cannuscio, "More Than Just an Eyesore: Local Insights and Solutions on Vacant Land and Urban Health," *Journal of Urban Health* 90, no. 3 (June 2013): 412–426.
63. Moyer et al., "Effect of Remediating Blighted Vacant Land on Shootings."
64. Herman Goldstein, *Problem-Oriented Policing* (Philadelphia, PA: Temple University Press, 1990); Anthony A. Braga, *Problem-Oriented Policing and Crime Prevention,* 2nd ed. (Boulder, CO: Rienner, 2008).
65. Moore, "The Police and Weapons Offenses"; Gary Kleck, *Point Blank* (New York, NY: Aldine de Gruyter, 1991).
66. Shaw, "Community Policing Against Guns"; McGarrell et al., "Reducing Firearms Violence Through Directed Police Patrol."

## Chapter 6

1. The names of the participants and some of the details of this incident were changed to ensure anonymity. See Andrew V. Papachristos, Anthony A. Braga, Eric L. Piza, and Leigh S. Grossman, "The Company You Keep? The Spillover Effects of Gang Membership on

Individual Gunshot Victimization in a Co-Offending Network," *Criminology* 53, no. 4 (2015): 624–649.

2. See. e.g., Devah Pager and Hana Shepherd, "The Sociology of Discrimination: Racial Discrimination in Employment, Housing, Credit, and Consumer Markets," *Annual Review of Sociology* 34 (2008): 181–209.
3. Andrew V. Papachristos, Christopher Wildeman, and Elizabeth Roberto, "Tragic, but Not Random: The Social Contagion of Nonfatal Gunshot Injuries," *Social Science & Medicine* 125 (January 2015): 139–150; Andrew V. Papachristos, Anthony A. Braga, and David M. Hureau, "Social Networks and the Risk of Gunshot Injury," *Journal of Urban Health* 89, no. 6 (2012): 992–1003.
4. David M. Kennedy, Anne M. Piehl, and Anthony A. Braga, "Youth Violence in Boston: Gun Markets, Serious Youth Offenders, and a Use-Reduction Strategy," *Law and Contemporary Problems* 59, no. 1 (1996): 147–196; Anthony A. Braga, David M. Hureau, and Christopher Winship, "Losing Faith? Police, Black Churches, and the Resurgence of Youth Violence in Boston," *Ohio State Journal of Criminal Law* 6, no. 1 (2008): 141–172.
5. Papachristos et al., "The Company You Keep?"
6. National Research Council, *Proactive Policing: Effects on Crime and Communities*, Committee on Proactive Policing: Effects on Crime, Communities, and Civil Liberties, eds. David L. Weisburd and Malay K. Majmunder (Washington, DC: The National Academies Press, 2018); Anthony A. Braga, David L. Weisburd, and Brandon Turchan, "Focused Deterrence Strategies and Crime Control: An Updated Systematic Review and Meta-Analysis of the Empirical Evidence," *Criminology & Public Policy* 17, no. 1 (2018): 205–250.
7. David M. Kennedy, *Don't Shoot: One Man, a Street Fellowship, and the End of Violence in Inner-City America* (New York, NY: Bloomsbury, 2011); Rod K. Brunson, "Focused Deterrence and Improved Police–Community Relations: Unpacking the Proverbial 'Black Box,'" *Criminology & Public Policy* 14, no. 3 (2015): 507–514; Tracey L. Meares, "The Legitimacy of Police Among Young African American Men," *Marquette Law Review* 92, no. 4 (2009): 651–666; Robin S. Engel, Nicholas Corsaro, and M. Murat Ozer, "The Impact of Police on Criminal Justice Reform: Evidence from Cincinnati, Ohio," *Criminology & Public Policy* 16, no. 2 (2017): 375–402.
8. Walter B. Miller, *Violence by Youth Gangs and Youth Groups as a Crime Problem in Major American Cities* (Washington, DC: U.S. Government Printing Office, 1975); Anthony A. Braga, *Gun Violence Among Serious Young Offenders*, Problem-Oriented Guides for Police, Problem-Specific Guides Series, no. 23 (Washington, DC: U.S. Department of Justice, Office of Community Oriented Policing Services, 2004); James C. Howell and Elizabeth Griffiths, *Gangs in America's Communities*, 3rd ed. (Thousand Oaks, CA: SAGE, 2019).
9. Terence P. Thornberry, Marvin D. Krohn, Alan J. Lizotte, Carolyn A. Smith, and Kimberly Tobin, *Gangs and Delinquency in Development Perspective* (New York, NY: Cambridge University Press, 2003).
10. Anthony A. Braga, David M. Kennedy, and George E. Tita. "New Approaches to the Strategic Prevention of Gang and Group-Involved Violence," in *Gangs in America*, 3rd ed., ed. C. Ronald Huff (Thousand Oaks, CA: SAGE, 2002), 271–286.
11. Carolyn Rebecca Block and Richard Block, *Street Gang Crime in Chicago*, National Institute of Justice, Research in Brief (Washington, DC: U.S. Department of Justice, December 1993).
12. George E. Tita, K. Jack Riley, Greg Ridgeway, Clifford Grammich, Allan F. Abrahamse, and Peter W. Greenwood, *Reducing Gun Violence: Results from an Intervention in East Los Angeles* (Santa Monica, CA: RAND Corporation, 2003).

13. Anthony A. Braga, Gregory M. Zimmerman, Lisa M. Barao, Chelsea Farrell, Rod K. Brunson, and Andrew V. Papachristos, "Street Gangs, Gun Violence, and Focused Deterrence: Comparing Place-Based and Group-Based Evaluation Methods to Estimate Direct and Spillover Deterrent Effects," *Journal of Research in Crime and Delinquency* 56, no. 4 (2019): 524–562.
14. Stephen Lurie, "There's No Such Thing as a Dangerous Neighborhood," *CityLab*, February 25, 2019, https://www.bloomberg.com/news/articles/2019-02-25/beyond-broken-windows-what-really-drives-urban-crime. Accessed January 26, 2021.
15. Anthony A. Braga, David M. Hureau, and Leigh S. Grossman, *Managing the Group Violence Intervention: Using Shooting Scorecards to Track Group Violence* (Washington, DC: U.S. Department of Justice, Office of Community Oriented Policing Services, 2014).
16. "Self-inflicted" shooting victimizations typically do not involve emotionally distraught individuals who were not successful in a suicide attempt. Investigators believe most of these shootings to be botched attempts at committing a violent crime and/or due to unsafe handling of a firearm. For instance, one of these shooting events involved a well-known gang member who was interviewed in a hospital emergency room with a bullet hole inside his pant-leg pocket and gunshot residue on his hands. Presumably, this gang member had accidently shot himself in the leg when reaching for his gun.
17. Papachristos et al., "The Company You Keep?"
18. Papachristos et al., "Tragic, but Not Random."
19. Braga et al., "Losing Faith?"
20. Papachristos et al., "Social Networks and the Risk of Gunshot Injury."
21. David M. Kennedy, Anthony A. Braga, and Anne M. Piehl, "The (Un)Known Universe: Mapping Gangs and Gang Violence in Boston," in *Crime Mapping and Crime Prevention*, Vol. 8, eds. David L. Weisburd and J. Thomas McEwen (Monsey, NY: Criminal Justice Press, 1997), 219–262; Jean M. McGloin, "Policy and Intervention Considerations of a Network Analysis of Street Gangs," *Criminology & Public Policy* 4, no. 3 (2005): 607–636.
22. Jillian J. Turanovic, Michael D. Reisig, and Travis C. Pratt, "Risky Lifestyles, Low Self-Control, and Violent Victimization Across Gendered Pathways to Crime," *Journal of Quantitative Criminology* 31, no. 2 (2015): 183–206; D. Wayne Osgood, Lloyd D. Johnston, Patrick M. O'Malley, and Jerald G. Bachman, "The Generality of Deviance in Late Adolescence and Early Adulthood," *American Sociological Review* 53, no. 1 (February 1988): 81–93. Wesley G. Jennings, Alex R. Piquero, and Jennifer M. Reingle, "On the Overlap Between Victimization and Offending: A Review of the Literature," *Aggression and Violent Behavior* 17, no. 1 (2012): 16–26.
23. Malcolm W. Klein, *The American Street Gang: Its Nature, Prevalence, and Control* (New York, NY: Oxford University Press, 1995).
24. California Partnership for Safe Communities, *Problem Analysis of Gun Homicides and Nonfatal Shootings in Oakland, California,* unpublished research report, 2018.
25. David M. Kennedy, *Deterrence and Crime Prevention: Reconsidering the Prospect of Sanction* (London, UK: Routledge, 2008); Braga et al., "Focused Deterrence Strategies and Crime Control."
26. David M. Kennedy, "Policing and the Lessons of Focused Deterrence," in *Police Innovation: Contrasting Perspectives* (2nd ed.), eds. David L. Weisburd and Anthony A. Braga (New York, NY: Cambridge University Press, 2019), 205–226.
27. Alfred Blumstein, "Youth Violence, Guns, and the Illicit Drug Industry," *Journal of Criminal Law and Criminology* 86 (1995): 10–36; Philip J. Cook and John H. Laub, "After

the Epidemic: Recent Trends in Youth Violence in the United States," *Crime and Justice* 29 (2002): 1–37.

28. Kennedy et al., "Youth Violence in Boston"; Anthony A. Braga, "Serious Youth Gun Offenders and the Epidemic of Youth Violence in Boston," *Journal of Quantitative Criminology* 19, no. 1 (2003): 33–54.
29. Kennedy et al., "Youth Violence in Boston."
30. Anthony A. Braga, Anne M. Piehl, and David M. Kennedy, "Youth Homicide in Boston: An Assessment of Supplementary Homicide Reports," *Homicide Studies* 3, no. 4 (1999): 277–299.
31. Kennedy et al., "Youth Violence in Boston"; see also Geoffrey Canada, *Fist, Stick, Knife, Gun* (Boston, MA: Beacon, 1995).
32. David M. Kennedy, Anthony A. Braga, and Anne M. Piehl, "Developing and Implementing Operation Ceasefire," in *Reducing Gun Violence: The Boston Gun Project's Operation Ceasefire* (Washington, DC: U.S. Department of Justice, September 2001).
33. Anthony A. Braga, Brandon Turchan, and Christopher Winship, "Partnership, Accountability, and Innovation: Clarifying Boston's Experience with Pulling Levers," in *Police Innovation: Contrasting Perspectives* (2nd ed.), eds. David L. Weisburd and Anthony A. Braga (New York, NY: Cambridge University Press, 2019), 227–250.
34. Christopher Winship and Jenny Berrien, "Boston Cops and Black Churches," *The Public Interest* 136 (Summer 1999): 52–68.
35. Kennedy et al., "Developing and Implementing Operation Ceasefire."
36. Kennedy et al., "Developing and Implementing Operation Ceasefire."
37. Kennedy et al., "Developing and Implementing Operation Ceasefire."
38. Kennedy et al., "Developing and Implementing Operation Ceasefire."
39. Kennedy et al., "Developing and Implementing Operation Ceasefire."
40. Kennedy et al., "Developing and Implementing Operation Ceasefire," 35.
41. Kennedy et al., "Developing and Implementing Operation Ceasefire," 37.
42. Kennedy et al., "Developing and Implementing Operation Ceasefire," 37.
43. Kennedy et al., "Developing and Implementing Operation Ceasefire," 37.
44. Kennedy et al., "Developing and Implementing Operation Ceasefire," 39.
45. Kennedy et al., "Developing and Implementing Operation Ceasefire," 40.
46. Kennedy et al., "Developing and Implementing Operation Ceasefire," 40.
47. Kennedy et al., "Developing and Implementing Operation Ceasefire," 40.
48. Kennedy et al., "Developing and Implementing Operation Ceasefire," 40.
49. Anthony A. Braga, David M. Kennedy, Elin J. Waring, and Anne M. Piehl, "Problem-Oriented Policing, Deterrence, and Youth Violence: An Evaluation of Boston's Operation Ceasefire," *Journal of Research in Crime and Delinquency* 38, no. 1 (2001): 195–225.
50. Braga et al., "Partnership, Accountability, and Innovation."
51. Braga et al., "Partnership, Accountability, and Innovation."
52. O'Ryan Johnson, "Program Seen as a Prevention Tool," *Boston Herald*, April 8, 2006, 2 (Newsbank Online). Accessed August 22, 2021.
53. Anthony A. Braga, David M. Hureau, and Andrew V. Papachristos, "Deterring Gang-Involved Gun Violence: Measuring the Impact of Boston's Operation Ceasefire on Street Gang Behaviour," *Journal of Quantitative Criminology* 30, no. 1 (2014): 113–139.
54. Braga et al., "Losing Faith?"
55. Braga et al., "Deterring Gang-Involved Gun Violence."
56. Braga et al., "Deterring Gang-Involved Gun Violence."

57. Anthony A. Braga, Robert Apel, and Brandon C. Welsh, "The Spillover Effects of Focused Deterrence on Gang Violence," *Evaluation Review* 37, no. 3–4 (2013): 314–342.
58. Andrew V. Papachristos, Tracey L. Meares, and Jeffrey Fagan, "Attention Felons: Evaluating Project Safe Neighborhoods in Chicago," *Journal of Empirical Legal Studies* 4, no. 2 (2007): 223–272.
59. Papachristos et al., "Attention Felons."
60. Papachristos et al., "Attention Felons."
61. Papachristos et al., "Attention Felons."
62. Danielle Wallace, Andrew V. Papachristos, Tracey L. Meares, and Jeffrey Fagan, "Desistance and Legitimacy: The Impact of Offender Notification Meetings on Recidivism Among High Risk Offenders," *Justice Quarterly* 33, no. 1 (2016): 1–28.
63. George Wood and Andrew V. Papachristos, "Reducing Gunshot Victimization in High-Risk Social Networks Through Direct and Spillover Effects," *Nature Human Behaviour* 3, no. 11 (2019): 1164–1170.
64. Papachristos et al., "Attention Felons."
65. David M. Kennedy, "Drugs, Race and Common Ground: Reflections on the High Point Intervention," *National Institute of Justice Journal* 262 (2009): 12–17.
66. Kennedy, *Don't Shoot.*
67. Kennedy, "Drugs, Race and Common Ground"; Kennedy, *Don't Shoot.*
68. Kennedy, "Drugs, Race and Common Ground."
69. Kennedy, "Drugs, Race and Common Ground."
70. David M. Kennedy and Sue-Lin Wong, *The High Point Drug Market Intervention Strategy* (Washington, DC: U.S. Department of Justice, Office of Community Oriented Policing Services, 2009), https://nnscommunities.org/wp-content/uploads/2017/10/e08097226-HighPoint.pdf.
71. Kennedy and Wong, *The High Point Drug Market Intervention Strategy.*
72. Nicholas Corsaro, Eleazer D. Hunt, Natalie Hipple, and Edmund F. McGarrell, "The Impact of Drug Market Pulling Levers Policing on Neighborhood Violence: An Evaluation of the High Point Drug Market Intervention," *Criminology & Public Policy* 11, no. 2 (2012): 167–199.
73. Corsaro et al., "The Impact of Drug Market Pulling Levers on Violence."
74. Jessica Saunders, Russell Lundberg, Anthony A. Braga, Greg Ridgeway, and Jeremy M. Miles, "A Synthetic Control Approach to Evaluating Place-Based Crime Interventions," *Journal of Quantitative Criminology* 31, no. 3 (2015): 413–434.
75. Braga et al., "Focused Deterrence Strategies and Crime Control."
76. Braga et al., "Focused Deterrence Strategies and Crime Control."
77. Braga et al., "Focused Deterrence Strategies and Crime Control."
78. Tita et al., *Reducing Gun Violence.*
79. Tita et al., *Reducing Gun Violence.*
80. Braga et al., "Street Gangs, Gun Violence, and Focused Deterrence."
81. Caterina G. Roman, Nathan W. Link, Jordan M. Hyatt, Avinash Bhati, and Megan Forney, "Assessing the Gang-Level and Community-Level Effects of the Philadelphia Focused Deterrence Strategy," *Journal of Experimental Criminology* 15, no. 4 (2019): 499–527.
82. Braga et al., "Street Gangs, Gun Violence, and Focused Deterrence."
83. National Research Council, *Firearms and Violence: A Critical Review*, Committee to Improve Research Information and Data on Firearms, eds. Charles F. Wellford, John V.

Pepper, and Carol V. Petrie (Washington, DC: National Academies Press, 2005); National Research Council, *Proactive Policing*.

84. Benjamin Hamilton, Richard Rosenfeld, and Aaron Levin, "Opting Out of Treatment: Self-Selection Bias in a Randomized Controlled Study of a Focused Deterrence Notification Meeting," *Journal of Experimental Criminology* 17, no. 1 (2018): 1–17.
85. In an unpublished New York State randomized experiment, Patrick Sharkey found individuals who were called in to attend the notification forums were substantially less likely to violate their parole, and this effect was driven primarily by reductions in violations due to absconding. However, the program did not affect individual arrest rates or neighborhood level gun violence. In communications with Braga, Sharkey speculated that gun violence levels in selected New York City neighborhoods were already so low during the study 2013–2014 time period that there wasn't much room for further improvement. Patrick Sharkey, *Evaluation of the New York State Gun Violence Reduction Program* (New York: Crime Lab New York, University of Chicago, 2014).
86. Thomas Abt and Christopher Winship, *What Works in Reducing Community Violence: A Meta-Review and Field Study for the Northern Triangle*, United States Agency for International Development (Bethesda, MD: Democracy International, February 2016), 13.
87. Jennifer S. Wong, Jason Gravel, Martin Bouchard, Carlo Morselli, and Karine Descormiers, *Effectiveness of Street Gang Control Strategies: A Systematic Review and Meta-Analysis of Evaluation Studies*, National Coordinating Committee on Organized Crime, Public Safety Canada (Ottawa, CA: Canadian Electronic Library, 2012), 29.
88. Daniel S. Nagin, "Deterrence in the Twenty-First Century," in *Crime and Justice: A Review of Research* (vol. 42), ed. Michael Tonry (Chicago, IL: University of Chicago Press, 2013), 199–263.
89. Franklin E. Zimring and Gordon J. Hawkins, *Deterrence: The Legal Threat in Crime Control* (Chicago, IL: University of Chicago Press, 1973).
90. Nagin, "Deterrence in the Twenty-First Century."
91. Edmund F. McGarrell, Steven Chermak, Jeremy M. Wilson, and Nicholas Corsaro, "Reducing Homicide Through a "Lever-Pulling" Strategy," *Justice Quarterly* 23, no. 2 (2006): 214–229.
92. Kennedy, *Don't Shoot*, 71.
93. Kennedy, *Don't Shoot*, 72.
94. Kennedy, *Don't Shoot*; see also Mark A. R. Kleiman, *When Brute Force Fails: How to Have Less Crime and Less Punishment* (Princeton, NJ: Princeton University Press, 2009).
95. David M. Kennedy, Mark A. R. Kleiman, and Anthony A. Braga, "Beyond Deterrence: Strategies of Focus and Fairness," in *Handbook of Crime Prevention and Community Safety* (2nd ed.), eds. Nick Tilley and Aiden Sidebottom (New York, NY: Routledge, 2017), 157–182.
96. Anthony A. Braga and David M. Kennedy, *A Framework for Addressing Violence and Serious Crime: Focused Deterrence, Legitimacy, and Prevention* (New York, NY: Cambridge University Press, 2020).
97. Robert J. Sampson, Stephen W. Raudenbush, and Felton Earls, "Neighborhoods and Violent Crime," *Science* 277, no. 5328 (1997): 918–924; Patrick Sharkey, *Uneasy Peace: The Great Crime Decline, the Renewal of City Life, and the Next War on Violence* (New York, NY: Norton, 2018).

98. Rod K. Brunson, Anthony A. Braga, David M. Hureau, and Kashea Pegram, "We Trust You, but Not That Much: Examining Police–Black Clergy Partnerships to Reduce Youth Violence," *Justice Quarterly* 32, no. 6 (2015): 1006–1036; Braga et al., "Street Gangs, Gun Violence, and Focused Deterrence."
99. Kennedy et al., "Beyond Deterrence: Strategies of Focus and Fairness."
100. National Network for Safe Communities, *Drug Market Intervention: An Implementation Guide* (Washington, DC: U.S. Department of Justice, Office of Community Oriented Policing Services, 2014), https://cops.usdoj.gov/RIC/Publications/cops-p303-pub.pdf.
101. Robin S. Engel, Marie Skubak Tillyer, and Nicholas Corsaro, "Reducing Gang Violence Using Focused Deterrence: Evaluating the Cincinnati Initiative to Reduce Violence (CIRV)," *Justice Quarterly* 30, no. 3 (2013): 403–439.
102. Kennedy, *Don't Shoot.*
103. Braga et al., "Focused Deterrence Strategies and Crime Control."
104. Kennedy, *Don't Shoot*; Braga et al., "Partnership, Accountability, and Innovation."
105. National Network for Safe Communities at John Jay College, https://nnscommunities.org. Accessed January 2, 2020.
106. Eugene Bardach, *Getting Agencies to Work Together: The Practice and Theory of Managerial Craftsmanship* (Washington, DC: Brookings Institution Press, 1998).
107. National Network for Safe Communities, *Implementing the Drug Market Intervention in Emerging Heroin Markets* (New York, NY: John Jay College of Criminal Justice, 2016).
108. Braga et al., "Street Gangs, Gun Violence, and Focused Deterrence."

## Chapter 7

1. Philip J. Cook, Anthony A. Braga, Brandon Turchan, and Lisa M. Barao, "Why Do Gun Murders Have a Higher Clearance Rate than Gunshot Assaults?" *Criminology & Public Policy* 18, no. 3 (2019): 549.
2. Analysis by Cook.
3. Sarah Ryley, Jeremy Singer-Vine, and Sean Campbell, "Shoot Someone in a Major US City, and Odds Are You'll Get Away With It," *The Trace,* January 24, 2019, https://www.thetrace.org/2019/01/murder-solve-rate-gun-violence-baltimore-shootings/. Accessed October 3, 2022.
4. Anthony A. Braga, Edward A. Flynn, George L. Kelling, and Christine M. Cole, "Moving the Work of Criminal Investigators Towards Crime Control," in *New Perspectives in Policing Bulletin* (Washington, DC: U.S. Department of Justice, National Institute of Justice, March 2011).
5. Jill Leovy, *Ghettoside: A True Story of Murder in America* (New York, NY: Spiegel & Grau, 2015), 8.
6. Conor Friedersdorf, "Criminal-Justice Reformers Chose the Wrong Slogan," *The Atlantic*, August 8, 2021, https://www.theatlantic.com/ideas/archive/2021/08/instead-of-defund-the-police-solve-all-murders/619672. Accessed August 17, 2021.
7. Peter W. Greenwood, Jan M. Chaiken, and Joan Petersilia, *The Criminal Investigation Process* (Lexington, MA: Lexington Books, 1977); Herman Goldstein, *Policing a Free Society* (Cambridge, MA: Ballinger, 1977); John E. Eck, *Solving Crimes: The Investigation of Burglary and Robbery* (Washington, DC: Police Executive Research Forum, 1983), https://www.ojp.gov/pdffiles1/Digitization/90569NCJRS.pdf. Accessed August 18, 2021.

8. Peter W. Greenwood and Joan Petersilia, *The Criminal Investigation Process, Volume I: Summary and Policy Implications* (Santa Monica, CA: RAND Corporation, October 1975), https://www.rand.org/content/dam/rand/pubs/reports/2007/R1776.pdf. Accessed August 18, 2021.
9. Greenwood and Petersilia, *The Criminal Investigation Process.*
10. Peter B. Bloch and James Bell, *Managing Investigations: The Rochester System* (Washington, DC: The Police Foundation, November 1976), https://www.ojp.gov/pdffiles1/34715.pdf. Accessed August 18, 2021; Peter B. Bloch and Donald R. Weidman, *Managing Criminal Investigations: Prescriptive Package* (Washington, DC: U.S. Government Printing Office, June 1975).
11. John K. Roman, Shannon E. Reid, Aaron Chalfin, and Carly R. Knight, "The DNA Field Experiment: A Randomized Controlled Trial of the Cost-Effectiveness of Using DNA to Solve Property Crimes," *Journal of Experimental Criminology* 5, no. 4 (2009): 345–369.
12. Braga et al., "Moving the Work of Criminal Investigators Towards Crime Control."
13. For example, see Charles Wellford and James Cronin, *An Analysis of Variables Affecting the Clearance of Homicides: A Multistate Study* (Washington, DC: Justice Research and Statistics Association, February 1999), https://www.ojp.gov/pdffiles1/nij/grants/181356.pdf. Accessed August 17, 2021; Charles Wellford, Cynthia Lum, Thomas Scott, Heather Vovak, and J. Amber Scherer. (2019). "Clearing Homicides: Role of Organizational, Case, and Investigative Dimensions," *Criminology & Public Policy* 18, no. 3 (2019): 553–600.
14. Franklin E. Zimring, "The Medium Is the Message: Firearm Caliber as a Determinant of Death from Assault," *Journal of Legal Studies* 1, no.1 (1972): 97–123; Anthony A. Braga and Philip J. Cook, "The Association of Firearm Caliber with Likelihood of Death from Gunshot Injury in Criminal Assaults," *JAMA Network Open* 1, no.3 (2018), https://doi.org/10.1001/jamanetworkopen.2018.0833.
15. Philip J. Cook, Jeffrey Ho, and Sara Shilling, *Criminal Investigations of Gun Assaults and Murders in Durham, 2015: The Challenge of Securing Victim and Witness Cooperation* (Durham, NC: Duke University, Sanford School of Public Policy, 2017).
16. Cook et al., "Why Do Gun Murders Have a Higher Clearance Rate than Gunshot Assaults?"
17. Cook et al., "Why Do Gun Murders Have a Higher Clearance Rate than Gunshot Assaults?"
18. Salmafatima S. Abadin and Mallory E. O'Brien, *2016 Annual Report: Homicides and Nonfatal Shootings in Milwaukee* (Milwaukee, WI: Milwaukee Homicide Review Commission, City of Milwaukee Health Department, September 2017), https://www.wpr.org/sites/default/files/2016%20MHRC%20Annual%20Report%209-29-2017%20FINAL.pdf. Accessed August 22, 2018.
19. Max Kapustin, Jens Ludwig, Marc Punkay, Kimberley Smith, Lauren Speigel, and David Weigus, *Gun Violence in Chicago, 2016* (Chicago, IL: University of Chicago Crime Lab, January 2017), https://urbanlabs.uchicago.edu/attachments/c5b0b0b86b6b6a9309ed88a9f5bbe5bd892d4077/store/82f93d3e7c7cc4c5a29abca0d8bf5892b3a35c0c3253d1d24b3b9d1fa7b8/UChicagoCrimeLab%2BGun%2BViolence%2Bin%2BChicago%2B2016.pdf. Accessed August 22, 2018.
20. Cook et al., *Criminal Investigations of Gun Assaults and Murders in Durham, 2015.*
21. Kailey White, Philip J. Cook, and Harold A. Pollack, "Gunshot-Victim Cooperation with Police Investigations: Results from the Chicago Inmate Survey," *Preventive Medicine* 143 (February 2021): https://doi.org/10.1016/j.ypmed.2020.106381; Cook et al., "Why Do Gun Murders Have a Higher Clearance Rate than Gunshot Assaults?"

22. Elise Schmelzer. "Denver Police Solved Less than Half of All Nonfatal Shootings Last Year. A New Solution Is Showing Promise," *The Denver Post*, November 13, 2020, https://www.denverpost.com/2020/11/13/nonfatal-shootings-denver. Accessed March 31, 2021.
23. Scott Phillips, Dae-Young Kim, Irshad Altheimer, and Greg Drake, "Implementing a Stand-Alone Investigative Unit to Clear Non-Fatal Shooting Cases," *Policing*, 16, no. 1 (2022): 204–217.
24. Anthony A. Braga and Desiree Dusseault, "Can Homicide Detectives Improve Homicide Clearance Rates?" *Crime & Delinquency* 64, no. 3 (2018): 283–315.
25. Braga and Dusseault, "Can Homicide Detectives Improve Homicide Clearance Rates?"
26. Anthony A. Braga, Brandon Turchan, and Lisa M. Barao, "The Influence of Investigative Resources on Homicide Clearances," *Journal of Quantitative Criminology* 35, no. 2 (2019): 337–364.
27. Philip J. Cook and Anthony Berglund, "More and Better Video Evidence for Police Investigations of Shootings: Chicago's Area Technology Centers," *Policing: An International Journal*, 44, no. 4 (2022): 655–668. https://doi.org/10.1108/PIJPSM-12-2020-0186; Brandon L. Garrett, *Autopsy of a Crime Lab: Exposing the Flaws in Forensics* (Berkeley, CA: University of California Press, 2021).
28. Jeffrey M. Jones, "Black, White Adults' Confidence Diverges Most on Police," Gallup, August 12, 2020, https://news.gallup.com/poll/317114/black-white-adults-confidence-diverges-police.aspx. Accessed August 22, 2021.
29. White et al., "Gunshot-Victim Cooperation with Police."
30. Rod K. Brunson and Brian A. Wade, "'Oh Hell No, We Don't Talk to Police': Insights on the Lack of Cooperation in Police Investigations of Urban Gun Violence," *Criminology & Public Policy* 18, no. 3 (2019): 637–638.

## Chapter 8

1. "Timeline of Events in Shooting of Michael Brown," Associated Press, August 8, 2019, https://apnews.com/article/shootings-police-us-news-st-louis-michael-brown-9aa32033692547699a3b61da8fd1fc62. Accessed September 29, 2021.
2. Nicholas Goldberg, "Ashli Babbitt Was Not a Peaceful Protester. It's Clear Why the Cop Who Shot Her Was Exonerated," *Los Angeles Times*, August 24, 2021, https://www.latimes.com/opinion/story/2021-08-24/officer-killed-ashli-babbitt. Accessed September 29, 2021.
3. Jerome H. Skolnick and James J. Fyfe, *Above the Law: Police and the Excessive Use of Force* (New York, NY: Free Press, 1993).
4. Franklin E. Zimring, *When Police Kill* (Cambridge, MA: Harvard University Press, 2017).
5. Rod K. Brunson, "Protests Focus on Over-Policing. But Under-Policing Is Also Deadly," *The Washington Post*, June 12, 2021, https://www.washingtonpost.com/outlook/underpolicing-cities-violent-crime/2020/06/12/b5d1fd26-ac0c-11ea-9063-e69bd6520940_story.html. Accessed September 29, 2021.
6. Zimring, *When Police Kill*; Colin Loftin, Brian Wiersema, David McDowall, and Adam Dobrin, "Underreporting of Justifiable Homicides Committed by Police Officers in the United States, 1976–1998," *American Journal of Public Health* 93, no. 7 (2003): 1117–1121.
7. Catherine Barber, Deborah Azrael, Amy Cohen, Matthew Miller, Deonza Thaynes, David E. Wang, and David Hemenway, "National Violent Death Reporting System, Vital Statistics, and Supplementary Homicide Reports,"

*American Journal of Public Health* 106, no. 5 (2016): 922–927; John K. Roman, *The State of Firearms Data in 2019* (Chicago, IL: NORC, September 2020), https://www.norc.org/PDFs/Firearm%20Data%20Infrastructure%20Expert%20Panel/State%20of%20Firearms%20Research%202019.pdf. Accessed September 29, 2021.

8. Daniel S. Nagin, "Firearm Availability and Fatal Police Shootings," *Annals of the American Academy of Political and Social Science* 687, no. 1 (2020): 49–57.
9. Kenneth Adams, "What We Know About Police Use of Force," in *Use of Force by Police: Overview of National and Local Data*, eds. Kenneth Adams, Lawrence A. Greenfield, Patrick A. Langan, Steven K. Smith, Joel H. Garner, Christopher D. Maxwell, Geoffrey P. Alpert, and Roger G. Dunham (Washington, DC: U.S. Department of Justice, Office of Justice Programs, October 1999), 1–14.
10. Roland G. Fryer, Jr., "An Empirical Analysis of Racial Differences in Police Use of Force," *Journal of Political Economy* 127, no. 3 (2019): 1210–1261.
11. Lawrence W. Sherman, "Causes of Police Behavior," *Journal of Research in Crime and Delinquency* 17, no. 1 (1980): 69–100.
12. Franklin E. Zimring, *The City That Became Safe* (New York, NY: Oxford University Press, 2011).
13. David Hemenway, Deborah Azrael, Andrew Connor, and Matthew Miller, "Variations in Rates of Fatal Police Shootings Across US States," *Journal of Urban Health* 96, no. 1 (2018): 63–73; Nagin, "Firearm Availability and Fatal Police Shootings."
14. Shane Bauer, "How a Deadly Police Force Ruled a City," *New Yorker*, November 23, 2020, https://www.newyorker.com/ magazine/2020/11/23/how-a-deadly-police-force-ruled-a-city. Accessed September 29, 2021.
15. James J. Fyfe, "Observations on Police Deadly Force," *Crime & Delinquency* 27, no. 3 (1981): 376–389.
16. William A. Geller and Kevin J. Karales, *Split-Second Decisions: Shootings of & by Chicago Police* (Chicago, IL: Chicago Law Enforcement Study Group, 1981).
17. Greg Ridgeway, "The Role of Individual Officer Characteristics in Police Shootings," *Annals of the American Academy of Political and Social Science* 687, no. 1 (2020): 58–66; Greg Ridgeway, "Officer Risk Factors Associated with Police Shootings: A Matched Case–Control Study," *Statistics and Public Policy* 3, no. 1 (2016): 1–6.
18. Christopher M. Donner, John Maskaly, Alex R. Piquero, and Wesley G. Jennings, "Quick on the Draw: Assessing the Relationship Between Low Self-Control and Officer-Involved Police Shootings," *Police Quarterly* 20, no. 2 (2017): 213–234.
19. Linda Zhao and Andrew V. Papachristos, "Network Position and Police Who Shoot," *The Annals of the American Academy of Political and Social Science* 687, no. 1 (2020): 89–112.
20. Abraham N. Tennenbaum, "The Influence of the Garner Decision on Police Use of Deadly Force," *Journal of Criminal Law & Criminology* 85, no. 1 (1994): 241–260.
21. Zachary A. Powell, Michele B. Meitl, and John L. Worrall, "Police Consent Decrees and Section 1983 Civil Rights Litigation," *Criminology and Public Policy* 16, no. 2 (2017): 575–605; Li Sian Goh, "Going Local: Do Consent Decrees and Other Forms of Federal Intervention in Municipal Police Departments Reduce Police Killings?" *Justice Quarterly* 37, no. 5 (2020): 900–929.
22. Zimring, *When Police Kill.*

23. James J. Fyfe, "Blind Justice: Police Shootings in Memphis," *Journal of Criminal Law & Criminology* 73, no. 2 (Summer 1982): 707–722; Lawrence W. Sherman, "Reducing Police Gun Use: Critical Events, Administrative Policy and Organizational Change," in *Control in the Police Organization,* ed. Maurice Punch (Cambridge, MA: MIT Press, 1983), 98–125; William Terrill and Eugene A. Paoline, III, "Police Use of Less Lethal Force: Does Administrative Policy Matter?" *Justice Quarterly* 34, no. 2 (2017): 193–216.
24. Samuel E. Walker and Carol A. Archbold, *The New World of Police Accountability*, 3rd ed. (Newbury Park, CA: Sage, 2020).
25. Joel H. Garner, Thomas Schade, John Hepburn, and John Buchanan, "Measuring the Continuum of Force Used by and Against the Police," *Criminal Justice Review* 20, no. 2 (1995): 146–158; William Terrill, "Police Use of Force: A Transactional Approach," *Justice Quarterly* 22, no. 1 (2005): 107–138.
26. George T. Williams, "Force Continuums: A Liability to Law Enforcement?" *FBI Law Enforcement Bulletin* 71, no. 6 (2002): 14–19; William Terrill and Eugene A. Paoline, III, "Force Continuums: Moving Beyond Speculation and Toward Empiricism," *Law Enforcement Executive Forum* 7, no. 4 (2007): 27–32.
27. International Association of Chiefs of Police, *National Consensus Policy and Discussion Paper on Use of Force* (Alexandria, VA: IACP, July 2020), https://www.theiacp.org/resources/document/national-consensus-policy-and-discussion-paper-on-use-of-force. Accessed September 29, 2021.
28. Bureau of Justice Statistics, *Local Police Departments: Policies and Procedures, 2016* (Washington, DC: U.S. Department of Justice, Office of Justice Programs, August 2020), https://bjs.ojp.gov/content/pub/pdf/lpdpp16.pdf. Accessed September 29, 2021.
29. Zimring, *When Police Kill.*
30. Lawrence W. Sherman, "Preventing Avoidable Deaths in Police Encounters with Citizens," *Annals of the American Academy of Political and Social Science* 687, no. 1 (2020): 216–227.
31. Geoffrey P. Alpert and Roger G. Dunham, *Understanding Police Use of Force: Officers, Suspects, and Reciprocity* (New York, NY: Cambridge University Press, 2004); Lawrence W. Sherman, "Reducing Fatal Police Shootings as System Crashes: Research, Theory, and Practice," *Annual Review of Criminology* 1 (2018): 421–429; David A. Klinger, "Social Theory and the Street Cop: The Case of Deadly Force," *Ideas in American Policing,* no. 7 (June 2005): https://www.policinginstitute.org/wp-content/uploads/2015/06/Klinger-2005-Social-Theory-and-the-Street-Cop.pdf; David A. Klinger, "Organizational Accidents and Deadly Police-Involved Violence," *Annals of the American Academy of Political and Social Science* 687, no. 1 (2020): 28–48.
32. Samuel Walker, "'Not Dead Yet': The National Police Crisis, a New Conversation About Policing, and the Prospects for Accountability-Related Police Reform," *University of Illinois Law Review* 5 (2018): 1795–1841.
33. Zimring, *When Police Kill*; Sherman, "Reducing Fatal Police Shootings as System Crashes."
34. Walker, "Not Dead Yet."
35. George L. Kelling and Robert B. Kliesmet, "Police Unions, Police Culture, the Friday Crab Club & Police Abuse of Force," in *And Justice for All: Understanding & Controlling Police Abuse of Force*, eds. William A. Geller and Hans Toch (Washington, DC: Police Executive Research Forum, 1995), 187–204.
36. Matthew J. Hickman, "Citizen Complaints About Police Use of Force," *Bureau of Justice Statistics Special Report* (June 2006), https://bjs.ojp.gov/content/pub/pdf/ccpuf.pdf. Accessed September 29, 2021.

37. Dhammika Dharmapala, Richard H. McAdams, and John Rappaport, "Collective Bargaining Rights and Police Misconduct: Evidence from Florida," *Journal of Law, Economics, & Organization* 38, no. 1 (2022): 1–41, https://doi.org/10.1093/jleo/ewaa025.
38. "Fired/Rehired," *The Washington Post*, August 3, 2017, https://www.washingtonpost.com/graphics/2017/investigations/police-fired-rehired/?itid=lk_inline_manual_25. Accessed September 29, 2021.
39. Dharmapala et al., "Collective Bargaining Rights and Police Misconduct"; Roman G. Rivera and Bocar A. Ba, "The Effect of Police Oversight on Crime and Allegations of Misconduct: Evidence from Chicago," *Faculty Scholarship at Penn Law*, University of Pennsylvania Law School (October 2019): 1–89.
40. Kelling and Kliesmet, "Police Unions, Police Culture."
41. Kelling and Kliesmet, "Police Unions, Police Culture."
42. Shelley S. Hyland, *Body-Worn Cameras in Law Enforcement Agencies, 2016* (Washington, DC: U.S. Department of Justice, Office of Justice Programs, November 2018), https://bjs.ojp.gov/content/pub/pdf/bwclea16.pdf. Accessed September 29, 2021.
43. See, e.g., Cynthia M. Lum, Christopher S. Koper, Linda M. Merola, J. Amber Scherer, and Amanda Reioux, *Existing and Ongoing Body Worn Camera Research: Knowledge Gaps and Opportunities*, Report for the Laura and John Arnold Foundation (Fairfax, VA: Center for Evidence-Based Crime Policy, George Mason University, 2015); Michael D. White, *Police Officer Body-Worn Cameras: Assessing the Evidence* (Washington, DC: U.S. Department of Justice, Office of Community Oriented Policing Services, 2014).
44. Cynthia M. Lum, Megan Stoltz, Christopher S. Koper, and J. Amber Scherer, "The Research on Body-Worn Cameras: What We Know, What We Need to Know," *Criminology & Public Policy* 18, no. 1 (2019): 93–118.
45. Morgan C. Williams, Jr., Nathan Weil, Elizabeth A. Rasich, Jens Ludwig, Hye Chang, and Sophia Egrari, "Body-Worn Cameras in Policing: Benefits and Costs," National Bureau of Economic Research, Working Paper 28622 (March 2021), https://www.nber.org/papers/w28622. Accessed September 29, 2021.
46. Anthony A. Braga, John M. MacDonald, and James McCabe, "Body Worn Cameras, Lawful Police Stops, and NYPD Officer Compliance: A Cluster Randomized Controlled Trial," *Criminology* 60, no. 1 (2022): 124–158.
47. Taeho Kim, "Facilitating Police Reform: Body Cameras, Use of Force, and Law Enforcement Outcomes," unpublished working paper, University of Pennsylvania (October 23, 2019), http://dx.doi.org/10.2139/ssrn.3474634.
48. Barak Ariel, Alex Sutherland, Darren Henstock, Josh Young, Paul Drover, Jane Sykes, Simon Megicks, and Ryan Henderson, "Wearing Body Cameras Increases Assaults Against Officers and Does Not Reduce Police Use of Force: Results from a Global Multisite Experiment," *European Journal of Criminology* 136, no. 6 (2016), 744–755.
49. Williams, Jr., et al., "Body-Worn Cameras in Policing."
50. Harold A. Pollack and Keith Humphreys, "Reducing Violent Incidents Between Police Officers and People with Psychiatric or Substance Use Disorders," *Annals of the American Academy of Political and Social Science* 687, no. 1 (2020): 166–186.
51. Michael S. Rogers, Dale E. McNiel and Renée L. Binder, "Effectiveness of Police Crisis Intervention Training Programs," *Journal of the American Academy of Psychiatry and the Law Online* 47, no. 4 (September 2019), http://jaapl.org/content/early/2019/09/24/JAAPL.003863-19.

52. Pew Charitable Trusts, "How to Transform the Response to Those Having a Mental Health Crisis," December 8, 2020, https://www.pewtrusts.org/en/research-and-analysis/articles/2020/12/08/how-to-transform-the-response-to-those-having-a-mental-health-crisis. Accessed September 29, 2021.
53. Pew Charitable Trusts, "How to Transform the Response to Those Having a Mental Health Crisis."
54. Rogers et al., "Effectiveness of Police Crisis Intervention Training Programs."
55. Pollack and Humphreys, "Reducing Violent Incidents Between Police Officers and People with Psychiatric or Substance Use Disorders."
56. Ian H. Stanley, Melanie A. Hom, and Thomas E. Joiner, "A Systematic Review of Suicidal Thoughts and Behaviors Among Police Officers, Firefighters, EMTs, and Paramedics," *Clinical Psychology Review* 44, no. 6 (2016): 25–44; James F. Ballenger, Suzanne R. Best, Thomas J. Metzler, David A. Wasserman, David C. Mohr, Akiva Liberman, Kevin Delucchi, Daniel S. Weiss, Jeffrey A. Fagan, Angela E. Waldrop, and Charles R. Marmar, "Patterns and Predictors of Alcohol Use in Male and Female Urban Police Officers," *American Journal on Addictions* 20, no. 1 (2011): 21–29.
57. Zimring, *When Police Kill.*
58. Sherman, "Reducing Fatal Police Shootings as System Crashes"; Sara F. Jacoby, Paul M. Reeping, and Charles C. Branas, "Police-to-Hospital Transport for Violently Injured Individuals," *Annals of the American Academy of Political and Social Science* 687, no. 1 (2020): 186–201.
59. Peter Rhee, Carlos Brown, Matthew Martin, Ali Salim, Dave Plurad, Donald Green, Lowell Chambers, Demetrios Demetriades, George Velmahos, and Hassan Alam, "QuikClot Use in Trauma for Hemorrhage Control: Case Series of 103 Documented Uses," *Journal of Trauma and Acute Care Surgery* 64, no. 4 (2008): 1093–1099.
60. Jacoby et al., "Police-to-Hospital Transport for Violently Injured Individuals."
61. Charles C. Branas, Ronald F. Sing, and Steven J. Davidson, "Urban Trauma Transport of Assaulted Patients Using Nonmedical Personnel," *Academic Emergency Medicine* 2, no. 6 (1995): 486–493; Roger A. Band, Rama A. Salhi, Daniel N. Holena, Elizabeth Powell, Charles C. Branas, and Brendan G. Carr, "Severity-Adjusted Mortality in Trauma Patients Transported by Police," *Annals of Emergency Medicine* 63, no. 5 (2014): 608–14.
62. Band et al., "Severity-Adjusted Mortality in Trauma Patients Transported by Police."
63. Branas et al., "Urban Trauma Transport of Assaulted Patients"; Band et al., "Severity-Adjusted Mortality in Trauma Patients Transported by Police."
64. Jacoby et al., "Police -to-Hospital Transport for Violently Injured Individuals."
65. Bureau of Justice Statistics, *Local Police Departments: Policies and Procedures, 2016.*
66. Michael R. Smith, Robert J. Kaminski, Geoffrey P. Alpert, Lorie A. Fridell, John M. MacDonald, and Bruce Kubu, *A Multi-Method Evaluation of Police Use of Force Outcomes* (Washington, DC; National Institute of Justice, July 2010), https://www.ojp.gov/pdffiles1/nij/grants/231176.pdf; John M. MacDonald, Robert J. Kaminski, and Michael R. Smith, "The Effect of Less-Lethal Weapons on Injuries in Police Use of Force Events," *American Journal of Public Health* 99, no. 12 (2009): 2268–2274.
67. Bocar A. Ba and Jeffrey Grogger, "The Introduction of Tasers and Police Use of Firearms: Evidence from the Chicago Police Department," *AEA Papers and Proceedings* 109 (May 2019): 157–160.
68. Smith, *A Multi-Method Evaluation of Police Use of Force.*

69. Stephen A. Bishopp, David A. Klinger, and Robert G. Morris, "An Examination of the Effect of a Policy Change on Police Use of TASERs," *Criminal Justice Policy Review* 26, no. 7 (2015): 727–746.
70. Zimring, *When Police Kill.*
71. David M. Bierie, "Assault of Police," *Crime & Delinquency* 63, no. 8 (2017): 899–925.
72. National Institute for Occupational Safety and Health, *Violence in the Workplace* (Morgantown, WV: U.S. Department of Health and Human Services, Public Health Service, Centers for Disease Control and Prevention, National Institute for Occupational Safety and Health, 1996).
73. Detis T. Duhart, *Violence in the Workplace, 1993–99*, Bureau of Justice Statistics Special Report (Washington, DC: U.S. Department of Justice, Office of Justice Programs, December 2001), https://bjs.ojp.gov/content/pub/pdf/vw99.pdf; Lorie A. Fridell, Don Faggiani, Bruce Taylor, Corina S. Brito, and Bruce Kubu, "The Impact of Agency Context, Policies and Practices on Violence Against Police," *Journal of Criminal Justice* 37, no. 6 (2009): 542–552.
74. Michael D. White, Lisa M. Dario, and John A, Shjarback, "Assessing Dangerousness in Policing: An Analysis of Law Enforcement Officer Deaths in the United States, 1970–2016," *Criminology and Public Policy* 18, no. 1 (2019): 11–35.
75. Zimring, *When Police Kill.*
76. White et al., "Assessing Dangerousness in Policing"
77. E.g., Heather MacDonald, *The War on Cops* (New York, NY: Encounter Books, 2016); Howard Safir. "The War on Police Hurts the War on Terror," *TIME*, January 9, 2015, https://time.com/3662529/howard-safir-the-war-on-police-hurts-the-war-on-terror-paris. Accessed September 29, 2021.
78. See Officer Down Memorial Page, https://www.odmp.org/search/year/2021. Accessed March 13, 2022.
79. Federal Bureau of Investigation, *Law Enforcement Officers Feloniously Killed, 2020*, Uniform Crime Report Series, Law Enforcement Officers Killed and Assaulted (LEOKA) (Washington, DC: U.S Department of Justice, Federal Bureau of Investigation, Spring 2021), https://ucr.fbi.gov/leoka/2019/topic-pages/tables/table-24.xls. Accessed August 1, 2021.
80. Bierie, "Assault of Police."
81. See, e.g., Fridell et al., "The Impact of Agency Context, Policies, and Practices on Violence Against Police"; Robert J. Kaminski, "Assessing the County-Level Structural Covariates of Police Homicides," *Homicide Studies* 12, no. 4 (2008): 350–380; John A. Shjarback and Michael D. White, "Departmental Professionalism and Its Impact on Indicators of Violence in Police–Citizen Encounters," *Police Quarterly* 19, no. 1 (2016): 32–62.
82. Patton N. Morrison and C. Kenneth Meyer, *A Microanalysis of Assaults on Police in Austin, Texas* (Norman, OK: Bureau of Government Research, University of Oklahoma, 1974), https://www.ojp.gov/pdffiles1/Digitization/27864NCJRS.pdf; James L. Regens, C. Kenneth Meyer, Cheryl G. Swanson, and Samuel G. Chapman, *An Analysis of Assaults on Municipal Police Officers in 46 South Central Cities* (Norman, OK: Bureau of Government Research, University of Oklahoma, 1974); Fridell et al., "The Impact of Agency Context, Policies, and Practices on Violence Against Police."
83. Antony M. Pate and Lorie A. Fridell, *Police Use of Force: Official Reports, Citizen Complaints, and Legal Consequences, Volumes I and II* (Washington, DC: The Police Foundation,

October 1993), https://www.ojp.gov/pdffiles1/Digitization/146825NCJRS.pdf. Accessed September 29, 2021.

84. Klinger, "Organizational Accidents and Deadly Police-Involved Violence."

## Chapter 9

1. Excerpted from James C. McKinley, Jr., "Couple Charged with Selling Illegal Guns in New York," *The New York Times*, April 26, 2016, https://www.nytimes.com/2016/04/26/nyregion/couple-charged-with-selling-illegal-guns-in-new-york.html. Accessed August 28, 2021.
2. Anthony A. Braga and Philip J. Cook, "The Criminal Records of Gun Offenders," *Georgetown Journal of Law and Public Policy* 14, no. 1 (Winter 2016): 1–16.
3. Braga and Cook, "The Criminal Records of Gun Offenders"; Anthony A. Braga, Philip J. Cook, David M. Kennedy, and Mark H. Moore, "The Illegal Supply of Firearms," in *Crime and Justice: A Review of Research*, vol. 29, ed. Michael Tonry (Chicago, IL: University of Chicago Press, 2000), 319–352; Philip J. Cook, "Gun Markets," *Annual Review of Criminology* 1 (2018): 359–377.
4. Emma E. McGinty, Daniel W. Webster, Jon S. Vernick, and Colleen L. Barry, "Public Opinion on Proposals to Strengthen U.S. Gun Laws: Findings from a 2013 Survey," in *Reducing Gun Violence in America: Informing Policy with Evidence and Analysis*, eds. Daniel W. Webster and Jon S. Vernick (Baltimore, MD: Johns Hopkins University Press, 2013), 239–258.
5. Philip J. Cook. "Gun Theft and Crime," *Journal of Urban Health* 95, no. 3 (2018): 305–312.
6. Anthony A. Braga, Garen J. Wintemute, Glenn L. Pierce, Philip J. Cook, and Greg Ridgeway, "Interpreting the Empirical Evidence on Illegal Gun Market Dynamics," *Journal of Urban Health* 89, no. 5 (2012): 779–793; see also U.S. Bureau of Alcohol, Tobacco and Firearms, *Following the Gun: Enforcing Federal Laws Against Firearms Traffickers* (Washington, DC: Bureau of Alcohol, Tobacco and Firearms, 2000).
7. Dale Armstrong, *Firearms Trafficking: A Guide for Criminal Investigators* (Saco, ME: Prudens Group Consulting, 2018).
8. Garen J. Wintemute, "Ghost Guns: Spookier Than You Think They Are," *Injury Epidemiology* 8 (2021): Article 13, https://doi.org/10.1186/s40621-021-00306-0. Accessed August 1, 2021.
9. Bureau of Alcohol, Tobacco, Firearms and Explosives, *Firearm Commerce in the United States* (Washington, DC: U.S. Department of Justice, 2022).
10. Philip J. Cook and Anthony A. Braga, "Comprehensive Firearms Tracing: Strategic and Investigative Uses of New Data on Firearms Markets," *Arizona Law Review* 43, no. 2 (2001): 277–309; Braga et al., "The Illegal Supply of Firearms."
11. Colleen Long and Jonathan Lemire, "Biden Targets Law-Breaking Gun Dealers in Anti-Crime Plan," Associated Press, June 23, 2021, https://apnews.com/article/joe-biden-health-coronavirus-pandemic-laws-crime-6e67362305041e7c889d8fd160e091e3. Accessed August 1, 2021.
12. Susan B. Sorenson and Katherine A. Vittes. "Buying a Handgun for Someone Else: Firearm Retailer Willingness to Sell," *Injury Prevention* 9, no. 2 (2003): 147–150; Garen J. Wintemute, "Firearm Retailers' Willingness to Participate in an Illegal Gun Purchase," *Journal of Urban Health* 87, no. 5 (2010): 865–878.

13. Garen J. Wintemute, "Comprehensive Background Checks for Firearm Sales: Evidence from Gun Shows," in *Reducing Gun Violence in America: Informing Policy with Evidence and Analysis*, eds. Daniel W. Webster and Jon S. Vernick (Baltimore, MD: Johns Hopkins University Press, 2013), 95–108.
14. Michael R. Weissner, "Isn't It About Time We Opened up That 'Secret' Gun Business?" July 19, 2021, https://mikethegunguy.social/2021/07/19/isnt-it-about-time-we-opened-up-that-secret-gun-business. Accessed August 1, 2021.
15. James B. Jacobs, *Can Gun Control Work?* (New York, NY: Oxford University Press, 2002).
16. Cook and Braga, "Comprehensive Firearms Tracing."
17. Braga et al., "Interpreting the Empirical Evidence on Gun Market Dynamics."
18. Anthony A. Braga, "Long-Term Trends in the Sources of Boston Crime Guns," *The Russell Sage Foundation Journal of the Social Sciences* 3, no. 5 (2017): 76–95.
19. Jens Ludwig and Philip J. Cook, "Homicide and Suicide Rates Associated with Implementation of the Brady Handgun Violence Prevention Act," *Journal of the American Medical Association* 284, no. 5 (2000): 585–591.
20. Philip J. Cook and Jens Ludwig, "The Limited Impact of the Brady Act: Evaluation and Implications," in *Reducing Gun Violence in America: Informing Policy with Evidence and Analysis*, eds. Daniel W. Webster and Jon S. Vernick (Baltimore, MD: Johns Hopkins University Press, 2013), 21–32.
21. Garen J. Wintemute, Mona A. Wright, Christiana M. Drake, and James J. Beaumont, "Subsequent Criminal Activity Among Violent Misdemeanants Who Seek to Purchase Handguns," *Journal of the American Medical Association* 265 (2001): 1019–1026.
22. Kerri M. Raissian, "Hold Your Fire: Did the 1996 Federal Gun Control Act Expansion Reduce Domestic Homicides?" *Journal of Policy Analysis and Management* 35, no. 1 (2016): 67–93.
23. Anthony A. Braga and David M. Hureau, "Strong Gun Laws Are Not Enough: The Need for Improved Enforcement of Secondhand Gun Transfer Laws in Massachusetts," *Preventive Medicine* 79 (2015): 37–42.
24. Mark H. Moore, "Achieving Discrimination in the Effective Price of Heroin," *American Economic Review* 63, no. 2 (1973): 193–206.
25. David M. Kennedy, "Can We Keep Guns Away from Kids?" *American Prospect* 18, no.1 (1): 74–80.
26. Philip J. Cook, Jens Ludwig, Sudhir Venkatesh, and Anthony A. Braga, "Underground Gun Markets," *Economic Journal* 117, no. 524 (2007): 558–588.
27. Philip J. Cook, Stephanie Molloconi, and Thomas B. Cole, "Regulating Gun Markets," *Journal of Criminal Law and Criminology* 86 (1995): 59–92.
28. Anthony A. Braga, Rod K. Brunson, Philip J. Cook, Brandon S. Turchan, and Brian Wade, "Underground Gun Markets and the Flow of Illegal Guns into the Bronx and Brooklyn: A Mixed Methods Analysis," *Journal of Urban Health* 98 (2021): 596–608, https://link.springer.com/article/10.1007/s11524-020-00477-z. Accessed August 28, 2021.
29. David M. Hureau and Anthony A. Braga, "The Trade in Tools: The Market for Illicit Guns in High-Risk Networks," *Criminology* 56, no. 3 (2018): 510–545.
30. Mark H. Moore, "The Police and Weapons Offenses," *Annals of the American Academy of Political and Social Science* 452, no. 1 (1980): 22–32; Mark H. Moore, "The Bird in Hand: A Feasible Strategy for Gun Control," *Journal of Policy Analysis and Management* 2, no. 2 (1983): 185–195.

31. Cook and Braga, "Comprehensive Firearms Tracing"; Glenn L. Pierce, Anthony A. Braga, Raymond R. Hyatt, and Christopher S. Koper, "The Characteristics and Dynamics of Illegal Firearms Markets: Implications for a Supply-Side Enforcement Strategy," *Justice Quarterly* 21, no. 2 (2004): 391–422.
32. Braga et al., "Underground Gun Markets and the Flow of Illegal Guns."
33. Braga et al., "Underground Gun Markets and the Flow of Illegal Guns."
34. Braga et al., "Underground Gun Markets and the Flow of Illegal Guns," 11.
35. Braga et al., "Underground Gun Markets and the Flow of Illegal Guns," 12.
36. Braga et al., "Underground Gun Markets and the Flow of Illegal Guns," 11.
37. Hureau and Braga, "The Trade in Tools."
38. Hureau and Braga, "The Trade in Tools"; Alexandra Ciomek, Anthony A. Braga, and Andrew V. Papachristos, "The Influence of Firearms Trafficking on Gunshot Injuries in a High-Risk Social Network," *Social Science & Medicine*, 259 (2020): 113114, https://doi.org/10.1016/j.socscimed.2020.113114. Accessed September 2, 2021.
39. International Association of Chiefs of Police, *Reducing Gun Violence in Our Communities: A Leadership Guide for Law Enforcement on Effective Strategies and Programs* (Alexandria, VA: International Association of Chiefs of Police, 2011), https://www.theiacp.org/sites/default/files/all/f-h/GunViolenceReductionGuide2011.pdf. Accessed September 2, 2021.
40. Peter L. Gagliardi, *The 13 Critical Tasks: An Inside-Out Approach to Solving More Gun Crime* (Quebec, CA: Ultra Electronics Forensic Technology, 2019).
41. Anthony A. Braga and Glenn L. Pierce, "Linking Gun Crimes: The Impact of Ballistics Imaging Technology on the Productivity of the Boston Police Department's Ballistics Unit," *Journal of Forensic Sciences* 49, no. 4 (July 2004): 701–706.
42. William King, William Wells, Charles Katz, Edward Maguire, and James Frank, *Opening the Black Box of NIBIN: A Descriptive Process and Outcome Evaluation of the Use of NIBIN and Its Effects on Criminal Investigations, Final Report* (Washington, DC: U.S. Department of Justice, National Institute of Justice, October 2013), https://www.ojp.gov/pdffiles1/nij/grants/243875.pdf. Accessed August 29, 2021.
43. Anthony A. Braga and Glenn L. Pierce, "Reconsidering the Ballistic Imaging of Crime Bullets in Gun Law Enforcement Operations," *Forensic Science Policy and Management* 2, no. 3 (2011): 105–117.
44. Braga and Pierce, "Reconsidering the Ballistic Imaging of Crime Bullets," 116.
45. David M. Kennedy, Anne M. Piehl, and Anthony A. Braga, "Youth Violence in Boston: Gun Markets, Serious Youth Offenders, and a Use-Reduction Strategy," *Law and Contemporary Problems* 59, no. 1 (1996): 147–196.
46. Summarized from David M. Kennedy, Anthony A. Braga, Anne M. Piehl, and Elin J. Waring, "Developing and Implementing Operation Ceasefire," in *Reducing Gun Violence: The Boston Gun Project's Operation Ceasefire* (Washington, DC: U.S. Department of Justice, National Institute of Justice, September 2001), https://www.ojp.gov/pdffiles1/nij/188741.pdf. Accessed August 29, 2021.
47. Anthony A. Braga and Glenn L. Pierce, "Disrupting Illegal Firearms Markets in Boston: The Effects of Operation Ceasefire on the Supply of New Handguns to Criminals," *Criminology & Public Policy* 4, no. 4 (2005): 717–748.
48. Greg Ridgeway, Glenn L. Pierce, Anthony A. Braga, George E. Tita, Garen J. Wintemute, and Wendell Roberts, *Strategies for Disrupting Illegal Gun Markets: A Case Study of Los Angeles* (Santa Monica, CA: RAND Corporation, 2008), https://www.rand.org/pubs/technical_reports/TR512.html. Accessed August 29, 2021.

49. Ridgeway et al., *Strategies for Disrupting Illegal Gun Markets.*
50. Greg Ridgeway, Anthony A. Braga, George E. Tita, and Glenn L. Pierce, "Intervening in Gun Markets: An Experiment to Assess the Impact of Targeted Gun Law Messaging," *Journal of Experimental Criminology* 7, no. 1 (2011): 103–109.
51. Anthony A. Braga and Peter L. Gagliardi, "Enforcing Federal Laws Against Firearms Traffickers: Raising Operational Effectiveness by Lowering Enforcement Obstacles," in *Reducing Gun Violence in America: Informing Policy with Evidence and Analysis*, eds. Daniel W. Webster and Jon S. Vernick (Baltimore, MD: Johns Hopkins University Press, 2013), 143–156.
52. Daniel W. Webster, April Zeoli, Maria Bulzacchelli, and Jon S. Vernick, "Effects of Police Stings of Gun Dealers on the Supply of New Guns to Criminals. *Injury Prevention* 12 (2006): 225–230.
53. Daniel W. Webster, Jon Vernick, and Maria Bulzacchelli. 2006. "Effects of a Gun Dealer's Change in Sales Practices on the Supply of Guns to Criminals." *Journal of Urban Health* 83: 778–787.
54. Daniel W. Webster and Jon S. Vernick, "Spurring Responsible Firearms Sales Practices Through Litigation: The Impact of New York City's Lawsuits Against Gun Dealers on Interstate Gun Trafficking," in *Reducing Gun Violence in America: Informing Policy with Evidence and Analysis*, eds. Daniel W. Webster and Jon S. Vernick (Baltimore, MD: Johns Hopkins University Press, 2013), 123–132.
55. National Research Council, *Firearms and Violence: A Critical Review*, Committee to Improve Research Information and Data on Firearms, eds. Charles F. Wellford, John V. Pepper, and Carol V. Petrie (Washington, DC: National Academies Press, 2005).
56. Anthony A. Braga and Garen J. Wintemute, "Improving the Potential Effectiveness of Gun Buyback Programs," *American Journal of Preventive Medicine* 45, no. 5 (2013): 668–671.
57. Carlo B. Morselli and Dominik Blais, "The Mobility of Stolen Guns in Quebec," *European Journal on Criminal Policy and Research* 20 (2014): 379–397.
58. Ronald V. Clarke, *Situational Crime Prevention*, 2nd ed. (New York, NY: Harrow & Heston, 1997); Michael S. Scott and Ronald V. Clarke, eds., *Problem-Oriented Policing: Successful Case Studies* (New York, NY: Taylor & Francis, 2020).
59. Michael Sutton, *Stolen Goods Markets*, Problem-Oriented Guides for Police, Problem-Specific Guides Series, No. 57 (Washington, DC: U.S. Department of Justice, 2010).
60. "LA County Sheriff Villanueva Calls for Ban on Selling, Manufacturing 'Ghost Gun' Kits," ABC 7 News, May 11, 2020, https://abc7.com/ghost-guns-california-gun-laws-kits-alex-villanueva/6172364. Accessed August 1, 2021.
61. Anthony A. Braga, Lisa M. Barao, Garen J. Wintemute, Steve Valle, and Jaimie Valente, "Privately Manufactured Firearms, Newly Purchased Firearms, and the Rise of Urban Gun Violence," *Preventive Medicine* (2022), https://doi.org/10.1016/j.ypmed.2022.107231

## Chapter 10

1. Emily Davies and Peter Herman, "Amid Rising Homicides, District Launches Effort to Target Hot Spots for Violence," *The Washington Post*, May 3, 2021, https://www.washingtonpost.com/local/public-safety/washington-gun-violence-bowser-/2021/05/03/cc74a06e-ac0c-11eb-b476-c3b287e52a01_story.html. Accessed August 10, 2021

# Index

*For the benefit of digital users, indexed terms that span two pages (e.g., 52–53) may, on occasion, appear on only one of those pages.*

Tables and figures are indicated by *t* and *f* following the page number


academic-police department collaboration, 53
Academy Homes gang, 101
accountability structures, 113
active shooter drills, 7, 15, 23
Adidas Tree, 94–95, 96–97
African Americans. *See* Blacks
"after action" reports, 142
age
  of gun homicide victims, 16, 17*f*
  of gun violence perpetrators, 16–17
  illegal gun ownership and, 40
  for legal gun purchase, 36
  of police shooting victims, 133
aggravated assault, 103
"Al Capone" punishment approach, 113–14
amnesties, 170
Annunciation Road gang, 101
AR-15s, 29
Armed Prohibited Persons System, 44–45
arrests
  deterrent effect of, 8
  for homicide, 116
  for shootings, 8–9, 117–18, 119–23, 174, 179
Asian police officers, 49–50
assassinations, 16, 22, 24–25, 27, 187n.28
assault
  aggravated, 103
  clearance rates for, 118–19
  decrease in, 17–18
  in hot spots, 78–79, 83
  on police officers, 149, 150
  Project Safe Neighborhoods impact on, 103
  rates of, 14*t*
assault weapons
  ban allowed to sunset, 28*t*, 29
  ban reinstatement called for, 30
  bans on, 28*t*, 29
  growth in sales of, 21–22
ATF. *See* Bureau of Alcohol, Tobacco, Firearms and Explosives
*Atlantic, The*, 117
Aurora movie theater shootings, 15

Babbitt, Ashli, 129–30
background checks, 10, 27–29, 37, 157
  bar on saving of successful, 31
  call for expansion of, 30
  gaps in databases, 36
  number of illegal transaction blocked by, 157–58
  for private transactions, 35–36
ballistics, 164–66, 165*f*
Baltimore, MD, 116
  focused deterrence in, 111–12
  gang violence in, 87–88
  hot spots in, 71
  officer-involved homicide in, 61
Barthelemy, Marvada, 65
Baton Rouge, LA, 149
Bayley, David, 53–54
Biden, Joe, 7, 156
Black Lives Matter, 61, 130
Blacks
  drug market intervention and, 104–5
  gun homicide victimization rate in, 16, 17*f*, 86–87
  gun ownership by, 34
  gun violence perpetrated by, 16–17
  hot spots in neighborhoods of, 67
  officer-involved homicide of, 61, 130, 134, 135*f*, 136*t*
  in police departments, 49–50, 139–40

Blacks (*cont.*)
police shootings of, 15–16, 133, 134, 134*t*, 135–36, 135*f*, 136*t*, 145, 180
public safety gap and, 11
shootings in neighborhoods of, 116–17
"stop, question, and frisk" and, 76–77, 79–80, 177
tensions between police and, 1–2, 6–7, 126–27, 131, 174
as victims of violence and crime, 4, 6, 174
Bloods, 65, 66
Bloomberg, Michael, 74–75, 76–77
body-worn cameras, 58–59, 61, 77, 145–46, 181
Boston, MA
fatal and nonfatal shootings in, 67, 68*f*, 122
gang violence in, 4–5, 8, 16–17, 58, 88, 88*f*, 89–90, 92–102
group yearly counts of shootings in, 70*f*
gun buybacks in, 170
gun carrying regulations in, 40
homicide clearance rate in, 123–25
hot spots in, 67, 79–83
prices of illegal guns in, 159
sources of illegal guns in, 157
types of guns used in, 21
underground gun market in, 163–64, 182
Boston Centers for Youth and Families, 99–100
Boston Common area, 81–82
Boston Community Centers' Streetworker program, 96
Boston Gun Project, 92–94, 166–67, 178
Boston Marathon shooting and bombing, 31
"Boston Miracle," 98
Boston Police Department (BPD), 4–5, 60–61, 166, 178
Boston Gun Project in, 92–94, 166–67, 178
homicide clearance rate in, 123–25, 179
Operation Ceasefire in (*see* Operation Ceasefire)
Safe Streets Teams in (*see* Safe Streets Teams)
shootings investigated by, 115, 122–23
"stop, question, and frisk" program in, 79–80
Youth Violence Strike Force in, 96, 98–99, 115
Boston Regional Intelligence Center (BRIC), 80–81, 99, 115
Bowdoin Street, Dorchester, 95, 96
Boyce, Robert K., 151
Boyle Heights, Los Angeles, 87–88
Brady Handgun Violence Prevention Act of 1993, 27–29, 28*t*, 37, 157
Braga, Anthony, 60–61, 69, 166
Boston Gun Project and, 92–93
clearance rate project and, 123–24
evaluation of body-worn cameras, 145–46
Operation Ceasefire and, 8, 98–99, 178
professional background of, 4–6
Safe Street Teams and, 79–81
study of shooting cases, 120, 122–23
underground gun market analysis by, 160–61, 163–64
Bragdon Street gang, 101
Bratton, William, 2, 47, 54–55, 56–57, 59, 74, 77–78
Brazil, officer-involved lethal shootings in, 131–33
BRIC. *See* Boston Regional Intelligence Center
broken-window theory, 56–57
Bronx, NY
gun availability in, 39
prices of illegal guns in, 159
underground gun market in, 160–63
Brooklyn, NY
gun availability in, 39
hot spots in, 74–75
police officers killed in, 149
prices of illegal guns in, 159
underground gun market in, 160–63
Brown, Michael, 9–10, 15–16, 129, 130
Brownsville, Brooklyn, 76
*Bruen* decision, *New York State Rifle & Pistol Association, Inc. v. Bruen,* 29–30
Buffalo, NY, 123
Bureau of Alcohol, Tobacco, Firearms and Explosives (ATF), 86–87, 152, 154, 157, 181
Crime Gun Intelligence Centers, 154, 159–60
history of, 30
licensed dealers regulated by, 32
price of illegal guns ignored by, 158
role of in enforcement, 30–31
tracing of gun transactions, 31–32, 40–42, 160–61, 164–66, 167
Bureau of Justice Statistics, U.S., 49
Bureau of Justice Statistics Law Enforcement Management and Administrative Statistics survey, 59–60

burglary, 36, 118–19

"cafeteria-style offending," 91
caliber, gun, 21–22
California, gun ownership disqualification in, 36, 44–45, 157–58
cameras. *See* body-worn cameras; surveillance cameras; video recordings
Canada, officer-involved lethal shootings in, 131–33
Cape Verdean, Boston, 89–90
Capone, Al, 26–27, 113–14
Caribbean
  guns smuggled to, 33
  officer-involved lethal shootings in, 131–33
Castile, Philando, 15–16
Center for Constitutional Rights, 77
Centers for Disease Control and Prevention, 131
Central America, officer-involved lethal shootings in, 131–33
Centre for Evidence-Based Policing (England), 137
CGICs. *See* Crime Gun Intelligence Centers
Chauvin, Derek, 48
Chicago, IL
  clearance rates for homicide in, 122
  enforcement in, 66
  focused deterrence in, 113–14
  gang violence in, 16–17, 87–88, 89–90
  gun availability in, 39
  gun carrying regulations in, 40
  homicide increase in, 9–10
  hot spots in, 177
  housing projects in, 12
  police shootings in, 15–16, 138*f*
  prices of illegal guns in, 159
  prisoner reentry and prevention of gun violence in, 102–4
  Project Safe Neighborhoods in, 102–4
  sources of illegal guns in, 157
  "stop, question, and frisk" program in, 7, 175
  supply-side interventions in, 169–70
  tracing of gun transactions in, 40
Chicago Inmate Survey, 39
Chicago Police Department (CPD), 5–6, 41, 102
  academic collaboration with, 59
  complaints against, 140–41
  police shootings in, 139–40
  shootings investigated by, 116
children, 22. *See also* school shootings
Cincinnati, OH, 111
Cincinnati Initiative to Reduce Violence (CIRV), 113
City University of New York, 112
clearance rates, 126–27
  defined, 117–18
  for homicide, 116, 123–25, 126*f*, 179–80
  for shootings, 116, 120, 121–22, 121*t*, 179–80
  for volume crimes, 118–19
clergy, 94, 98, 111, 178
Codman Square, Dorchester, 81–82
Columbine shootings, 15
community engagement, 62–63
community policing, 53, 64, 175
  explained, 56
  in hot spots, 81, 82
  police-academic collaboration in, 59
  prevalence of, 59–60
CompStat, 60–61, 64, 74, 75–76, 81
  development of, 199n.26
  explained, 55
concealed carrying, 43
conducted-energy devices (CEDs), 148–49
"Constitutional carry," 43
contingent valuation method, 23–24
co-offenders and gun violence, 87–91
Cook, Philip, 4–5, 23
  professional background of, 5–6
  study of gun confiscation, 41
  study of shootings cases, 120
  underground gun market analysis by, 160–61
Cooper housing project (New Orleans), 12
cost of illness (COI) approach, 24
COVID-19 pandemic, 1, 4–5, 11, 13–14, 24–25, 43, 78, 131
crack cocaine epidemic, 1, 19, 27–29, 47, 53–54, 92, 93–95
crime. *See also violent crime*; *specific types of crimes*
  comprehensive intelligence on gun-related, 164–66
  decrease in, 4, 6, 17–19, 47, 173, 183
  evolution of police strategy for controlling, 53–59
  police innovation and decline in, 54–59
  "root causes" perspective, 2, 4, 19

crime (*cont.*)
sources of guns for, 36–42, 38*t*
traditional mechanisms for prevention of, 51–53
Crime Gun Intelligence Centers (CGICs), 154, 159–60
criminal records (gun ownership prohibited by), 27–29, 32–33
Crisis Intervention Teams (CITs), 146–47

Dallas, TX
police officers killed in, 149
police shootings in, 6–7, 137–38, 138*f*, 139*f*, 141, 180
Dallas Police Department, 137–38, 141
Davis, Abdul, 151
Davis, Edward F., 5, 60–61, 79–81, 99, 123–24
DEA. *See* Drug Enforcement Administration
de Blasio, Bill, 77
"defund the police" movement, 1–2, 61, 117, 173
Democrats, 27–29
Denver Police Department, 123
Department of Justice, California, 168
Department of Justice, U.S., 32, 74, 92–93, 143–44, 159–60
Department of the Treasury, U.S., 30
Department of Youth Services (DYS) of Boston, 95, 97
deterrence, 2–3, 63, 71–72, 175. *See also* focused deterrence
policing impact on, 51
of violent crime, 52–53
Detroit, MI, 169–70
diffuse sources, 156, 168–69
disarming (of court-identified dangerous people), 44–45
disorder policing, 54–55, 57, 59
disqualification from gun ownership. *See* gun ownership disqualification
diversion of guns, illegal, 153–56, 160, 167, 169–70, 181
DMI. *See* drug market intervention
DNA evidence, 52–53, 58–59, 118–19, 126, 164
domestic violence, 88
gun ownership disqualification for, 29, 36, 157–58
homicide resulting from, 17, 29, 36, 157–58
Dorchester, Boston, 67, 79–80, 93–94, 95, 99
Downtown Crossing, Boston, 81–82
Drug Enforcement Administration (DEA), 94–95, 96–97, 99–100, 158
drug market intervention (DMI), 104–6, 107
drug offenses, 88, 96–98, 104–6
Duke University, 5–6
Durham, NC, 122
Durham, North Carolina, Police Department (DPD), 120
DYS. *See* Department of Youth Services

education level
gun ownership and, 34
of police officers, 50–51
effective price, 158
Egleston Square gang, 101
enforcement
controversy over, 66
of federal law, 30–32
in hot spots, 66
regulation and, 26
England, lethal violence against police in, 149
Equal Protection Clause of 14th Amendment, 60, 76–77
ERPO. *See* Extreme Risk Protection Orders
Eterno, John A., 75–76
Extreme Risk Protection Orders (ERPO), 44, 45

fatal shootings, 8–9, 116–17, 174, 182. *See also* gun homicide
in Boston, 67, 68*f*
clearance rates for, 116, 179–80
gang involvement in, 89–90
in hot spots, 83
nonfatal shootings compared with, 119–23
by police (*see* police shootings, fatal)
FBI Supplementary Homicide Reports, 16–17
Federal Bureau of Investigation (FBI), 30–31, 131, 149–50
Federal Firearms Act of 1938, 28*t*
federal law
enforcement of, 30–32
history of regulation, 26–30
federally licensed dealers, 27–29, 152–53
ATF regulation of, 32
illegal gun transactions and, 154–56, 157–58, 161–63, 170, 181–82
percentage of transactions involving, 35–36, 37

requirement to refuse disqualified buyers, 36
federal prison sentences, 102, 103, 104
federal prosecutions, 96–97, 102, 103, 104
felony convictions (gun ownership disqualification for), 27, 36, 44–45, 153, 157–58
Ferguson, MO, 9–10, 15–16, 61, 129, 130, 131
"Ferguson effect," 9–10, 64, 130
FFLs (Federal Firearms Licensees). *See* federally licensed dealers
field interrogations, 78
fingerprints, 58–59, 126, 164
Firearm Owners ID (Illinois), 37, 41
Firearm Owners Protection Act of 1986, 28*t*, 30
Firearms Compliance Inspections, 32
firearms industry, immunization against civil suits, 28*t*, 29–30
firearms regulation, 3
efficacy of, 157–58
enforcement and, 26
history of, 26–30
permissive *vs.* restrictive, 20
time line of, 28*t*
firearms trafficking, 10–11, 40–42, 152, 153–54, 163–64, 181–82
geographical trends in, 40–41
indicators for, 161–63, 161*t*
interstate, 41
intrastate, 167
investigations of, 154–56
obtaining intelligence on, 164–66
pathways for, 154–56, 155*t*
regulation efficacy against, 157
Florida, 41
police unions and officer misconduct in, 144
underground gun market in, 161–63
*Floyd, et al. v. City of New York, et al.*, 77
Floyd, George, 1–2, 9–10, 15–16, 48, 61, 78, 130
focused deterrence, 3, 7–8, 52, 54–55, 58, 87, 91–106, 113–14, 178–79
basic framework of, 91–92
drug market intervention and, 104–6, 107
explained, 58
growing evidence of violence reduction via, 106–9
implementation challenges, 111–13
Operation Ceasefire and (*see* Operation Ceasefire)
optimizing, 109–11
Project Safe Neighborhoods and, 102–4
randomized controlled trial of, 108
foreign-made handguns, 27
Fourteenth Amendment, 60, 76–77
Fourth Amendment, 60, 74–75, 77, 141
4th Precinct (Newark), 88–89, 89*f*
French, Gary, 96, 98
Friedersdorf, Conor, 117
Fryer, Roland G., Jr., 136
fully automatic weapons, 26–27
Funderberk, Shelita, 151

Gacrama, Praxedo, 26
Gallup Polls, 126–27
gangs, 4–5, 8, 86–87, 178–79
controlling gun violence by, 92–102
focused deterrence and, 58, 106–7, 109–10, 178–79 (*see also* Operation Ceasefire)
hot spots and, 65
prevalence of gun violence driven by, 87–91
prices of illegal guns purchased by, 159
rates of deadly violence in, 16–17
underground gun market connections of, 163–64
vicariously treated, 101–2, 108
GCA. *See* Gun Control Act of 1938
General Social Survey (GSS), 23–24, 33
Georgia, underground gun market in, 161–63
Germany, lethal violence against police in, 149
*Ghettoside* (Leovy), 116–17
ghost guns, 26, 152–53, 154, 171–72, 181–82
Glasgow, Scotland (focused deterrence program in), 106–7
Gottfredson, Michael, 53–54
*Graham v. Connor,* 141
Great Crime Drop (1993-2014), 4, 6, 17–19, 47, 173, 183
greening of vacant lots, 83–84
G-Shine Bloods, 86
GSS. *See* General Social Survey
*Guardian, The,* 131
gun buybacks, 170
gun carrying, 44
concealed, 43
deregulation of, 177
illegal, 3, 66, 71–74, 173–74
permitless laws, 71–72
regulation of, 3, 20, 42–44
targeted patrol to reduce illegal, 71–74

gun confiscations. *See* gun seizures/confiscations
gun control, 3, 26, 173–74
Gun Control Act (GCA) of 1938, 27, 28*t*, 30, 36, 37, 41
gun exchange programs, 170
gun homicide, 6. *See also* fatal shootings
  clearance rates for, 116
  decrease in, 74
  gang involvement in, 89–90
  negligible impact of regulation on, 157–58
  by police (*see* police shootings, fatal)
  Project Safe Neighborhoods impact on, 103
  rates of, 14–15, 14*t*, 15*f*, 17*f*
  risk of, 86–87
gun ownership. *See also* gun possession
  demographics of, 34
  geographic trends in, 36
  prevalence of, 33–34, 34*f*
gun ownership disqualification, 29, 32–33, 37, 44–45, 157–58
  "lie and buy" curtailed, 27–29
  price of obtaining a weapon and, 36
  reasons for, 36
gun possession. *See also* gun ownership
  disarming of dangerous people, 44–45
  in the general population, 32–36
  use and, 42–45
gun recoveries, 40, 102, 104, 164. *See also* gun buybacks; gun seizures/confiscations
guns
  assault weapons (*see* assault weapons)
  availability of, 38–40
  fully automatic weapons, 26–27
  ghost guns, 26, 152–53, 154, 171–72, 181–82
  handguns, 27, 33, 160–61, 167
  long guns, 33
  number of in circulation, 38–39
  pistols, 33
  revolvers, 21–22, 33
  rifles, 33
  Saturday night specials, 28*t*
  semiautomatic pistols, 21–22, 160–61, 166
  shotguns, 33
  sources of to criminal use, 36–42, 38*t*
  taxes on, 33
gun sales
  annual number of, 152–53
  illegal (*see* illegal gun transactions)
  increase in, 1, 3
  private, 35–36, 157–58, 181–82
  retail (*see* retail gun sales)
gun seizures/confiscations, 41, 71–74, 73*f*, 103
gun shows, 35–36, 154–55
gun transactions, 32–36. *See also* illegal gun transactions
gun violence. *See also* shootings
  characteristics of shooters, 16–17
  concentration of, 67–71
  decrease in, 17–19
  economic cost of, 23–24
  impact of threat of, 13, 22–23
  increase in, 4, 19
  portfolio of effective reduction programs, 176–82
  prisoner reentry and prevention of, 102–4
  regulation impact on extent of, 157–58
  risk factors, 86–87
  social cost of, 22–24
  types of guns used in, 21–22
  victimization rates, 14–17, 14*t*, 17*f*

handguns, 27, 33, 160–61, 167
Harlem, NY, 22
Harvard University, 4–5, 92–94
Hawaii, gun ownership in, 38–39
H-Block gang, 101
Heath Street gang, 101, 101*f*
Heinrich, Ted, 96
*Heller v. District of Columbia*, 28*t*, 29–30
High Point, NC, drug market intervention in, 104–6
Hirschi, Travis, 53–54
Hispanics
  gun homicide victimization rate in, 17*f*
  gun ownership by, 34
  officer-involved homicide of, 135*f*, 136*t*
  in police departments, 49–50
  police shootings of, 133, 134*t*, 135–36, 135*f*, 136*t*, 180
  "stop, question, and frisk" and, 76–77
Hollenbeck, Boyle Heights, 107
homelessness, 81–82, 146
homicide. *See also* gun homicide
  arrest rates for, 116
  clearance rates for, 123–25, 126*f*, 179–80
  decrease in, 4, 17–18, 47, 54–55, 98, 100–1, 173, 183
  domestic, 17, 29, 36, 157–58

gang involvement in, 87–89
in hot spots, 67
increase in, 1, 17–18, 78, 98
officer-involved, 6–7, 15–16, 61, 130, 131, 132*f*, 134, 134*t*, 135*f*, 136*t*, 137–39, 138*f*, 139*f*, 180
Operation Ceasefire impact on, 98, 100–1
police role in preventing, 48
police victims of, 149–50
Project Safe Neighborhoods impact on, 103–4, 104*f*
solvability of, 119
total (firearm and non-firearm) rates, 18*f*, 19–20
youth, 92–102, 93*f*
hot spots, 3, 5, 7–8, 52, 54–55, 56, 57, 59, 60–62, 63, 65–85, 173, 176–78
description of phenomenon, 67
police-academic collaboration and, 59
prevalence of policing in, 59–60
problem-oriented policing in, 66–67, 78–84, 85, 176–77
"stop, question, and frisk" programs in, 74–78, 79–80, 84
targeted patrol to reduce illegal carrying in, 71–74
housing projects, 12–13, 65, 77–78
Houston, TX
hot spots in, 67–69
police shootings in, 136, 138*f*, 139*f*
Howard Houses (Brooklyn), 65, 66, 78
hunting, 34–35
Hureau, David, 159

IACP. *See* International Association of Chiefs of Police
illegal gun transactions, 151–72. *See also* diversion of guns, illegal; firearms trafficking; straw purchases; theft (of guns); underground gun markets
police actions to reduce, 159–71, 182
price of guns and, 36, 158–59, 167, 182
sources of, 152–56
source states for, 161–63, 162*f*
supply-side interventions, 152, 166–70, 182
Venn diagram of, 153, 153*f*
Illinois
Firearm Owners ID in, 37, 41
firearms trafficking in, 40
Impact Zones, 74–75, 76
incapacitation, 2–3, 51–52, 63, 175
incarceration, 51–52
in federal prison, 102, 103, 104
increase in rates of, 19
state prison inmate survey, 37, 38*t*
Indiana, firearms trafficking in, 40
Indianapolis, IN hot spots, 73–74, 79–80, 84–85
instant check system, 27–29, 30–31
instrumentality, 19–22, 186n.10
International Association of Chiefs of Police (IACP), 62, 142
intersections, 69–71, 80–81
Interstate 95 (I-95), 40, 161–63, 166
Intervale Posse, 94–95, 96–98
Irvington, NJ, 67

January 6 insurrection, 7, 42–43, 129–30
Jersey City, NJ, 59, 78–79
John Jay College of Criminal Justice, 112

Kansas City, KS hot spots, 59, 79–80, 84–85
Kansas City Gun Project, 72–74
Kelling, George, 59
Kelly, Raymond, 74–76
Kennedy, David, 92–93, 178
Kennedy, John, 16, 27
Kennedy, Robert, 16
Kennedy School of Government (Harvard University), 4–5, 92–93
King, Martin Luther, Jr., 16
knives (used in crimes), 19–20, 21

larceny, 118–19
Las Vegas Strip shootings, 15
Lautenberg Amendment of 1996, 28*t*, 29
Law Enforcement Officers' Bill of Rights, 144
Law Enforcement Officers Killed and Assaulted reports, 149–50
lawsuits
firearms industry immunized against, 28*t*, 29–30
against out-of-state gun dealers, 169–70
against "stop, question, and frisk," 77
legal intervention deaths, 131
Lenox Street gang, 101
Leovy, Jill, 116–17
"lessons learned" reports, 142
letter campaign (for gun purchasers), 168–69, 169*f*
licensed dealers. *See* federally licensed dealers

Lithcutt, Tracy, 96
Loehmann, Timothy, 144
long guns, 33
Los Angeles, CA
  disorder policing in, 59
  gang violence in, 16–17
  ghost gun recovery in, 171–72
  gun carrying regulations in, 40
  Operation Ceasefire in, 107
  police shootings in, 138*f*, 139*f*
  South, 167–69
  "stop, question, and frisk" program in, 7, 175
Los Angeles Police Department (LAPD), 47, 143
  diversity in, 49–50
  supply-side interventions in, 167–69
*Los Angeles Times*, 116
Louisville, KY, 15–16
Lowell, MA, 5, 79
Lowell Police Department, 79
Lucerne Street Doggz, 99–101, 100*f*
Ludwig, Jens, 23

mail-order shipment of guns, 26–27, 41
Malcolm X, 16
Malvo, Lee Boyd, 117
Maple, Jack, 74
Marjory Stoneman Douglas High School shootings, 15
Maryland, due-process protections for police in, 144
Massachusetts, 166
  gun ownership rates in, 36
  homicide clearance rates in, 126*f*
  illegal gun transactions in, 166–67
  requirements for gun ownership in, 37
  robberies involving gun use in, 38–39
mass shootings, 44. *See also* school shootings
  defined, 15
  as a percentage of all gun violence, 7, 15
  social cost of, 23
  types of guns used in, 21–22, 29
Master Settlement Agreement, 29–30, 189n.10
Mattapan, Boston, 67, 79–80, 93–94, 99
McCulloch, Bob, 129
McDonald, Laquan, 9–10, 15–16, 144
*McDonald v. City of Chicago*, 29–30
media
  gang activity covered by, 97
  police shootings tabulated by, 131
men
  gun homicide victimization rate in, 16, 17*f*
  gun ownership by, 33, 34
  gun violence perpetrated by, 16–17
  illegal gun transactions by, 161–63
  police shootings of, 133, 134, 134*t*
mental illness (in police shooting victims), 133, 134*t*, 146–47, 180
mental incompetence (gun ownership disqualification for), 36
Mexico, gun smuggling to, 33
Miami-Dade County, FL, 146–47
Michigan, gun carrying in, 43
Milwaukee, WI, 122, 169–70
Minneapolis, MN, 1–2, 111–12
  hot spots policing in, 59
  police shootings in, 15–16
Minneapolis Police Department, 9–10
minority communities. *See also* racial disparities
  gun ownership in, 34
  gun violence risk in, 86–87
  heightened tensions with police in, 61–63, 174–75
  increased safety in, 4
  public safety gap in, 1
  shootings in, 116
  "stop, question, and frisk" in, 175
  violence concentrated in, 11, 16
misdemeanor convictions (gun ownership disqualification for), 36, 157–58
Mississippi, gun ownership rates in, 36
Montgomery County Police Department, 50*f*
Muhammed, John Allen, 117
murder. *See* homicide

National Firearms Act (NFA) of 1934, 26–27, 28*t*, 29
National Firearms Survey, 33, 35–36
National Instant Check System. *See* instant check system
National Institute of Justice, 118–19
National Integrated Ballistics Information Network (NIBIN), 164–66
National Network for Safe Communities (NNSC), 112
National Opinion Research Center, 33
National Policing Improvement Agency (UK), 124
National Rifle Association, 43

National Tracing Center of ATF, 40
National Violent Death Reporting System, 131
National Vital Statistics System, 131
network of capacity, 112–13
Newark, NJ
  co-offending network in, 90*f*
  gang violence in, 86, 88–89, 89*f*
  hot spots in, 67
New Jersey, robberies involving gun use in, 38–39
New Orleans, LA, 12
New Orleans Police Department, 50*f*
New York, firearms trafficking in, 41, 163
New York City
  body-worn cameras used in, 145–46
  crime decrease in, 6, 22, 54–55, 55*f*, 56
  disorder policing in, 59
  gun carrying regulations in, 40
  homicide decrease in, 54–55, 74
  homicide increase in, 78
  hot spots in, 74–78, 177
  officer-involved homicide in, 61
  police shootings in, 137–38, 138*f*, 139*f*
  prices of illegal guns in, 159
  shootings decrease in, 74
  shootings increase in, 1, 65, 78
  supply-side interventions in, 169–70
  underground gun market in, 160–64, 182
New York City Housing Authority (NYCHA), 65
*New Yorker, The,* 138–39
New York Police Department (NYPD), 47
  gun buyback program of, 170
  key steps in crime prevention strategy, 54–55
  police shootings in, 139–40, 141
  problem-oriented policing in, 56–57
  "stop, question, and frisk" program in, 5, 7, 48, 60, 64, 74–78, 79–80, 175, 177
  Street Crime Unit, 78
  underground gun market analysis by, 160–64
  *New York State Rifle & Pistol Association, Inc. v. Bruen,* 29–30
*New York Times,* 12, 49
NFA. *See* National Firearms Act of 1934
NIBIN (National Integrated Ballistics Information Network), 164–66
Nicaragua, officer-involved lethal shootings in, 131–33
nonfatal shootings, 6, 8–9, 13, 119, 174, 182
  in Boston, 67, 68*f*
  clearance rates for, 116, 179–80
  fatal shootings compared with, 119–23
  gang involvement in, 89–90
  in hot spots, 83
  Operation Ceasefire and, 99
  rates of, 14–15, 14*t*
North Carolina, 41
  prices of illegal guns in, 159
  requirements for gun ownership in, 37
  underground gun market in, 161–63
North Charleston, SC, 61
Northeastern states, 34, 40, 182
Northeastern University, 5
"no snitching" norm, 1–2, 64, 127, 175

Oakland, CA
  focused deterrence in, 108, 113–14, 178
  gang violence in, 87–88, 91
  Operation Ceasefire in, 111, 113
Obama, Barack, 30, 62
objective reasonableness standard, 141, 142
Occhipinti, Frank, 42
offender notification meetings, 102–3, 108, 109, 110
Officer Down Memorial Page, 149
Ohio, underground gun market in, 163
one-gun-a-month regulation, 157
O'Neill, James, 77–78
Operation Ceasefire, 4–5, 8, 79, 94–102, 109–10, 178
  challenges in sustaining, 111–12
  development of, 94
  halting of, 98, 111–12
  key elements of gun market disruption strategy, 166–67
  in Los Angeles, 107
  in Oakland, 111, 113
  relaunching of, 99
  vicariously treated gangs and, 101–2, 108
Operation Impact, 74–75, 76
Operation Trident, 74–75
Orchard Park, Boston, 82–83, 101
Oswald, Lee Harvey, 27
O'Toole, Kathleen, 98–99

Part I index crimes, 49
"pattern and practice" investigations, 141–42, 143–44
pawnbrokers, 155–56

Peel, Sir Robert, 2–3, 8–9
Pennsylvania, underground gun market in, 161–63
people in behavioral crisis (PBCs), 146–47
PERF. *See* Police Executive Research Forum
permitless carry laws, 71–72
"permit to purchase" requirement, 37
Pew Research Center, 34
Philadelphia, PA
  disorder policing in, 57
  focused deterrence in, 108, 113–14
  greening vacant lots in, 83–84
  hot spots in, 67–69, 71, 78, 83–84
  police shootings in, 138*f*, 139*f*, 140, 148
Philadelphia Police Department, 140, 148
Phoenix, AZ, police shootings in, 6–7, 137–38, 138*f*, 139*f*, 141, 180
Phoenix Police Department, 137–38, 141
Piehl, Anne, 92–93, 178
pistols, 33
Pittsburgh, PA, 73–74, 79–80
PL 109-92 (Protection of Lawful Commerce in Arms Act), 29–30
point sources, 156
police
  allocation of time, 50*f*
  complaints against, 140–41, 144, 145–46
  "defund" movement, 1–2, 61, 117, 173
  diversity in employment, 49–50
  evolution and persistent challenges in, 174–76
  excessive use of force by, 48, 63, 174–75
  growth of resources and employment, 48–51
  homicide by (*see* homicide, officer-involved)
  importance of in crime prevention, 1, 2–4, 47–48, 182–83
  "irrelevancy" argument, 2, 47, 53–54
  lack of confidence in, 126–28
  lethal violence against, 149–50
  motivating to do the right thing, 9–10
police chiefs, 49–50, 176
Police Executive Research Forum (PERF), 59–60, 143
Police Foundation survey, 50–51
police shootings, 129–50
  accountability and, 143–45
  circumstances of, 133, 134*t*, 136*t*
  community and organizational factors in, 137–39
  defining the problem, 131–37
  fatal, 6–7, 15–16, 130, 131, 132*f*, 134, 134*t*, 135*f*, 136*t*, 137–39, 138*f*, 139*f*
  individual and situational factors in, 139–41
  law and police department policy, 141–43
  legally justified, 133, 180
  patterns in, 137–41
  people in behavioral crisis and, 146–47
  as a percentage of all shooting deaths, 132*f*, 134, 135*f*
  per year fatalities, 132*f*
  police disengagement in aftermath of, 9–10
  racial disparities in, 133–37, 135*f*, 136*t*
  reducing, 141–49, 180–81
  reducing fatality rates from, 147–48
policing
  academic collaboration and, 59
  challenges remaining for, 63–64
  community (*see* community policing)
  cost *vs.* value of, 48
  disorder, 54–55, 57, 59
  evolution of crime control strategy, 53–59
  hot spots (*see* hot spots)
  illegal gun transaction reduction and, 159–71
  innovation and declining crime rates, 54–59
  precision, 52, 77–78, 177
  predictive, 59
  primary approaches in, 7–9
  proactive, 3, 7–8, 63, 175
  problem-oriented (*see* problem-oriented policing)
  professional (reform), 53–54
  reactive, 2–3, 63, 175, 176–77
  renaissance in, 47
  resistance to change in, 60–61
  strategic thinking about deterrence, 52–53
  technologies in, 58–59, 64
  unintended harms, legitimacy crises, and move toward 21st century, 59–63
  value of investing in improved, 173
political era, 53
political violence, 7, 16
precision policing, 52, 77–78, 177
precursor activities, 52, 63, 175
predictive policing, 59
preemption laws, 43
prices (of guns to criminals), 36, 158–59, 167, 182

prisoner reentry, 102–4
private gun sales, 35–36, 157–58, 181–82
privately manufactured firearms. *See* ghost guns
proactive policing, 3, 7–8, 63, 175
probable cause standard, 71–72
problem analyses, 113
problem-oriented policing, 54–55, 57, 60
 explained, 56
 in hot spots, 66–67, 78–84, 85, 176–77
 for illegal gun transaction reduction, 160, 171
 police-academic collaboration in, 59
 prevalence of, 59–60
procedural justice, 53, 61–62, 64, 110, 174, 175, 178–79
professional (reform) policing, 53–54
Prohibition Era, 26–27
Project Safe Neighborhoods (PSN), 58, 102–4, 159–60
property crime decrease, 55*f*, 56
Protection of Lawful Commerce in Arms Act (PL 109-92), 29–30
PSN. *See* Project Safe Neighborhoods
public health perspective, 2, 3
public safety
 economic value of, 23–24
 gap in, 1, 11
Public Safety Canada, 108–9
"pulling-levers policing," 58, 91. *See also* focused deterrence
Pulse Nightclub shootings, 15

quality of life offenses, 56–57

racial disparities. *See also* minority communities; specific racial/ethnic groups
 in gun homicide victimization rates, 16
 in police shootings, 133–37, 135*f*, 136*t*
 in public safety, 1
 in "stop, question, and frisk," 76–77, 79–80
Ramsey, Charles H., 145
RAND Corporation, 106, 118, 167–68
reactive policing, 2–3, 63, 175, 176–77
Reagan, Ronald, 16
reasonable suspicion standard, 71–72, 77
red flag laws, 44, 147
reform policing. *See* professional policing
regulation. *See* firearms regulation
relationship-intensive interventions, 112–13
retail deterrence, 86–114, 173, 178. *See also* focused deterrence; gangs
retail gun sales, 33, 35*f*. *See also* federally licensed dealers
revolvers, 21–22, 33
Rice, Tamir, 144
Ridgeway, Greg, 140
rifles, 33
"risky people, risky places" approach, 99
robbery
 clearance rates for, 118–19
 decrease in, 17–18, 47
 in hot spots, 78–79, 80–83
 instrumentality and, 20, 21
 percentage of involving guns, 38–39
 street, 79, 81–83, 88
"root causes" perspective on crime, 2, 4, 19
routine violence, 6–7
Roxbury, Boston, 67, 79–80, 93–95, 99
Rutgers University, 5

Sacramento Police Department, 50*f*
Safe Street Teams (SST), 79–83
 evaluation of crime trends, 83
 identification of problems and their causes by, 81–82
 selection of treatment areas, 80
sales of guns. *See* gun sales
San Antonio, TX, police shootings in, 138*f*, 139*f*
San Diego, CA, police shootings in, 138*f*, 139*f*
Sandy Hook Elementary School shootings, 15, 30, 32
San Francisco, CA, 111–12
San Jose, CA, police shootings in, 138*f*, 139*f*
Saturday night specials, ban on import of, 28*t*
Schelling, Thomas, 23
school shootings, 7, 15, 23, 30, 32
"scoop and run," 147–48
screening of gun buyers, 27–29. *See also* background checks
Second Amendment, 3, 29–30, 45, 173–74, 182
self-inflicted shootings, 88, 203n.16
semiautomatic pistols, 21–22, 160–61, 166
September 11 terrorist attacks, 30
 793 Bloods, 86
 75th Precinct (Brooklyn), 74–75
 77th Street Policing District (South Los Angeles), 167–68
Sherman, Lawrence, 59, 137
Shilling, Sara, 120

shipments of new guns, 33, 35*f*
shootings, 115–28. *See also* fatal shootings; gun violence; mass shootings; nonfatal shootings; police shootings
  challenges and opportunities in investigations, 125–28
  decrease in, 74
  group yearly counts in Boston, 70*f*
  improving investigative practices, 118–19, 173, 179–80
  increase in, 1, 65, 78
  obtaining intelligence on, 164–66
  school, 7, 15, 23, 30, 32
  self-inflicted, 88, 203n.16
  solvability of, 117–19
shotguns, 33
Skogan, Wes, 59
social media, 52–53, 64, 126, 130
social service provisions, 8, 102–3, 111
solvability, 117–19, 125
South Carolina, underground gun market in, 161–63
Southern states, 166
  firearms trafficking in, 40, 157, 161–63
  gun ownership in, 34
  supply-side interventions in, 166–67
"sporting purposes" test, 27
sports, gun, 34–35
SST. *See* Safe Street Teams
St. Louis, MO, 9–10
  focused deterrence in, 108
  hot spots in, 73–74
  police shootings in, 138–39
stabbings, 19–20
state prison inmates, survey of, 37, 38*t*
Stern, Donald, 97–98
Stewart, Billy, 95–96
"stop, question, and frisk" programs, 5, 7, 48, 60, 64, 79–80, 84, 175, 177
  constitutional laws grounding, 71–72
  criticism of, 74–75
  decrease in number of NYPD stops, 77
  described, 74–78
  increase in number of NYPD stops, 74–77, 75*f*
"stop shooting" protocol, 142–43
Strategic Alternatives to Community Safety Initiative, 58
straw purchases, 37, 41, 152, 154, 163, 181–82
  defined, 41
  difficulty in detecting patterns of, 31
  difficulty of making cases against, 41
  interventions, 168–70
  investigations of, 154–55
Street Crime Unit, 74
street robbery, 79, 81–83, 88
street segments, 69–71, 80–81
suicide, 44
  instrumentality and, 186n.10
  rates of, 14–15, 14*t*
  social cost of, 23
Supplementary Homicide Reports, 131
supply-side interventions, 152, 166–70, 182
Supreme Court, U.S.
  on personal right to keep guns, 3, 29–30, 156, 173–74
  on police use of deadly force, 141
  on stop and frisk practice, 71–72
surveillance cameras, 126
sustainability plans, 113

tactical decision-making, 143
targeted patrol, 71–74
TASERs, 148–49, 181
Task Force on 21st Century Policing, 62
taxes on guns, 33
Taylor, Breonna, 15–16
technologies in policing, 58–59, 64
*Tennessee v. Garner,* 141–42
Ten Point Coalition, 94, 98, 99–100
*Terry* stops, 71–72, 74, 79–80
*Terry v. Ohio,* 71–72
theft (of guns), 41–42, 152–54, 164
  extent of, 42
  percentage of investigations involving, 154–55
  question of importance of in crime, 170–71, 181
  reporting requirements, 42
Tiahrt, Todd, 31–32
Tiahrt Amendments of 2004, 31–32
tobacco industry lawsuits, 29–30, 189n.10
tracing of gun transactions, 40–42
  process of, 40
  restrictions on use of data from, 31–32
  useful intelligence acquired from, 40, 164–66
trafficking. *See* firearms trafficking
transactions costs, 39, 45
Tremont/Stuart, Boston, 81–82
Trump, Donald, 7

underground gun markets, 10–11, 152, 153–54, 164
  analyzing, 160–64
  as a byproduct of regulation, 26

disrupting, 156–59, 181–82
Uniform Crime Report, 56
unintentional shooting injuries, 14*t*
unions, police, 60–61, 138–39, 144–45, 181
United Kingdom, 124
University of Chicago, 5–6
University of Pennsylvania, 5, 83
U.S. Agency for International Development, 108–9
use-of-force continuum, 142–43

vacant lots, greening, 83–84
Vailsburg, Newark, 86, 88–89
Vallejo, California, Police Department (VPD), 138–39, 144
Vamp Hill Kings, 95–97
Vance, Cyrus R., Jr., 151
Van Dyke, Jason, 144
Venezuela, officer-involved lethal shootings in, 131–33
Vermont
ERPO in, 44
gun carrying in, 43
vicariously treated gangs, 101–2, 108
video recordings, 174–75
of crimes, 52–53, 58–59
of police shootings, 15–16
Vietnam War era, 17–18, 53–54
violent crime
decrease in, 55*f*, 56, 106
drug market intervention impact on, 106
focused deterrence impact on, 106–9
optimizing prevention mechanisms against, 109–11
strategic thinking about deterrence of, 52–53
Virginia
firearms regulation in, 157
underground gun market in, 161–63
Virginia Tech shootings, 15
Vollmer, August, 53
volume crimes, 118–19

Wales, lethal violence against police in, 149
Walnut Park gang, 101
Washington, DC
gun carrying regulations in, 40, 42–43
hot spots in, 71, 176
prices of illegal guns in, 159
Washington Beltway sniper attacks, 117
*Washington Post, The,* 15–16, 131, 133, 145
Weisburd, David, 59
Western Europe, officer-involved lethal shootings in, 131–33
*When Police Kill* (Zimring), 141–42
Whites
gun homicide victimization rate in, 17*f*
gun ownership by, 34
gun violence victimization in, 174
officer-involved homicide of, 134, 135*f*, 136*t*
in police departments, 49–50, 139–40
police shootings of, 133, 134, 134*t*, 135–36, 135*f*, 136*t*, 180
Wilson, Darren, 129
Wilson, James Q., 71–72
Wilson, O. W., 53
Windley, Jamal, 65
Wisconsin, firearms trafficking in, 40
witnesses to crimes, 9, 121–22, 126–27, 179
women
gun homicide victimization rate in, 17, 17*f*
gun ownership by, 33, 34
in police departments, 49–50
police shootings of, 134*t*
Woods, Daniel, 26
Wyoming, gun ownership in, 38–39

youth homicide, 92–102, 93*f*
Youth Opportunity Unlimited, 99–100
Youth Violence Strike Force (YVSF) of BPD, 96, 98–99, 115

Zimring, Franklin, 19–20, 141–42